# America
## *Needs* Human
## Rights

Edited by Anuradha Mittal and Peter Rosset

**FOOD FIRST BOOKS**
OAKLAND, CALIFORNIA

The editors would like to thank the following individuals for the support and assistance that made this book possible: Marilyn Borchardt (you know why!), our editor Sal Glynn, Martha Katigbak, Martin Bourque, Jonathan Hudec, Tracy Lingo, Wylie Liu, Ravi Rajan, María Elena Martínez, and DeWayne Boyd. We also thank the following donors whose generosity made our work possible: Ford Foundation, California Wellness Foundation, Fritz Pappenheim Fund, Evangelical Lutheran Church, Boehm Foundation, and A Better World Fund; and the thousands of Food First members who support our work on an on-going basis.

Text and cover design by Colored Horse Studios. Set in Adobe Garamond with Adobe Jenson Headings. Front cover adapted from video cover design by i·arte. Index by Ken DellaPenta.

Library of Congress Cataloging-in-Publication Data

America needs human rights / edited by Anuradha Mittal and Peter Rosset.
     p.  m.
    Includes index.
    ISBN 0-935028-72-2 (pbk.)
      1. Poverty—United States.   2. Poor—United States.   3. United States—Economic conditions—1981–   4. United States—Economic policy—1993–
    5. Economic security—United States.   I. Mittal Anuradha, 1967–   .
    II. Rosset, Peter.
    HC110.P6A677   1999
    362.5'8'0973—dc21

                                     99—43435
                                       CIP

Food First Books are distributed by:
LPC Group
1436 West Randolph Street
Chicago, IL 60607
(800) 243-0138

Printed in Canada

10 9 8 7 6 5 4 3 2 1

# TABLE OF CONTENTS

# INTRODUCTION

## A CALL TO ACTION: WHY AMERICA
## NEEDS HUMAN RIGHTS

*One has to speak out and stand up for one's convictions. Inaction at a time of conflagration is inexcusable.*
—Gandhi

"It isn't that I never worked," said Katherine Engels, "I've worked since I was fourteen years old." Engels, a grandmother and president of the Kensington Welfare Rights Union, was testifying at a congressional hearing on the human rights implications of increasing hunger, poverty, and economic insecurity in America. "With the jobs that are out there you're not making enough to live. When you're hungry, it's really hard. Sometimes I psyche myself up to a cup of tea and try to make myself feel as though I just ate a full course meal, even though I didn't. Sometimes I roll bread up into little dough balls to try to fill myself up. Mothers go hungry at night so their children can eat. You have to find a way to feed your kids no matter what it takes. And if it takes going in people's trash cans, hey, I have no pride when it comes to my kids."[1]

Despite glowing media reports on our booming economy, hunger afflicts thirty million Americans today, at least twelve million of whom are children. One in five children under the age of five lives in poverty—the highest rate among industrialized countries—and as many as seven million Americans are homeless. In San Francisco, health department figures show that a record 157 people died on the streets in 1998. Their deaths were attributed to the lack of shelter beds and affordable housing.[2]

It doesn't have to be that way in a nation like ours. The wealth and resources clearly exist for every man, woman, and child to have a roof over their heads, food in their bellies, and access to decent education, health care, and a job that pays a living wage. The sad truth is that our economy puts corporate profits before people's lives; it places economic efficiency over opportunity and compassion for all. This book is a call to reverse those priorities. This book is about human rights.

It is a systematic and widespread violation of the most basic of human rights for so many to go without, amid so much plenty. Human rights are the birthright of everyone: no one has the right to deny them, and everyone has the right to fight for their own rights. A human rights perspective builds on the civil and women's rights struggles that came before, and extends them into the 'food, shelter, and jobs' arena of economics.

It matters to Americans whether or not our nation lives up to the international human rights standards to which we subscribe. Given the opportunity, all Americans *can* make a decent living and take care of themselves. Americans *do* believe in fairness and justice, and the power of the individual. Whether the nation lives up to its beliefs matters morally, in terms of right and wrong, and also in terms of the spirit and quality of life that a nation and its people enjoy.

*America Needs Human Rights* is inspired by the daily struggles of mothers on welfare, homeless people, low wage workers, and many others who find themselves poor in America. In 1997 Food First launched the *Economic Human Rights: The Time Has Come!* campaign, and in 1998 organized congressional hearings which documented the day-to-day struggles of poor people, who testified in their voices. Katherine Engels was one of them. In this book, we provide a vision that places their experience in a larger, more meaningful context. It is our deep-rooted desire for equality and fairness that calls for their stories to be heard and their struggles recognized.

A triumphant view of the U.S. economy dominates media coverage: the lowest yearly unemployment rate in a quarter century, rising profits, a balanced budget, and declining numbers of Americans classified as poor. While all this can be considered a cause for national celebration, Katherine Engels knows that the problem is bigger then her personal struggle. The present economic optimism masks the deepening erosion of the American dream.

The number of hungry people in the U.S. grew by fifty percent between 1985 and 1990, from twenty million to thirty million—twelve percent of the population.[3] By 1995 the number was estimated at almost thirty-five million.[4] In 1997, the first year of 'welfare reform,' a survey by the U.S. Conference of Mayors found an additional sixteen percent increase.[5]

This hunger is not caused by a shortage of food, but rather by political and economic factors which result in unfair distribution and access. So many Americans are hungry because they are poor and cannot afford adequate food, a result of long-term decline in the real wages of the average worker and cutbacks in social welfare spending. According to official statistics, in 1994 there were more than thirty-eight million Americans living below the poverty line.[6]

The primary reason for growing poverty among Americans is declining wages, despite falling unemployment figures. Official statistics count people as employed if they hold any job—whether for ten hours or forty hours a week; and whether paying $7.00 or $70.00 an hour. That is misleading, because many need full-time jobs but can't find them, and many are unable to support themselves and their families on the low wages they earn. In 1996, four million workers were employed part-time, though they wanted to work full-time but could not find such jobs. Nearly ten million more worked full-time year-round for less than $7.00 an hour. These two groups of workers, all counted as employed, did not earn a sufficient income to house and feed a family of four.[7] They are the new 'working poor.' They amount to twice the seven million workers who held no job and were classified as unemployed in official statistics. Together, the un- and under-employed totaled twenty-one million people.

In August 1996 President Clinton signed the 'welfare reform' bill, mandating $54 billion in cuts, eliminating the Aid to Families with Dependent Children (AFDC) program that provided monthly cash benefits to 12.8 million people, including more than 8 million children. More than half of the $54 billion in welfare cuts ($27.7 billion) came from the food stamps that twenty-five million poor Americans depend on. (Over eighty percent of food stamps go to families with children.) It is likely that' welfare reform' has pushed millions of Americans into desperation.[8]

The 1999 federal budget proposed by the Clinton Administration included a $112 billion increase for the military over a six year period.

The majority of federal discretionary spending over the next decade—tax dollars that aren't automatically allocated to mandatory entitlement programs like Social Security or Medicare, or to interest on the debt—will go to the Pentagon. When a fifth of America's children are raised in poverty, it is a national disgrace to place the interests of military contractors at the top of our national priorities. Some might say we are making "war on the poor."

To appreciate this fundamental lack of human values in American social policy, one need only look back and compare our time to earlier decades. Where Roosevelt's New Deal and Johnson's Civil Rights Act and 'War on Poverty' promised *some* future for all Americans, the legacy of the past two decades—welfare reform, the 'Contract with America,' and balanced budget mania—have snatched away that promise. Today we face terrible challenges: the growing rift between the rich and poor; the tearing apart of our social fabric; the drive to privatize Social Security and Medicare; the decay of inner cities; and the decline in civic participation and public trust.

In 1944, President Franklin Roosevelt told Americans that true individual freedom cannot exist without economic security and independence. He argued that people who are hungry and out of work are the stuff of which dictatorships are made. He called for a 'second bill of rights' covering economic life, under which a new basis of security and prosperity could be established for all. Both he and Eleanor Roosevelt, the first chair of the United Nations Commission on Human Rights, provided leadership in the adoption of the Universal Declaration of Human Rights (UDHR), which is the primary formulation of the fundamental and inalienable rights of all members of the human family. The Universal Declaration was adopted by the United Nations General Assembly on December 10, 1948, and represented the first comprehensive agreement among nations on the specific rights and freedoms of all human beings.

Originally intended as a "common standard of achievement for all peoples and all nations," over the past fifty years, the Universal Declaration has become the cornerstone of human rights. It guarantees civil and political rights, such as equal protection under the law; protection against arbitrary arrest, torture, and punishment; and the right to participate in government through periodic elections. The Universal

Declaration also guarantees a full range of economic human rights including the right to a standard of living adequate for the health and well-being of oneself and one's family.9 This does not mean that governments must feed everyone or give them a home, but rather that they must assure, through policy, that those rights are not denied.

The guarantees in the Universal Declaration include an inextricable link between different categories of rights. Civil and political rights are meaningless when the majority of the citizens remain economically disenfranchised. Likewise, exercising one's economic rights becomes impossible against a backdrop of political repression and exploitation.

While the Universal Declaration is not legally binding on governments, it does provide them with a 'guiding set of principles,' and has been codified by numerous covenants and conventions that make portions of it legally binding. In 1976, President Carter signed both the International Covenant on Civil and Political Rights (ICCPR) and the International Covenant for Economic, Social, and Cultural Rights (ICESCR). The Senate ratified the ICCPR in 1992. It also ratified the Convention on the Elimination of all Forms of Racial Discrimination (CERD) and the Convention Against Torture (CAT) in 1994. The U.S. is currently bound to uphold the ICCPR, CERD, and CAT, and can be held in violation of them before the UN Human Rights Committee. The ICESCR still awaits ratification by the Senate. All of these documents, both ratified and to be ratified, should be the guiding principles for our country's policies.

Rights spelled out on paper, even legally binding paper, are meaningless if people do not demand their enforcement. In this context the Universal Declaration for Human Rights has become the foundation of a movement that has grown to include human rights organizations in nearly every country of the world. Some, like Amnesty International, safeguard the civil and political rights of people. Others, like the Food First Information and Action Network (FIAN), and Survival International, are working to ensure the economic and cultural survival of the poor, and of indigenous peoples struggling to feed themselves in the face of a global economy pushing them to the margins.

Food First's *Economic Human Rights: The Time Has Come!* campaign demands economic human rights for every person right here in America. Because the Senate is stalling on ratification of the

International Covenant for Economic, Social and Cultural Rights, we are counting on pressure from grassroots movements. Already several city councils have adopted resolutions declaring themselves "human rights cities." In Oakland, Berkeley, San Francisco, Chicago, and Arcata, they have adopted the Covenant, and "resolved that the City affirms its stand for human rights by pledging to oppose any legislation or action that impinges on the fundamental human rights of human beings as stated in the UDHR...." Not only is that a message to the Senate, but activists can now hold those cities accountable to the UDHR and the Covenant. When the San Francisco Board of Supervisors voted to ban sleeping and camping by the homeless in some of the last public spaces that were still left in which to sleep, many in San Francisco, including the American Friends Service Committee, were quick to remind the Supervisors of their commitment to universal human rights.

When we think of human rights violations, we think of Kosovo, Indonesia, or Rwanda, yet using the lens of economic and social human rights, we find widespread and growing violations right here at home. Kate Engels' testimony and endless similar stories show how far the U.S. has fallen short of its commitments under the UDHR, and how far from acceptable our social conditions and social policies really are.

In the international arena, the U.S. government stood alone in rejecting the right to housing at the Habitat Conference in Istanbul in 1996, and the right to food at the World Food Summit in Rome in November 1996. Melinda Kimble, the head of the United States government delegation to the Food Summit, said that the U.S. could not support language around the right to food in the Summit's Plan of Action because the new welfare reform law would then be in violation of international law.[10] The U.S. tried to downgrade the right to food, calling it "a goal or aspiration to be realized progressively..., [which] does not give rise to any international obligations."[11] In other words, go ahead and say we aspire to a world where everyone eats, but don't hold us to it.

In December 1998, against the backdrop of the 50th anniversary celebrations of the UDHR, the U.N. General Assembly adopted a resolution that urged all countries to eliminate obstacles to development by protecting not just political and civil rights, but also economic, social, and cultural rights. In the text of the resolution, its drafters argued that the existence of widespread poverty inhibits the full and effective enjoyment of human rights, and renders democracy and popular participation fragile. The resolution, supported by all of the developing nations in the world body, had only one negative vote: the United States.[12]

In the past, the U.S. government has applied the framework of human rights selectively to mostly Third World countries, and focused only on political rights, to the exclusion of economic, social, and cultural rights. Now we must call our country to task for its own record on human rights. The time has come to say that human rights are indivisible—civil and political rights cannot be separated from economic and social human rights—and they are universal, applying just as much here at home as anywhere else in the world. Human rights are a basic way of conceptualizing and implementing concepts of right and wrong.

The human rights discourse is a powerful means to counter Republican-style casting of social issues like hunger as questions of mere economic efficiency and numerical cost/benefit analysis. It is profoundly different to talk about hunger in terms of human rights. When we speak in numbers we might decide that while thirty million hungry are too many, eighteen million might be an acceptable policy goal. But if we say that food is a human right, that we all have the inalienable right to be able to feed ourselves and our families, then to have even one hungry family in the richest nation on Earth constitutes a human rights violation, and must be fully addressed.

We must necessarily view options very differently if we use cost/benefit analysis, versus human rights, as the policy filter. Under the former we might find policies that encourage job flight and privatized social services to be acceptable, while under the latter we would have to discard such options because they do not pass the human rights filter, as they lead to growing and persistent hunger. And why not use a human rights policy filter? We reject out of hand any political system which practices torture. The same is true for genocide—killing 100,000 and killing one million are both totally unacceptable. Why should we view hunger in a different light? It is after all a quiet violence in which hunger-related diseases take the lives of many.

If we don't stand up now for our human rights and those of all Americans, the safety net for the poor will be further weakened or may even be abolished outright. Homelessness and hunger will continue to increase. The prison industry will grow, constituting the only form of public service that is fully and willingly funded. The gap between the rich and poor, already the largest in the industrialized world, will widen. Unregulated industries will require employees to work in increasingly unsafe conditions at lower wages, and cut back worker's health and retirement benefits.

Those of us concerned about growing economic insecurity are still awaiting U.S. ratification of the International Covenant on Economic, Social, and Cultural Rights. Until we legally endow all people with the inalienable rights to not just liberty, but freedom from want, the U.S. cannot rightfully claim moral authority as a human rights leader. This is not a radical proposal for the late twentieth century. All other major industrialized countries have embraced these economic and social human rights through ratification of the Covenant.

Mere ratification of an international treaty will not ensure these rights any more than the Fourteenth Amendment to the U.S. Constitution ended racial discrimination in this country, or ensured political rights for all Americans. Human rights may be inalienable, but realization requires that people demand them and that there be constant vigilance. Adopting economic human rights as constitutional standards through treaty law will make them an explicit goal for the U.S., providing new tools in the struggle to obtain these basic human rights for all Americans.

The very survival of our democratic system depends on breaking out of the narrow confines of conventional political views. We need to focus on public policy issues affecting increasing hunger and poverty in America, using the framework of social and economic human rights. We need to challenge the social ills of contemporary America, like growing hunger and poverty, as human rights abuses, to lay the basis for a powerful movement for fundamental change. Organizing ourselves, creating new alliances, and reframing the basic terms on which

America's public debate takes place, using the framework of human rights, is the hope that guides us into the new century.

Our objective is to show what we can do. Human rights are secured and strengthened by public pressure. Economic and political oppression are our common enemies, whether in the industrialized countries or in the Third World. We must therefore all begin to speak the same language, educate others about human rights and actively work to make our voices heard. Only then will it be possible for a coherent new political vision for America to emerge where human rights are guaranteed for all.

We have organized this book in four parts. In Part One, "The New American Crisis," we show just how serious unemployment, hunger, homelessness and poverty are in today's America—despite record earnings in the stock market and low levels of official unemployment. In Part Two, "Root Causes," we look at how we have gotten to this dismal state of affairs, highlighting policy changes and economic globalization as key forces driving poverty. Part Three, "What's Wrong With Welfare," is a guide to how anti-poverty policies have gone wrong, from when we were a British colony through President Clinton's welfare reform. In the last part, "Human Rights for America," we reflect on the values we share as Americans, and build the case for a human rights movement based on those values, a movement to end hunger and extreme poverty once and for all in this nation of ours.

In the appendices we provide the full text of the Universal Declaration of Human Rights and the International Covenant on Economic, Social, and Cultural Rights, together with selections from two key speeches by Franklin Delano Roosevelt, and a resource guide of organizations that are working on ensuring economic and social human rights for all.

NOTES

1. This Congressional Hearing was organized on September 23, 1998 at Capitol Hill, by Food First in collaboration with the Institute for Policy Studies and the Progressive Challenge.

2. "New Welfare and Medicaid Bill Bad for Children," *Children's Defense Fund Reports*, 1996, Vol. 17, No. 7/8

3. *Hunger 1995: Causes of Hunger, Fifth Annual Report on the State of the World Hunger* (Washington, DC: Bread for the World Institute, 1995).

4. *The Changing Politics of Hunger: Hunger 1999* (Washington, DC: Bread for the World Institute, 1998), pg. 84.

5. Ibid., pg. 57.

6. Schwarz, J. "The Hidden Side of the Clinton Economy," *The Atlantic Monthly*, October 1998.

7. Ibid.

8. Edelman, P. "The Worst Thing Bill Clinton Has Done," *The Atlantic Monthly*, March 1997.

9. Universal Declaration of Human Rights (UDHR), Article 25.

10. Mittal, Anuradha. "Report from the World Food Summit," *Food Rights Watch*, December 1996.

11. Ibid.

12. Thalif, Dean. "U.S. Votes Against Development," *Development Bulletin-Rights*, IPS, December 12, 1998.

## PART ONE

# The New American Crisis

Once the social programs of the New Deal and the defense industries of World War II had pulled America out of the Great Depression, the President of the United States wanted to put guarantees in place so that social desperation on a grand scale could never again become a feature of American life. In his 1944 State of the Union address, Franklin D. Roosevelt called for a "Second Bill of Rights." Recognizing that the original Bill of Rights with its emphasis on civil liberties was not enough to ensure freedom and equality for all, he argued that true freedom cannot exist without economic human rights:

> *This Republic had its beginning, and grew to its present strength, under the protection of certain inalienable political rights... our rights to life and liberty. As our nation has grown in size and stature, as our industrial economy expanded, [these political rights to life and liberty] proved inadequate to assure us equality in the pursuit of happiness.... We have come to a clear realization of the fact that true individual freedom cannot exist without economic security and independence....*
> *Necessitous men are not free men.*[1]

The idea of a second bill of rights eventually moved beyond our borders and gave birth to the Universal Declaration of Human Rights (UDHR) in 1948. While the next thirty years did see an unprecedented across-the-board improvement in the living standards of most Americans, our government's never-very-strong commitment to economic opportunity for all disintegrated in the 1980s and 1990s. At the turn of the century, amidst the illusion of broad-based economic prosperity, we once again find ourselves in a crisis of barely-hidden, widespread desperation and structural poverty. That is the new American crisis outlined in Part One.

Millions in today's America are deprived of their basic human right to food, housing, health care and meaningful work opportunities. U.S. infant mortality rates, poverty rates, and illiteracy rates are among the world's worst for industrialized nations. While the number of million-aires in the U.S. has tripled, the ranks of the homeless have doubled.[2] Some estimate that more American children die each month because of poverty than the total U.S. combat deaths in the entire Vietnam war.[3]

In the first chapter of Part One, "Illusions of Opportunity: The American Dream in Question," John Schwarz questions the American dream which binds us together as a single society: the belief that every American can get ahead by virtue of hard work. He asks if the deteri-oration of that dream is due, as Conservative commentators would suggest, to a decline in the work ethic, or if there is another force at work. With a deficit of sixteen million adequate jobs, nearly a quarter of American families cannot find the work they need to sustain themselves with dignity. In today's America, it is just not true that everyone who works hard can support a family and improve their living conditions.

While America is increasingly a wealthier country, it is also a hun-grier one. In Chapter Two, Janet Poppendieck looks at "Hunger in the Land of Plenty." Beginning with the varied ways that hungry people can be counted, she leaves us with best estimates that put the number of hungry Americans at some thirty million people. In examining the causes of this pervasive hunger, she analyzes the failure of our economy to generate jobs that pay livable wages, cutbacks in social programs and the erosion in the value of the benefits they provide, and the sharp increase in housing costs which place many families in the dilemma of having to choose between a roof over their heads versus adequate food. In Chapter Three, "The Inner City: When Work Disappears," distin-guished social critic William Julius Wilson paints a vivid picture of neighborhoods without jobs, places where poor African-Americans find no way out of deepening poverty. He outlines the policies and social forces that have created such desperate landscapes.

In the following chapter, Paul Koegel, M. Audrey Burnam, and Jim Baumohl take up the logical consequence of this dilemma: the nation-wide epidemic of homelessness that began in the 1980s. In "The Causes of Homelessness" they use an integrated perspective to demon-strate how structural factors like the decline in affordable housing, and the growing ranks of the vulnerable poor have interacted to produce blatant human rights violations.

In Chapter Five, "Slavery in the Fields," Daniel Rothenberg takes us to rural America, revealing the conditions of modern day quasi-slavery faced by many farm workers, our nation's poorest and most disadvantaged group of laborers. Part One closes with "The State of America's Children," a warning about the future of our nation. With more than fourteen million children—one in five—living in poverty, we face immense moral and social costs as a society. With the exception of Somalia, which for part of the 1990s lacked a legally constituted government, the U.S. stands alone among nations in failing to ratify the Convention on the Rights of the Child. The authors question our refusal to guarantee our children the adequate health care, food, shelter, and education that should be every child's birthright.

In reading Part One we urge our readers to keep the principles of human rights foremost in their minds. As a nation we must see the human rights implications of this crisis. Too often the lives of millions of poor Americans appear strange, distant and impossible to understand. Yet the tragedy of our nation's poor does not lie in some fundamental difference that sets them apart from other Americans, but rather in our shared humanity. Human rights standards of economic and social justice give every human being and every community a powerful tool for struggle. If there is any silver lining in the cloud of the new American crisis, it is surely that a real commitment to human rights for all may emerge from the struggles it engenders.

NOTES

1. Roosevelt, Franklin D. "Annual Message to Congress," January 11, 1944, in *The Public Papers and Addresses of Franklin D. Roosevelt 1944–45*, ed. Samuel I. Rosenman (New York: Harper and Brothers, 1950), pp. 32–44.
2. Chomsky, Noam. "Roll Back" in *The New American Crisis*, eds. Greg Ruggiero and Stuart Sahulka (New York: New Press, 1995).
3. Ibid.

# I

## ILLUSIONS OF OPPORTUNITY:
## THE AMERICAN DREAM IN QUESTION

*John E. Schwarz*

Disquieting doubts have crept into America's consciousness over the past thirty years. Mounting social pathologies, troubling economic uncertainties, and rising political disillusion have left many feeling that something is wrong, that the nation's bright luster has become tarnished, that the nation has somehow lost its way. To ascertain the root of our fears, recover our moral bearings, and renew the nation's sense of purpose, we must begin at the beginning: with our fundamental principles, with our basic creed.

The nation's creed asserts the moral equality of all. Belief in it connects each of us to the whole and thus to one another. It gives us a sense of shared fate, despite the centrifugal forces of our many ethnic, racial, and religious differences, and the great importance we attach to individuality. The glue that binds us is a shared idea that supplies us with a common sense of our responsibilities to one another. Out of our enormous array of differences, it is what makes us one people.

A central component of this creed is called the American Ethos, or the American Dream. Every American today instinctively knows the ethos: that every individual should be able to get ahead and gain some measure of success through actions and means that are under his or her own control.[1] The ethos is that everyone who steadfastly practices certain practical virtues will find a place at the table. No one need be left out, unless he or she voluntarily chooses to be. These virtues—self-control, discipline, effort, perseverance, and responsibility—stand at the core of our sense of morality and our idea of good character, and are essential to the success and safety of a good society. To fail to reward them would be to diminish and devalue them as virtues. No value survives forever on incantations alone.

That America should be a land of opportunity where every hard-working person who perseveres can find a respected place is an idea whose roots run so deep in American history that it dates back to the Declaration of Independence and the very founding of the Republic. So universally is it accepted among Americans as a moral foundation that it transcends politics and party identification—Democrat, Republican, Libertarian, religious right, Perotista—independent of voters and non-voters alike, no matter their age, gender, race, or ethnic background. It is what unites us in the present and, in turn, unites the present with the past.

The ethos also sets forth a standard of justice that holds each individual accountable, for it assumes that one's fate is in large measure under one's own control. With this belief in mind, Congress named its landmark welfare reform bill of 1996, "The Personal Responsibility Act." Yet a community in which individuals lack control over their own fate loses the moral right to apply an authentic notion of personal accountability.

To many Americans, the very idea of being wholly human dissolves if we have little or no control over our own fate. If it is true that absolute power corrupts, so can absolute powerlessness. The ability to exercise a reasonable level of control over one's own future is essential, in the American way of thinking, not simply due to the virtues it will affirm or the sense of justice it permits but because it defines our idea of fully realized humanity itself.

As a result, the notion that people do have a capacity to control their own destinies is an enormously strong, almost insistent feature of our American culture. The stories of penniless immigrants who came to these shores and became successful are as legion as they are inspiring, fostering a belief that anyone can start anew in this country and succeed. America is a land, in the fashion of Horatio Alger, Jr., where "God helps those who help themselves."

Nonetheless, many people believe that over the past three decades a dangerous anti-ethos has arisen: the idea that the individual American is not responsible for his or her own fate. From the point of view of these observers, too many individuals have come to see themselves as victims rather than as agents, to feel sorry for themselves instead of working to pick themselves up—a mentality that government assistance programs helped to spawn and now continue to reinforce. With the expansion of government has come a feeling of entitlement and an

emphasis on rights over responsibilities. The creed of personal accountability so important to the American ethos has withered, and with that
has come a rise in welfare, illegitimacy, crime, and other social pathologies—the price the society has paid for the abandonment of character.
In the end, William Bennett reminds us, "the state of the union
depends on the character of its citizens."[2]

Or has something gone wrong with the ethos itself? The premise
that individuals can control and so be personally responsible for their
own lives presumes that the opportunity to do so exists. Generations
of Americans have called this "the land of opportunity." But is it, still?
Does opportunity remain available and adequate to the needs of the
American people, sufficient to enable them to take control of their own
lives? Are the problems troubling society today due to the disintegration of values and character, or to a genuine lack of opportunity that
prevents individuals and families from being able to determine their
own futures?

The answers we are offered rely on little more than intuitive sense
and anecdotal information. Some say good jobs are there for the asking, all a worker needs to do is to look in the daily newspapers;[3] others
tell of employers who have so many applications on file for jobs that
they can easily keep wages low and, if necessary, rid themselves of
workers.[4] One scholar says that the very brief time individuals stay
unemployed before finding a new job stands as compelling testimony
to the availability of opportunity,[5] yet a news story reports that 1,000
people lined up and waited for hours to apply for a handful of temporary jobs with no benefits at a General Motors plant.[6] The chairman
of Pacific Telesis informs us that over half of the 6,400 workers applying for 700 operator jobs at $7 per hour with his company were not
qualified and could not read at the seventh grade level. But 2,700
applicants *were* qualified for the 700 jobs.[7] One person points to the
welfare queen who cheats the taxpayer, and a series of private sector
programs that have gotten good jobs for welfare recipients who are
willing to work. Another tells the story of a welfare recipient who tries
and perseveres but has gotten nowhere.

These contradictory narratives, each resulting from a cobbling
together of bits and pieces of evidence, have become central to our politics. Each side routinely exploits its narrative for political gain. The

debate doesn't move us forward, however. Instead, it polarizes and ultimately shackles us.

The struggle between left and right infusing our politics, played out particularly in our social and economic policies, isn't mainly a battle between different world views of morality or the good society. Looking beneath the surface, however, it is even more a conflict about the degree to which a society that every side perceives as essentially good—a society that provides enough opportunity for all—actually exists. Each side of the political debate fundamentally agrees that the deserving should be helped, and that those who try and cannot help themselves *are* the deserving. The American ethos is common currency; in the end, all sides concur that there are certain entitlements, and that foremost among them is the right to opportunity.

What, then, does economic opportunity mean according to American thinking? To what extent does opportunity commensurate with American standards that exist in the nation, both now and in the recent past? What implications do the answers to these questions have for an understanding of the troubles presently facing the nation? What do the answers teach us about our policies now—and what they must become in the future—with respect to job creation, welfare, child support, health care measures, minimum wage laws, education, job training, and labor organization, among others? What are the implications in terms of the role government should play in the economy, and in terms of what it means to say that the economy is a success or a failure? Do today's measures of the economy accurately inform us or fundamentally mislead us? If there isn't enough opportunity, why not?

NOTES

1. Hochschild, Jennifer. "The Political Contingency of Public Opinion, or What Shall We Make of the Declining Faith of Middle Class African-Americans?," *PS: Political Science and Politics*, vol. 27, no. 1 (March 1994): pg. 36.

2. Bennett, William J. *The Moral Compass* (New York: Simon and Schuster, 1995), pg. 694.

3. Ronald Reagan expressed this view, pointing out once in a speech that the Washington Sunday paper had thirty-four full pages of help wanted ads and the Los Angeles paper fifty-two such pages. See Office of the Federal Register, *U.S. Weekly Compilation of Presidential Documents,* vol. 18 (September–December 1982).

4. Horwitz, Tony. "Minimum Wage Jobs Give Many Americans Only a Miserable Life," *Wall Street Journal,* November 12, 1993, pg. A4.

5. Mead, Lawrence M. *The New Politics of Poverty: The Nonworking Poor in America* (New York: Basic Books, 1992), pp. 93–94.

6. *Arizona Daily Star,* April 12, 1995, pg. 12A.

7. Bracey, Gerald W. "The Assessor Assessed: A 'Revisionist' Looks at a Critique of the Sandia Report," *Journal of Educational Research,* vol. 88, no. 3 (January/February 1995): pp. 141–142.

# 2

## HUNGER IN THE LAND OF PLENTY

*Janet Poppendieck*

### THE HUNGER PROBLEM NOW: SIZE AND SCOPE

In the United States, there have generally been three broad approaches to the measurement of hunger: inference from statistical information on income, behavioral indicators and surveys, and self-reports. Over time, the *inferential* approach has probably been the most frequently used. We know the amount of money required to purchase a minimally adequate diet. We have figures on the numbers of people living on incomes below levels that would reasonably permit them to allocate that amount to food purchase. Thus we can infer the number of people who are hungry or 'at risk' of hunger. In the United States, this may be easier than it is in some other first world nations because the entire U.S. system of poverty income thresholds, the so-called poverty line, is derived directly from the cost of a minimally adequate diet, the Economy Food Plan (EFP), a subsistence diet for emergency use developed by dieticians at the Agriculture Department. The logic by which this system was constructed sheds further light upon the challenges of measurement.

In short, household consumption surveys from the 1950s showed that, on average, U.S. households spent about a third of their income on food. Casting about for an operational definition of poverty in the early 1960s, Molly Orshansky of the Social Security Administration reasoned that a family could be considered poor if a third of its income was not sufficient to purchase a subsistence diet for its household size. She established poverty income thresholds for households of various sizes by multiplying the cost of the EFP by three. They are updated annually for inflation, but they do not change to reflect the declining share of income that the society as a whole spends on food purchases. That is, the poverty line embodies an absolute rather than a relative definition of poverty. Over time, the officially poor have fallen steadily further from the median.[1]

The federal poverty line remains a topic of controversy among academics and advocates concerned with poverty, but it makes estimates of inadequate food purchasing power relatively easy to compute. This was the approach used by the U.S. Senate Select Committee on Nutrition and Human Needs in the aftermath of the 1960 discovery of hunger.[2] The Committee, in a study that became a prototype for subsequent inferential assessments, reported that approximately 5.1 million people lived on total incomes less than the cost of the economy food plan, and another 9.3 million had incomes less that twice the cost of the plan for their household size. These 14.4 million people, the Committee concluded, had incomes so low that they would almost certainly suffer hunger and malnutrition unless they received food assistance; another 10.4 million officially poor people were at risk, and yet another thirteen million 'near poor' had incomes low enough to make hunger a real possibility. The Committee went on to point out that the patently inadequate family food assistance programs were serving only a combined total of 6.4 million persons and that their aggregate expenditure fell far short of meeting the gap between poor people's incomes and the cost of the economy food plan.[3] More recently, the inferential approach was used by the Tufts University Center on Hunger, Poverty, and Nutrition Policy to come up with an estimate of twenty-eight million hungry Americans in 1991.[4]

A second approach to measurement might be labeled 'behavioral.' We conclude that people are hungry if we observe them engaging in activities to obtain food that we believe most people would find distasteful: foraging in dustbins and skips, waiting in long lines under unpleasant conditions for a meal at a soup kitchen, taking food from plates left on tables at restaurants. In essence, we believe that most people would not do these things unless they were hungry, so we use them as behavioral indicators of hunger. In the early 1980s, in the aftermath of the Reagan administration budget cuts, the U.S. Conference of Mayors began conducting surveys of growing numbers at soup kitchens and food pantries. In subsequent years, the mayors issued annual updates on hunger and homelessness in American cities, reporting each year an overall growth in the numbers of people seeking emergency food. In 1994 the behavioral approach culminated in the release of a report by Second Harvest, the national food bank network. A consulting firm that conducted a massive study of thirty-four member banks and then projected the results to the organization's total membership of 185 banks, reported that twenty-six million people had received food from soup kitchens and food pantries supplied by Second Harvest member food banks. Assuming that some of them had used more than one such program, Second Harvest projected the 'unduplicated count' of emergency food clients to be in the vicinity of 21.8 million individual persons.[5] Since Second Harvest does not collect statistics on agencies supplied by food banks that are not Second Harvest members, and since no one familiar with the haphazard nature of the emergency food network would claim that it reaches all who are hungry, the Second Harvest report of nearly twenty-two million people makes the Tufts estimate of twenty-eight million appear quite credible, if one assumes that going to a soup kitchen or food pantry is an indicator of hunger.

For the advocates of the food security approach, resort to an emergency food provider, as noted above, is *prima facie* evidence of hunger. On the other hand, many observers question whether all clients at soup kitchens and food pantries would actually go hungry without this emergency food assistance; some would simply have less money to spend on other portions of the household budget. Ed Meese, an adviser to President Ronald Reagan, made his skepticism famous when he told reporters questioning him about growing lines at Washington area soup kitchens that the Reagan administration had received "considerable information that people go to soup kitchens because the food is free and that's easier than paying for it."[6] The Reagan administration's contention that there were no reliable measures of hunger and that reports of hunger were based upon 'anecdotal stuff' led hunger activists to collaborate with social scientists and public health professionals to construct more reliable and convincing measures.

The largest of these efforts has been the Community Childhood Hunger Identification Project (CCHIP). The CCHIP relies upon a point-prevalence survey in which members of households with at least one child and incomes below 18.5 percent of the federal poverty line are asked a series of questions about household food supply and strategies for coping with household food shortages, that is, "Thinking about the past thirty days, how many days was your household out of money to buy food to make a meal?"7 Households are designated as 'hungry' if their answers on five of eight key dimensions indicate inadequate food resources.

The CCHIP approach was carefully designed and meticulously tested before local studies were conducted in seven sites across the nation, and, although it has its critics, its findings have received wide acceptance in both government circles and the medical and public health community. Based on its findings from 2,335 interviews in seven low income communities, CCHIP estimated in 1991 that there were approximately 5.5 million hungry children under the age of 12 and that another six million children were at risk of hunger because they lived in households experiencing food insufficiency due to inadequate resources. A far simpler survey approach was taken by Dr. Vincent Breglio whose conservative credentials as a 'Republican Pollster' with clients including the *Wall Street Journal* gave special credibility to his efforts in some circles. Breglio, repeating a technique used a decade earlier by Louis Harris, simply asked the 1000 respondents in his random phone survey if they knew anyone who was hungry. He produced an estimate of thirty million hungry people.8

The Second Harvest study looked at the housing situation of respondents as well as such standard demographic variables as age, sex, family structure and race and ethnicity. Second Harvest found that 18.1 percent of clients served by its network were homeless and another 5.4 percent live in marginal housing situations. Children age 17 or younger account for more than two-fifths (42.9 percent) of all emergency food clients but make up 25.9 percent of the total U.S. population; while 8.1 percent of all Second Harvest clients are elderly, a figure that rises to twenty-two percent of soup kitchen clients, as compared with 12.5 percent of the general U.S. population. Women comprise more than two-thirds of adult pantry clients; while men comprise sixty-two percent of soup kitchen clients. Single-parent households comprise 26.8 percent of all households served by the Second Harvest network and 55.5 percent of those households with children. A majority of food recipients are white (50.9 percent of clients as compared with 75.6

percent of the American population), but minority groups are over-represented. African-Americans constitute nearly a third (32.9 percent) of food recipients as compared to 11.7 percent of the U.S. population. Native Americans are substantially over-represented and Latinos are slightly over-represented, while Asian-Americans are under-represented, in comparison with their numbers in the total population. The study also collected data on employment and income and found that 17.2 percent of all clients are disabled; nearly a third (31.6 percent) of all client households have someone employed. Finally, nearly three-quarters of all client households have incomes under $10,000 annually and 87.9 percent have annual household incomes below $14,000.[9]

## EXPLANATIONS FOR HUNGER

Poverty has virtually always been the prime suspect in explaining hunger in the U.S. When reports of hunger began to appear with increasing frequency in the early 1980s, the search for explanations focused upon two related questions: Why were more people poor? And why were the food assistance programs that advocates had worked so hard to expand and reform during the 1970s not preventing hunger among those who fell into poverty? On a day-to-day basis, these questions surfaced primarily in attempts to explain the rising demand for emergency food at soup kitchens and food pantries. As providers and advocates surveyed applicants in an effort to understand the rapid expansion of demand, there emerged a portrait of people caught between declining income and rising costs. Four factors were generally identified as contributors to the growing need for emergency assistance in the 1980s, and to varying degrees they all continue to explain the persistence of need in the 1990s: (1) cutbacks in food assistance programs, (2) deterioration of the ability of the economy to generate jobs and incomes, (3) erosion of the value of public assistance benefits, and (4) sharp increases in shelter and other costs.

Cutbacks in food assistance are listed first, not because they are the primary explanation but because they were the trigger that put hunger on the public agenda. Ronald Reagan was elected in 1980 claiming a mandate to cut domestic social spending. By including food assistance programs among those targeted for cuts, the administration almost guaranteed that the issue would be framed in terms of hunger, since food assistance had so active a network of dedicated advocates. The Congressional Budget Office has estimated that over the period encompassed by fiscal years 1982 to 1985, $12.2 billion less was available for food aid than would have been true had the laws remained unchanged. Added to the effects of other cuts in social spending, and implemented in the midst of a particularly deep recession, the nutrition cuts hurt poor people and enraged advocates. Frustrated in their attempts to expand programs or even resist cuts, anti-hunger activists threw themselves into the task of documenting the growth of hunger and specifying the social circumstances that led so many people to the soup kitchen and food pantry door.

The reality they found, however, was not simply the fallout from budget cuts. Writing in the early 1980s, Michael Harrington, whose book *The Other America* had aroused the nation to the plight of the poor in the 1960s, summarized the matter this way: "the new American poverty is not...the creation of Ronald Reagan. He made the worst of a bad thing, to be sure, scapegoating the poor for imaginary wrongs. But the structures of misery today are not simply the work of the ideological rigidity of a President.... They are the results of massive economic and social transformations...."[10]

In short, as the economies of Europe and the Pacific developed and markets internationalized, U.S. industries found themselves in competition with the products of a powerful combination of advanced technology and low wage workers. Multinational corporations with little or no loyalty to particular societies moved capital around the globe to find its most profitable application, leaving behind empty smokestacks and ruined communities in the industrial heartland of the U.S. Even those firms that remained in the U.S. adapted to the new reality in ways that hurt workers: they automated, streamlined, downsized, and engaged in a frenzy of leveraged buyouts and hostile takeovers.

Recessions in both the early 1980s and the early 1990s intensified the pace of these trends and made them more visible. Average unemployment rates have been rising for the last quarter century in virtually all Western industrialized nations.[11] In the U.S., unemployment averaged

4.6 percent in the 1968–1973 period and 7.2 percent in the 1980–1989 period, reaching well over nine percent in the recession of the early 1980s and climbing to 7.7 percent in the milder recession of the early 1990s. Coupled with a reduction in the proportion of the unemployed who received unemployment compensation and a drop in the fraction who ever got their old jobs back, these rates spelled disaster for many once independent.[12]

The recession of the early 1980s hit particularly hard at workers who had held manufacturing jobs that paid relatively high wages and provided health insurance. These were the among the people who acquired the label 'new poor;' the General Accounting Office described them in a 1983 survey of clients at emergency food centers as "the breed of 'new poor,' members of families, young and able-bodied with homes in the suburbs. They now find themselves without work, with unemployment and savings accounts exhausted, and with diminishing hopes of being able to continue to meet their mortgages, automobile, and other payments."

When the new poor of the early 1980s did find new jobs, they countered other aspects of the global restructuring of the economy, aspects that continue in full force today. The new jobs were less likely to be in manufacturing, less likely to provide comprehensive fringe benefits and very likely to pay lower wages. The proportion of the labor force employed in the manufacturing sector fell by nearly a quarter between 1975 and 1990. Real wages, adjusted for inflation, dropped in private non-agricultural industries between 1973 and 1993, and adjusted average weekly earnings during the same period declined by nearly a fifth.[13] The decline in purchasing power has been even more pronounced at the very bottom, for workers earning the minimum wage. Despite increases in the national minimum in 1990 and 1991, the minimum wage has fallen steadily in its ability to protect a family from poverty. Throughout most of the 1960s and 1970s, the income earned by a person working full time at a minimum wage job was sufficient to keep a family of three out of official poverty. By 1994, a minimum wage job, forty hours a week, 52 weeks a year would not even keep a household of two above the poverty threshold; figured on the more typical thirty-five-hour week, the minimum wage does not now pay enough to keep a single individual above the poverty line.[14]

Wages are not the only source of income that has declined in value in recent decades. The erosion of the purchasing power of public assistance benefits is even more pronounced. By 1989, the average monthly AFDC benefit per family, adjusted for inflation, was worth only two-thirds of what it had been in 1970.[15] The decline in welfare benefits is not the result of a unified national policy; rather, it reflects the decisions of the fifty state legislatures. AFDC is a combined federal-state program, with each state defining its own standard of need (the amount of money that the state believes that families need in order to subsist) and establishing its own benefit level, generally considerably below its declared standard of need. The erosion of public assistance benefits that has been in progress for several decades generally reflects the states' failure to adjust benefits to keep up with inflation. Even in the federal income transfer program for elderly and disabled persons, Supplemental Security Income (SSI), which is indexed to inflation, state supplements are not tied to rising costs and most have failed to keep pace with prices. Single adults who do not qualify for either SSI or AFDC can turn to whatever state or local programs exist under the rubric of General Assistance, called by a variety of different names in different localities, but these programs are providing less support and are harder to obtain than in earlier years. The states of Michigan and Illinois recently ended general assistance altogether, and in the current assault on welfare, several other states are considering similar moves.

Inflation is the other side of the squeeze that has sent so many Americans to emergency food providers in the last fifteen years. As studies of the growing demand for emergency food piled up, one fact emerged with startling clarity: a sharp rise in shelter costs was forcing many impoverished Americans, both the working poor and those supported by public income transfers, into a dilemma often labeled 'heat or eat.' With shelter costs consuming an ever greater share of the household budget, more and more families were finding themselves without adequate resources for food. In 1980, the federal government set a benchmark of thirty percent of family income as the appropriate ceiling for rents; higher figures were defined as excessive.[16] A 1985 Census Bureau survey found twenty-two million families paying rents in excess of this standard; forty-five percent of all households with incomes below the official poverty threshold spent seventy percent or more of their income for rent and utilities. No wonder they could not afford to purchase adequate food!

For some the escalating burden of shelter became too much to bear, and homelessness joined hunger as both symbol and symptom of the escalation of poverty. Once a person becomes homeless, he or she almost automatically joins the ranks of the hungry, or at least the ranks of those dependent upon soup kitchens and other emergency providers for food. Without access to kitchen facilities, any hope of economical eating vanishes, and although food stamps can be used in restaurants under certain circumstances, they were never designed to cover the costs of eating out on a full-time basis. Since 'the homeless' constitute a fairly large segment of 'the hungry,' nearly anything that causes homelessness contributes to the rise of hunger.

Taken together, these factors—the underlying deterioration of the economy, the impact of recession, the erosion of public assistance benefits, and the rise in shelter costs—go a long way toward explaining why more Americans are poor, but they do not immediately explain why the public food assistance programs that grew out of the New Deal of the 1930s and the War on Poverty of the 1960s have not been sufficient to prevent hunger among poor people. More specifically, they do not explain why the food stamp program, the nation's first line of defense in any war against hunger, has permitted so many casualties.

Many of the nation's first emergency food pantries were established primarily to provide families experiencing a 'food emergency' with a three-day supply of food which would tide them over during the waiting period for expedited (emergency) food stamps. Once they were in business, however, many pantries began to see the same families returning month after month. Inquiring as to what had become of the food stamps, they received a simple answer: they ran out. Other applicants whose need was convincing to pantry operators reported that they were unaware of the stamp program, did not know how to apply for it, did not believe they were eligible, had applied and been turned down, or did not want to apply. Some were food stamp dropouts who had given up the attempt to secure the benefits, discouraged by the lengthy paperwork requirements and the demanding application and certification process, or unable for logistical reasons (hours of operation, location) to access a food stamp office.[17]

Several factors combine to explain why food stamps run out before the month is over, why so many needy people are not eligible for the stamps and why others believe they are ineligible or do not want to apply. First, food stamps were never designed to provide a full month's supply of food, except for families with no cash income whatsoever. Benefit levels are calculated on the assumption that families can allocate thirty percent of their income (after certain deductions) to food purchase. The stamp allotment is set at the cost of the Thrifty Food Plan (TFP), discounted by thirty percent of household income. When the program was first designed, the thirty percent assumption, derived from the same information used to set the poverty line, may have made sense. Families could allocate thirty percent of income for food when they could secure shelter for a quarter of their income, when fuel was cheap, when VCRs, faxes, and home computers had not yet been invented. Households now struggling to allocate thirty percent of income to food are struggling against much greater odds. With rent consuming sixty percent or more of income for well over half of poor renters, it is not surprising that they cannot find cash to supplement their food stamps up to the TFP level.

What about those who simply don't apply? Studies of eligible nonparticipants have generally identified three contributing factors: people were unaware of their eligibility, did not believe that they needed the stamps, or felt that the costs of participation in terms of stigma, travel to the program office or the rigors of the certification process outweighed the benefits. In general, participation rates decline with the size of the expected benefits. Thus, while only sixty percent of eligible households were participating in August 1984, nearly eighty percent of the benefits payable if all eligible households had participated were disbursed.[18]

Food stamps are the only food assistance program that might be expected to prevent hunger across the board. None of the other programs is a general entitlement. Most are limited to specific groups, children or the elderly, for example. Several, like the WIC program, are limited by available funding, they are not entitlements at all. Others are entitlements only if some local agency chooses to make the program available. Free and reduced price school meals, for example, are an entitlement for income eligible children who attend schools that offer the programs, but schools are not required to do so. And finally, none of these programs is intended to provide access to a basic diet; all are supplemental in nature, providing a particular meal, or a meal and a snack. Packaged together, the school meal, child and adult care feeding, senior meals, and WIC programs can certainly help a poor household stretch its food dollars—and its food stamps—and it is probable that they provide a margin of safety that helps many families avoid hunger. Both the school meal programs and WIC set eligibility ceilings at a more realistic 18.5 percent of poverty, enabling them to assist families not eligible for food stamps.

Reprinted from "The USA: Hunger in the Land of Plenty" in *First World Hunger: Food Security and Welfare Politics,* edited by Graham Riches (New York: St. Martin's Press, 1997). Copyright ©1997 Macmillan Press Ltd. Used with permission of the publisher.

NOTES

1. Bell, Winifred. *Contemporary Social Welfare, second edition* (New York: Macmillan, 1987).
2. U.S. Senate Select Committee on Nutrition and Human Needs, 91st Congress, First Session. *The Food Gap: Poverty and Malnutrition in the United States* (Washington, DC: U.S. Government Printing Office, 1969).
3. Assuming that food assistance benefits reduced the incidence of actual hunger, the Committee calculated what it called a 'food income gap.' It estimated that the total aggregate income of households below the poverty level fell ten billion dollars short of what they would need to avoid poverty, and that a third of that gap should be allocated to food, and it subtracted total spending on food assistance benefits from this figure to come up with a total figure by which the income of poor households, including food assistance as in-kind income, fell short of the minimum they would need to purchase the economy food plan (*The Food Gap*, pg. 22).
4. Center on Hunger, Poverty, and Nutritional Policy. *Summary of U.S. Hunger Estimates: 1984 to the Present* (Medford: Tufts University, March 1993).
5. VanAmburg Group. *Second Harvest 1993 National Research Study* (Erie, PA: VanAmburg Group, 1994).

6. Newton, E. "All the Hungry People," *New York Daily News Magazine*, March 9, 1986, pg. 12.

7. Wheler, C.A. and R.I. Scott and J.J. Anderson. "The Community Childhood Hunger Identification Project: A Model of Domestic Hunger—Demonstration Project in Seattle, Washington," *Journal of Nutritional Education*, vol. 24 no. 1, 1992 supplement, pg. 31S.

8. *Summary of U.S. Hunger Estimates*, op. cit.

9. Second Harvest 1993 National Research Study.

10. Harrington, Michael. *The New American Poverty* (New York: Penguin Books, 1985).

11. McFate, K. "Introduction: Western States in the New World Order," in K. McFate, R. Lawson, and W.J. Wilson (eds.), *Poverty, Inequality, and the Future of Social Policy* (New York: Russell Sage Foundation, 1995) pg. 3.

12. Burt, Martha R. *Over the Edge: The Growth of Homelessness in the 1980s* (New York: Russell Sage Foundation, 1992), pp. 99–100; Center on Hunger, Poverty, and Nutritional Policy, *Statement on Key Welfare Reform Issues: Empirical Evidence*, (Medford: Tufts University, 1995) pg. 17.

13. *Statement on Key Welfare Reform Issues*, pg. 15.

14. *Over the Edge*, pp. 73–75.

15. Ibid., pp. 84–85.

16. Chelf, Carl P. *Controversial Issues in Social Welfare Policy: Government and the Pursuit of Happiness* (Newbury Park, CA: Sage Publications, 1992) pg. 57.

17. Physicians Task Force on Hunger in America. *Hunger in America: The Growing Epidemic* (Middletown, CT: Wesleyan University Press, 1985); A.L. De Havenon, *The Tyranny of Indifference and the Re-Institutionalization of Hunger, Homelessness, and Poor Health* (New York: East Harlem Interfaith Welfare Committee, 1988), K. Clancy, J. Bowering, and J. Poppendieck, "Characteristics of a Random Sample of Emergency Food Program Users in New York: I. Food Pantries," *American Journal of Public Health* no. 81, 1991, pp. 153–174.

This overview, culled from local reports and extended interviews with emergency food providers, was recently confirmed by a large-scale study of emergency food clients conducted on behalf of Second Harvest, the food bank network (*Second Harvest 1993 National Research Study*, pp. 150–156). The Second Harvest study found that just under half of the more than 6000 pantry clients interviewed for the study were currently receiving food stamps; of those, sixty-five percent had been receiving them for a year or more. Interviewers asked clients who received food stamps how long their stamps usually lasted; more than four-fifths reported that they ran out by the end of the third week of the food stamp month. Among those not receiving stamps, close to half had ever applied for them. Of these, 43.2 percent were awaiting approval, 37.6 percent had been rejected and another 16.8 percent had previously received them but were no longer doing so at the time of the interview. Among the slightly larger group who had never applied, 28.6 percent believed that they did not qualify and another 28.6 percent did not want to apply, while approximately eleven percent did not know about the program or did not know enough about it to apply and additional, smaller percentages were deterred by logistical reasons such as lack of transportation to a program office.

18. Allin, S. and H. Beebout, P. Doyle and C. Trippe. "Current Perspectives on Food Stamp Program Participation," in C. Trippe, N. Heiser, and H. Beebout (eds.), *Food Stamp Policy Issues: Results from Recent Research* (Washington DC: U.S. Department of Agriculture, 1990) pp. 23–35.

# 3

## THE INNER CITY: WHEN WORK DISAPPEARS

### William Julius Wilson

Joblessness and declining wages are closely related to the recent growth in ghetto poverty. The most dramatic increases in ghetto poverty occurred between 1970 and 1980, and they were mostly confined to the large industrial metropolises of the Northeast and Midwest regions that experienced massive industrial restructuring and loss of blue collar jobs during that decade. But the rise in ghetto poverty was not the only problem. Industrial restructuring had devastating effects on the social organization of many inner city neighborhoods in these regions. The fate of the West Side black community of North Lawndale vividly exemplifies the cumulative process of economic and social dislocation that has swept through Chicago's inner city.

After more than a quarter century of continuous deterioration, North Lawndale resembles a war zone. Since 1960, nearly half of its housing stock has disappeared; the remaining units are mostly run down or dilapidated. Two large factories anchored the economy of this West Side neighborhood in its good days—the Hawthorne plant of Western Electric, which employed over 43,000 workers; and an International Harvester plant with 14,000 workers. The world headquarters for Sears, Roebuck and Company was located there, providing another 10,000 jobs. The neighborhood also had a Copenhagen snuff plant, a Sunbeam factory, and a Zenith factory, a Deli Farm food market, an Alden's catalog store, and a U.S. Post Office bulk station. But conditions rapidly changed. Harvester closed its doors in the late 1960s. Sears moved most of its offices to the Loop in downtown Chicago in 1973; a catalog distribution center with a workforce of 3,000 initially remained in the neighborhood but was relocated outside the state of Illinois in 1987. The Hawthorne plant gradually phased out its operations and finally shut down in 1984.

The departure of the big plants triggered the demise or exodus of the smaller stores, the banks, and other businesses that relied on the wages paid by the large employers. To make matters worse, scores of stores were forced out of business or pushed out of the neighborhoods by insurance companies in the wake of the 1968 riots that swept through Chicago's West Side after the assassination of Dr. Martin Luther King, Jr. Others were simply burned or abandoned. It has been estimated that the community lost seventy-five percent of its business establishments from 1960 to 1970 alone. In 1986, North Lawndale, with a population of over 66,000, had only one bank and one super-market; but it was also home to forty-eight state lottery agents, fifty currency exchanges, and ninety-nine licensed liquor stores and bars.

The impact of industrial restructuring on inner city employment is clearly apparent to urban blacks. A survey posed the following question: "Over the past five or ten years, how many friends of yours have lost their jobs because the place where they worked shutdown—would you say none, a few, some, or most?" Only twenty-six percent of the black residents in the sample reported that none of their friends had lost jobs because their workplace shut down. Nearly half of the employed black fathers and mothers in the survey stated that they considered themselves to be at high risk of losing their jobs because of plant shutdowns.

Some of the inner city neighborhoods have experienced more visible job losses then others. Residents of the inner city are keenly aware of the rapid depletion of job opportunities. A 33-year-old unmarried black male of North Lawndale who is employed as a clerical worker stated: "Because of the way the economy is structured, we're losing more jobs. Chicago is losing jobs by the thousands. There just aren't any starting companies here and it is harder to find a job compared to what it was years ago."

A similar view was expressed by a 41-year-old black female, also from North Lawndale, who works as a nurse's aide:

*"Chicago is really full of people. Everybody can't get a good job. They don't have enough good jobs to provide for everybody. I don't think they have enough jobs period.... And all the factories and the places, they closed up and moved out of the city and stuff like that, you know. I guess it's one of the reasons they haven't got too many jobs now, 'cause a lot of the factories and business have moved out. So that way it's less jobs for a lot of people."*

Respondents from other neighborhoods also reported on the impact of industrial restructuring. According to a 33-year-old South Side janitor:

*"The machines are putting a lot of people out of jobs. I worked for* Time *magazine for seven years on a videograph printer and they come along with the A.B. Dick printer, it cost them half a million dollars: they did what we did in half the time, eliminating two shifts."*

"Jobs were plentiful in the past," stated a 29-year-old unemployed black male who lives in one of the poorest neighborhoods on the South Side. "You could walk out of the house and get a job. Maybe not what you want but you could get a job. Now, you can't find anything. A lot of people in this neighborhood, they want to work but they can't get work. A few, but a very few, they just don't want to work. The majority they want to work but they can't find work."

Finally, a 41-year-old hospital worker from another impoverished South Side neighborhood associated declining employment opportunities with decreasing skill levels:

*"Most of the jobs have moved out of Chicago. Factory jobs have moved out. There are no jobs here. Not like it was twenty, thirty years ago. And people aren't skilled enough for the jobs that are here. You don't have enough skilled and educated people to fill them."*

Blacks living in central cities have less access to employment, as measured by the ratio of jobs to people and the average travel time to and from work, than do central-city whites. Moreover, unlike most other groups of workers across the urban/suburban divide, less educated central city blacks receive lower wages than suburban blacks who have similar levels of education. And the decline in earnings of central city blacks is related to the decentralization of employment—the movement of jobs from cities to the suburbs—in metropolitan areas.

The African-Americans surveyed clearly recognized a spatial mismatch of jobs. Both black men and black women saw greater job prospects outside the city. For example, only one-third of black fathers from areas with poverty rates of at least thirty percent reported that their best opportunities for employment were to be found in the city. Getting to suburban jobs is especially problematic for the jobless individuals in the survey because only twenty-eight percent have access to an automobile. This rate falls even further to eighteen percent for those living in the ghetto areas.

Among two-car middle class and affluent families, commuting is accepted as a fact of life; but it occurs in a context of safe school environments for children, more available and accessible day care, and higher incomes to support mobile, away-from-home lifestyles. In a multi-tiered job market that requires substantial resources for participation, most inner city minorities must rely on public transportation systems that rarely provide easy and quick access to suburban locations. A 32-year-old unemployed South Side welfare mother described the problem this way:

> *"There's not enough jobs. I think Chicago's the only city that does not have a lot of opportunities opening in it. There's not enough factories, there's not enough work. Most all the good jobs are in the suburbs. Sometimes it's hard for the people in the city to get to the suburbs, because everybody don't own a car. Everybody don't drive."*

An unemployed South Side black male had this to say: "Most of the time…the places be too far and you need transportation and I don't have none right now. If I had some I'd probably be able to get one (a job)."

But the problem is not simply one of transportation and the length of commuting time. There is also the problem of the travel expense and of whether the long trek to the suburbs is actually worth it in terms of the income earned—after all, owning a car creates expenses far beyond the purchase price, including insurance, which is much more costly for city dwellers than it is for suburban motorists. "If you work in the suburbs you gotta have a car," stated an unmarried welfare mother of three children who lives on Chicago's West Side, "then you gotta buy gas. You spending more getting to the suburbs to work than you is getting paid, so you still ain't getting nowhere."

One unemployed 36-year-old black man from the West Side of Chicago actually quit his suburban job because of the transportation problem. "It was more expensive going to work in Naperville, transportation and all, and it wasn't worth it.... I was spending more money getting to work than I earned working."

If transportation poses a problem for those who have to commute to work from the inner city to the suburbs, it can also hinder poor ghetto residents' ability to travel to the suburbs just to seek employment. For example, one unemployed man who lives on the South Side had just gone to O'Hare Airport looking for work with no luck. His complaint: "The money I spent yesterday, I could have kept that in my pocket. 'Cause you know I must have spent about $7 or somethin'. I could have kept that."

Finally, in addition to enduring the search-and-travel costs, inner city black workers often confront racial harassment when they enter suburban communities. A 38-year-old South Side divorced mother of two children who works as a hotel cashier described the problems experienced by her son and his coworker in one of Chicago's suburbs:

*"My son, who works in Carol Stream, an all-white community, they've been stopped by a policeman two or three times asking them why they're in the community. And they're trying to go to work. They want everyone to stay in their own place. That's what society wants. And they followed them all the way to work to make sure. 'Cause it's an all-white neighborhood. But there are no jobs in the black neighborhoods. They got to go way out there to get a job."*

These informal observations on the difficulties and cost of travel to suburban employment are consistent with the results of a recent study by the labor economists Harry J. Holzer, Keith R. Ihlandfeldt, and David L. Sjoquist. In addition to finding that the lack of automobile ownership among inner city blacks contributed significantly to their lower wages and lower rate of employment, these authors also reported that African-Americans "spend more time traveling to work than whites," that "the time cost per mile traveled is significantly higher for blacks," and that the resulting gains are relatively small. Overall, their results suggest that the amount of time and money spent in commuting, when compared with the actual income that accrues to inner city blacks in low-skill jobs in the suburbs, acts to discourage poor people from seeking employment far from their own neighborhoods. Holzer and his colleagues concluded that it was quite rational for blacks to reject these search-and-travel choices when assessing their position in the job market.

Changes in the industrial and occupational mix, including the removal of jobs from urban centers to suburban corridors, represent external factors that have helped to elevate joblessness among inner city blacks.

The increase in the proportion of jobless adults in the inner city is also related to changes in the class, racial, and age composition of such neighborhoods—changes that have led to greater concentrations of poverty. Concentrated poverty is positively associated with joblessness. That is, when the former appears, the latter is found as well. Poor people today are far more likely to be unemployed or out of the labor force than in previous years. In addition to the effects of joblessness, inner city neighborhoods have experienced a growing concentration of poverty for several other reasons, including (1) the out-migration of non-poor black families; (2) the exodus of non-poor white and other non-black families; and (3) the rise in the number of residents who have become poor while living in these areas. Additional research on the growth of concentrated poverty suggests another factor: the movement of poor people into a neighborhood. And one more factor should be added to this mix: changes in the age structure of the community.

One of the important demographic shifts that had an impact on the upturn in the jobless rate has been the change in the age structure of inner city ghetto neighborhoods. In the three Bronzeville neighborhoods of Douglas, Grand Boulevard, and Washington Park, the proportion of those ages 20–64 that roughly approximate the prime-age workforce has declined in all three neighborhoods since 1950, whereas the proportion of people age 65 and over has increased. Of the adults age 20 and over, the proportion of prime-age people declined by seventeen percent in Grand Boulevard, sixteen percent in Douglas, and twelve percent in Washington Park between 1950 and 1990. The smaller the percentage of prime-age adults in a population, the lower the proportion of residents who are likely to be employed. The proportion of residents aged 5–19 increased sharply in each neighborhood from 1950 to 1990, suggesting that the growth in the proportion of teenagers also contributed to the rise in the jobless rate. However, if we consider the fact that male employment in these neighborhoods declined by a phenomenal forty-six percent between 1950 and 1990, these demographic changes obviously can account for only a fraction, albeit a significant fraction, of the high proportion of the area's jobless adults.

The rise in the proportion of jobless adults in the Bronzeville neighborhoods has been accompanied by an incredible depopulation—a decline of sixty-six percent in the three neighborhoods combined—that magnifies the problems of the new poverty neighborhoods. As the population drops and the proportion of non-working adults rises, basic neighborhood institutions are more difficult to maintain: stores, banks, credit institutions, restaurants, dry cleaners, gas stations, medical doctors, and so on lose regular and potential patrons. Churches are experiencing dwindling numbers of parishioners and shrinking resources; recreational facilities, block clubs, community groups, and other informal organizations also suffer. As these organizations decline, the means of formal and informal social control in the neighborhood becomes weaker. Levels of crime and street violence increase as a result, leading to further deterioration of the neighborhood.

The more rapid the neighborhood deterioration, the greater the institutional disinvestment. In the 1960s and 1970s, neighborhoods plagued by heavy abandonment were frequently 'red-lined' (identified as areas that should not receive or be recommended for mortgage loans or insurance); this paralyzed the housing market, lowered property values, and further encouraged landlord abandonment. The enactment of federal and state community reinvestment legislation in the 1970s curbed the practice of open redlining. Nonetheless, prudent lenders will exercise increased caution in advancing mortgages, particularly in neighborhoods marked by strong indication of owner disinvestment and early abandonment.

As the neighborhood disintegrates, those who are able to leave depart in increasing numbers; among these are many working and middle class families. The lower population density creates additional problems. Abandoned buildings increase and often serve as havens for crack use and other illegal enterprises that give criminals footholds in the community. Precipitous declines in density also make it even more difficult to sustain or develop a sense of community. The feeling of safety in numbers is completely lacking in such neighborhoods.

Also, since 1980, a fundamental shift in the federal government's support for basic urban programs has aggravated the problems of joblessness and social organization in the new poverty neighborhoods. The Reagan and Bush administrations—proponents of the New Federalism—sharply cut spending on direct aid to cities, including general revenue sharing, urban mass transit, public service jobs and job training, compensatory education, social service block grants, local public works, economic development assistance, and urban development action grants. In 1980, the federal contribution to city budgets was eighteen percent; by 1990 it had dropped to 6.4 percent. In addition, the economic recession which began in the Northeast in 1989 and lasted until the early 1990s sharply reduced those revenues that the cities themselves generated, thereby creating budget deficits that resulted in further cutbacks in basic services and programs along with increases in local taxes.

For many cities, especially the older cities of the East and Midwest, the combination of the New Federalism and the recession led to the worst fiscal and service crisis since the Depression. Cities have become increasingly under-serviced, and many have been on the brink of bankruptcy. They have therefore not been in a position to combat effectively three unhealthy social conditions that have emerged or become prominent since 1980: (1) the prevalence of crack cocaine addiction and the violent crime associated with it; (2) the AIDS epidemic and its escalating public health costs; and (3) the sharp rise in the homeless population not only for individuals but for whole families as well.

Although drug addiction and its attendant violence, AIDS and its toll on public health resources, and homelessness are found in many American communities, their impact on the ghetto is profound. These communities, whose residents have been pushed to the margins of society, have few resources with which to combat these social ills that arose in the 1980s. Fiscally strapped cities have watched helplessly as these problems—exacerbated by the new poverty, the decline of social organization in the jobless neighborhoods, and the reduction of social services—have made the city at large seem a dangerous and threatening place in which to live. Accordingly, working and middle class urban residents continue to relocate in the suburbs. Thus, while joblessness and related social problems are on the rise in inner city neighborhoods, especially in those that represent the new poverty areas, the larger city has fewer and fewer resources with which to combat them.

Finally, policymakers indirectly contributed to the emergence of jobless ghettos by making decisions that have decreased the attractiveness of low-paying jobs and accelerated the relative decline in wages for low income workers. In particular, in the absence of an effective labor market policy, they have tolerated industry practices that undermine worker security, such as the reduction in benefits and the rise of involuntary part-time employment, and they have allowed the minimum wage to erode to its second-lowest level in purchasing power in forty years. After adjusting for inflation, the minimum wage is twenty-six percent below its average level in the 1970s. Moreover, they virtually eliminated AFDC benefits for families in which a mother is employed at least half-time. In the early 1970s, a working mother with two children whose wages equaled seventy-five percent of the amount designated as the poverty line could receive AFDC benefits as a wage supplement in forty-nine states; in 1995 only those in three states could. Even with the expansion of the earned income tax credit (a wage subsidy for the working poor) such policies make it difficult for poor workers to support their families and protect their children. The erosion of wages and benefits force many low income workers in the inner city to move or remain on welfare.

# 4

## THE CAUSES OF HOMELESSNESS

### Paul Koegel, M. Audrey Burnam, and Jim Baumohl

Imagine the children's game of musical chairs, but played with both an individual aim to keep a chair and a collective goal to keep everyone seated. Imagine as well that in this game not only are seats gradually removed, but the number of players is progressively increased.

At the start of the game, adjustments are made easily enough, and for a short time the collective goal is achieved. True, the number of seats decreases and the pool of individuals competing for them gets bigger, but those sitting down accommodate the others by sharing their chairs or allowing onto their laps. The seats are small, however, and there are limits to how much weight people can bear. Inevitably, some people find themselves standing, their numbers growing as time passes.

As the game continues, many small dramas unfold. Some of those seated on laps are pushed off, then allowed back again. Seats are periodically relinquished, and the appearance of an empty seat precipitates a scramble among those outside the circle. Indeed, many people move back and forth between standing up and sitting down, but the total number of people standing continues to grow, and the collective goal of the game becomes untenable.

Who gets left standing is not determined merely by chance. Some players are fast and strong; some are impaired. Some are unpleasant and disruptive, and others are very heavy: these players are unlikely to be invited onto an occupied chair. Some are timid, ashamed to enlist help, or perhaps just don't know any of the other players. Still others don't understand the rules of the game and wander through the scene.

The grossly disadvantaged are the first to lose their seats and the least likely to grab replacements; they are disproportionately present among those on their feet, particularly at the early stages of the game. Later, as there are fewer and fewer chairs and more and more people vying for them, they are joined by players whose disadvantages are more subtle. Inevitably, as the competition becomes more fierce, they share the floor with large numbers of the hale, hearty, and sociable.

So it has been with homelessness. A host of problems in society's needs-meeting mechanisms established the context in which homelessness was inevitable. Those affected first and profoundly were drawn from the most vulnerable of the poor. They were single minority males with little education and few occupational skills; they were those with severe mental illnesses and habits of substance abuse; they were those whose early childhood experiences left them ill prepared to take their place in a competitive world; they were those without friends and family to help them, or whose kith and kin were no better off. And more often than not, they did not have just one of these vulnerabilities.

## THE CAUSES OF HOMELESSNESS:
## AN INTEGRATED PERSPECTIVE

When widespread homelessness emerged in the early 1980s, explanations were of two sorts. On the one hand, the large numbers of troubled and troublesome people among the homeless poor suggested to some observers that homelessness was best explained by the personal limitations of those who became homeless. According to this perspective, people were homeless because something was wrong with them. They were severely mentally ill, for instance, or end-of-the-line substance abusers—people incapable of caring for themselves, unable to keep themselves housed, and newly visible because of drastic changes in policies that had previously kept them institutionalized in hospitals or jails. Or, they had trouble maintaining relationships and therefore lacked the protective buffer of supportive family and friends. Or, worst of all, they rejected conventional responsibilities and had chosen homelessness.

Liberal advocates of this perspective tended to see homeless people sympathetically: as victims of circumstances over which they had little control. Emphasis was placed on the role of failed mental health and substance abuse treatment policies, and advocates pressed for rehabilitation programs and better networks of community care. On the other hand, conservatives were more likely to impute willfulness and choice to homeless people. To press people to shoulder responsibility, they advocated policies designed to make homelessness less attractive, such as controlling the availability of subsistence services and stepping up legal sanctions against being homeless.

The other explanation put forward was that pervasive and rising homelessness was caused by structural factors; that is, that it was a function of the way our society's resources are organized and distributed. Those who favored this explanation emphasized a dramatically widening gap between the availability of low-cost housing and the income-generating ability of those on the lowest rungs of the housing ladder. They observed that the number of available low income housing units was rapidly diminishing just as the population of poor people in need of such housing was growing. Their equation was simple: too few housing units for too many poor people meant that growing numbers of the poor were unable to afford housing. The solution that was proposed was to expand the supply of low income housing.

Public rhetoric in the 1980s about the causes of homelessness was characterized by strident and generally sterile debate between defenders of these two positions. Many on the political left dismissed personal problems as inconsequential to the creation of homelessness, branding as apologists for inequality those who focused on the causal contributions of mental illness and substance abuse. In their view, this medicalized—or, worse, moralized—a fundamentally economic problem. While conceding that some among the homeless had serious personal problems, they denied that most homeless people were anything other than well-adjusted people who had fallen on hard times. Homeless people were 'just like you and me,' except that they were suffering the consequences of a breakdown in the needs-meeting structures of society. The rest of us were 'just a paycheck away.'

Their opponents cited the existence of a large proportion of homeless people with severe mental health, substance abuse, or behavioral problems as evidence that the structural arguments must be flawed. Many homeless people, they claimed, were fundamentally different from ordinary citizens. Pointing to studies documenting high rates of these debilitating conditions, they argued that the structuralists 'normalized' homeless people in order to elicit public sympathy and advance a policy agenda that had far more to do with eliminating poverty among housed individuals than with providing needed help to the homeless.

In fact, neither of these positions independently could accommodate a growing body of evidence. Narrowly defined structuralist arguments did not satisfactorily explain the high rates of mental disorder and substance abuse documented in carefully designed studies. But by the same token, arguments claiming that individual limitations caused homelessness turned a blind eye toward a well-developed body of scholarship suggesting a close historical relationship between homelessness and broader economic conditions, and ignored the changing social contexts in which poor people—including poor, non-institutionalized mentally ill, and substance-abusing adults—lived their lives. Moreover, they could not explain the distinctive demographics of contemporary homelessness, which did not resemble the broader group of those troubled by mental health and substance abuse problems, but instead, those groups at greatest disadvantage in our socioeconomic system. While acknowledging the contributing influences of structural events like deinstitutionalization (without necessarily recognizing their structural character), they continued to frame their explanations of homelessness largely in terms of the limitations of people. They ignored one of history's clear lessons: that the lives of all people, disabled or not, are embedded in circumstances shaped as much by structural factors as personal and biographical ones, and that in a permissive environment full of cheap flops and undemanding work, even outcasts largely remain housed.[1]

This article offers a structural explanation of homelessness that gives individual limitations their due. We will be concerned with the effects of the patterned deployment of society's resources, and within this framework will suggest why the ranks of the homeless are disproportionately filled with troubled and troublesome people.

PERVASIVE HOMELESSNESS: THE STRUCTURAL BASIS

The rise in homelessness over the last fifteen years has accompanied two broad trends, each of which has exacerbated the impact of the other. First, there has been steady erosion of the supply of rental housing affordable to those falling at or below the poverty level. Second, the pool of poor people competing for these increasingly scarce units has swelled at precisely the same time.

## THE DECLINE IN LOW-COST HOUSING

The nation's supply of low-cost rental housing has been shrinking for over twenty years. During the 1980s, changes in the federal tax structure, rising interest rates, and new financing practices removed incentives for private investors to produce new low-cost housing, and this occurred as the federal government dramatically scaled back the production and maintenance of public housing. Simultaneously, first-time buyers faced substantial difficulty in purchasing single family homes and thus remained renters. This intensified competition in the rental market and rapidly drove up rents. Further, low income housing units were lost to demolition, conversion, abandonment, and arson as redevelopment and gentrification reclaimed some inner city areas previously ceded to the poor. Others were lost as it became fiscally prudent for owners to disinvest and warehouse low income properties, especially in blighted areas. Contemporary building codes and land use regulation have made their replacement an ever more costly and arduous affair.

While there is room to question the precise mechanics of these processes and their relative importance, the end result is uncontroversial. Ample growth took place in the national housing stock throughout the 1980s, but not at the lower end of the market. The number of units renting for more than $800 per month (in 1987 dollars) increased by eighty-six percent between 1981 and 1987, but those renting for less than $300 *fell* by more than thirteen percent.[2] This continued a trend begun in the 1970s, when six percent of units renting for less than $300 were lost. Making a bad situation worse, the rental market was *tightest* among units renting for less than $300.[3] The vacancy rate among units renting for less than $150 stood at 3.8 percent in 1987, well below the five percent threshold that housing analysts usually consider essential to the normal functioning of the market.

This dismal situation was somewhat mitigated by a marked increase during this period in the number of renters receiving housing subsidies from the federal government, despite the draconian cuts experienced by the Department of Housing and Urban Development. Still, approximately two-thirds of poor renters received no such subsidies and remained extremely vulnerable to the impact of rising housing costs.

National figures mask extremes and local scarcities, of course. The availability of surplus elsewhere in and of itself is no incentive to move. (Generally speaking, a vacancy in Houston does no good for someone queued up for public housing in San Francisco or New York.) For instance, in Los Angeles, the cost of housing shifted to a much greater degree than national figures would suggest. After correcting for inflation, the proportion of units renting for more than $500 in Los Angeles County grew from fourteen percent in 1974 to forty-five percent in 1985. But this occurred at the expense of low-end units, which fell from thirty-five percent of the rental stock in 1974 to only sixteen percent by 1985. While the number of units renting for upwards of $750 per month rose by 320 percent in this time period, the number of units renting for $300 or less fell by forty-two percent, with vacancy rates in this low-end sector hovering around one percent. This bleak picture continued throughout the 1980s, during which time no net additions to the public housing stock occurred, and approximately 4,000 low-cost housing units (which had cost less than $350 per month) were demolished or converted annually.[4]

Not only the stock of multi-room units typically inhabited by poor families suffered significant losses during this period. Even more precipitous losses befell the stock of single room occupancy (SRO) hotels, the housing of last resort for those on society's margins, and a particularly important source of housing for poor single persons, including the severely mentally ill and down-and-out substance abusers.[5] This was especially the case in large cities. New York lost eighty-seven percent of its $200 per month or less SRO stock between 1970 and 1982. Chicago, in addition to experiencing sharp losses in SROs, experienced the complete eradication of cubicle hotels that had previously housed thousands of near-homeless individuals in its skid row area. By 1985, more than half the SRO housing that had existed in Los Angeles's downtown area had been destroyed, a process that was arrested only when the city's Community Redevelopment Agency placed a moratorium on downtown SRO demolition.[6]

## A GROWING POOL OF THE VULNERABLE POOR

A decrease in the supply of housing units at the lower end of the market is not necessarily bad, of course. Were the absolute number of people falling below the poverty level shrinking, a decline in low-end housing units could be interpreted as a healthy response of the housing market to changing demand. This was nor the case in the 1970s and 1980s, however, when just as the supply of low-cost housing began to decrease, the demand began to rise. Between 1970 and 1988, the number of poor people grew from 25.4 million to 31.9 million, an increase of almost twenty-six percent.

Several factors were responsible for increasing poverty during these years. For one, this period coincided exactly with the coming of age of those born during the 'baby boom,' the post-World War II birth explosion that lasted through 1964. But during the 1970s and 1980s, when huge numbers of good new jobs were required to absorb the boomers successfully, the American occupational structure was transformed by intensification of an older process called 'de-industrialization.' De-industrialization refers to a shift from a predominance of relatively high-paying, often unionized manufacturing jobs to lower-paying, often part-time or temporary service jobs that lack the same level of benefits and security. Ultimately, de-industrialization created a growing pool of young workers, particularly poorly educated women and people of minority status, who became mired in chronic unemployment or in jobs that kept them below the poverty line. Wages, work opportunities, and employment levels for these individuals fell precipitously between 1979 and 1993, even during periods of economic recovery.

A steady erosion of the real dollar value of public entitlements other than Social Security also contributed to growing poverty in the 1970s and 1980s. For instance, the monthly purchasing power of a family receiving Aid to Families with Dependent Children (AFDC) fell by almost one-third, from $568 in 1970 to $385 in 1984, a time during which rents increased significantly. A related development was the systematic tightening, particularly during the Reagan administration, of eligibility requirements for federal entitlements, which are more generous than aid provided by states and counties. This process left almost 500,000 previous recipients of AFDC without access to benefits in 1981 and an additional 300,000 with reduced benefits.[7] It also resulted in almost a half million disabled individuals being removed from the Supplemental Security Income (SSI) and Social Security Disability Insurance (SSDI) programs between 1981 and 1984.[8]

Yet another factor underlying the growing numbers of the poor was deinstitutionalization, which during the 1960s and 1970s propelled into the community a severely mentally ill population—once housed in state institutions—and foreclosed the option of prolonged hospitalization for their present day counterparts. The reliance of these individuals on public entitlements for income consigned most to poverty. Thus, a new and socially marginal population of poor individuals entered the pool of those competing for low-cost housing. Similarly, the decriminalization of public drunkenness in many states ensured that public inebriates, most of whom had previously spent considerable time in county jails and state hospitals, now sought housing in their communities.[9] Both of these groups made heavy use of the SRO hotels that, at the time of deinstitutionalization, were sufficiently plentiful to house them. But the rapid erosion of this housing in the 1970s did not bode well for such people or their successors.

Nor did the changing urban landscape. The skid row neighborhoods that had previously served as zones of tolerance for such people increasingly shrank. Moreover, loss of physical space was accompanied by a decimation of the *vocational* space they occupied. Day labor, which allows people to work intermittently as their functioning and motivation permit, was increasingly in short supply. At the same time, changes wrought by de-industrialization and both legal and illegal immigration created a larger, more competent, and more tractable pool of individuals vying for spot work. The growth of the temporary help industry meant that an increasing amount of temporary light industrial work—traditionally important to poor people and skid row denizens—was controlled by agents who screened out the least presentable job seekers.[10]

## INCREASING RENT BURDEN AND ITS CONSEQUENCES

The inevitable consequence of sharply rising housing prices and simultaneously decreasing wages and benefits was a growing mismatch between the supply of low-cost housing and the demand for it. By 1989 there was a deficit of five million units—2.8 million units for 7.8 million bottom-quartile renter households. In other words, there were nearly three poor households for every one unit affordable to them (costing thirty percent of their income, or less).

Because of the dearth of low-cost housing, poor households began to spend more of their income on rent, increasingly becoming 'shelter poor.'[11] By 1978, seventy-two percent of poor renter households were spending at least thirty-five percent of their income on rent. By 1985, this percentage rose to almost eighty percent. Even more disturbing, sixty-four percent spent more than half their income on rent. Again, these national averages mask regional extremes. In areas of the country where the low income housing market was particularly tight, the situation was worse. By 1985, seventy-four percent of poor households in Los Angeles spent more than half their income on rent.[12]

As their situations worsened, poor households increasingly experienced many of the problems that leave people most vulnerable to homelessness (such as substance abuse and domestic violence). Over time, too, the strain reduced their capacity to support unproductive household members. This latter point is worth highlighting. In good times, when households are less crowded, when budgets are less tight, and when levels of stress are low, it is far easier for an unemployed relative or friend to feel welcome on the couch, or for a severely mentally ill relative to feel comfortable within the household, just as it is easier for household members to accommodate them. Under adverse conditions, such makeshift arrangements are prone to unravel, either because the tense household climate prompts such peripheral household members to leave, or because the household's diminished capacity to provide support leads to their expulsion.

Throughout the 1970s and 1980s, poor people—particularly the impaired among them—faced a growing set of pressures that included a dearth of affordable housing, a disappearance of the housing on which the most unstable had relied, and a diminished ability to support themselves either through entitlements or conventional or makeshift labor. Households barely making do increasingly found themselves under financial and interpersonal stress that only made a bad situation worse. Such pressures have a cumulative impact, culminating in the pervasive homelessness we have begun to take for granted.

Once homelessness became an established phenomenon, it fed on itself, not only because the structural forces responsible for it were intensifying, but because the very pervasiveness of homelessness robbed it of some stigma. Public shelters increasingly became incorporated into the coping strategies of poor individuals and households, particularly African-American households. For a young, unemployed man struggling against an uneasy welcome in a relative's household, a municipal shelter could provide an alternative that lessened the possibility of permanently exhausting an important resource. For a woman with young children, cramped in her mother's apartment and unable to afford market housing, a few months in a homeless shelter might provide access to public or subsidized housing, offering her a chance to form her own household. With the establishment of homelessness as a social reality, then, new possibilities were added to the myriad makeshifts upon which poor people always had relied for survival. From safety valve to resource in times of transition, the function of shelter was changing.

## CONCLUSION

Given a structural context that fosters homelessness, people may be at risk because of their economic situations, their demographic characteristics, their disabilities, their childhood histories, their access to family and friends, their personalities, or their experience of any number of situational crises. Conceivably, any of these alone can trigger homelessness. Most often, however, they act in combination, probably because they are all so interrelated. Risk factors, in other words, are almost invariably bundled; very rarely does one alone cause homelessness. And the chances that one will acquire such bundles are not evenly distributed at the outset of the game. Nor do they even out over time.

The lesson here is that there are no simple solutions to the problem of homelessness. Effective policy responses must at a minimum address both the vulnerabilities that leave certain individuals at risk for homelessness and the structural conditions that differentially distribute such vulnerabilities and make their consequences more serious. Thus, rehabilitative and economic responses must be paired so that affordable housing is provided along with the jobs, services, and supports that will allow vulnerable people to stay housed. More challenging still would be to address the terrific imbalance of resources and opportunity in the starting gate.

The political task is to recognize that homelessness is not an isolated crisis requiring an independent set of solutions, but is one of many symptoms—like the crack epidemic or the foster care debacle—which point to the growing failure of the needs-meeting structures of our society. We cannot address homelessness at it sources until we recognize that it is inextricably connected to other social ills—as the biographies of homeless people amply attest. As Rosenheck and Fontana recently noted, we would be wise to view homelessness as "the proverbial miner's canary."[13]

NOTES

1. Baumohl, Jim. "A Dissent from the Manichees," *Contemporary Drug Problems* 20 (1993): pp. 333–334.
2. Apgar, William C., Jr, Denise DiPasquale, Nancy McArdel, and Jennifer Olson. *The State of the Nation's Housing* (Cambridge, MA: Joint Center for Housing Studies of Harvard University, 1989).
3. As we use the term, a 'tight' market is one with high demand relative to supply. This is the typical lay understanding. Many housing economists use the term to mean precisely the opposite, however; that is, a market is 'tight' when demand is readily absorbed, when there is no slack.

4. Wolch, Jennifer R. and Michael Dear. *Malign Neglect: Homelessness in an American City* (San Francisco: Jossey-Bass, 1993)

5. See Paul Groth, *Living Downtown* (Berkeley: University of California Press, 1994); Charles Hoch and Robert A. Slayton, *New Homeless and Old: Community and the Skid Row Hotel* (Philadelphia: Temple University Press, 1989); Robert Hamburger, *All the Lonely People: Life in a Single Room Occupancy Hotel* (New York: Ticknor and Fields, 1983); Ellie Winberg and Tom Wilson, *Single Rooms* (Cambridge, MA: Schenkman, 1981); Joyce Stephens, *Loners, Losers, and Lovers: Elderly Tenants in a Slum Hotel* (Seattle: University of Washington Press, 1976); and Joan Hatch Shapiro, *Communities of the Alone* (New York: Association Press, 1971).

6. Hopper, Kim, and Jill Hamberg. "The Making of America's Homeless: From Skid Row to New Poor, 1945–1984" in *Critical Perspectives on Housing*, edited by Rachel G. Bratt, Chester Hartman, and Ann Meyerson (Philidelphia: Temple University Press, 1986). See also Peter H. Rossi, *Down and Out in America: The Origins of Homelessness* (Chicago: University of Chicago Press, 1989); *Malign Neglect*; and *New Homeless and Old* for the experiences of other cities.

7. Burt, Martha R. *Over the Edge: The Growth of Homelessness in the 1980s* (New York: Russell Sage Foundation, 1992).

8. Subsequent studies indicated that most of these latter individuals, among whom the mentally ill were over-represented, were terminated largely because their impairments made it difficult for them to challenge erroneous decisions, not because they were ineligible for benefits. About half of those who managed to mount appeals were eventually successful in having their entitlements reinstated ("The Making of America's Homeless," pg. 27).

9. Drunks and addicts were among the first groups to be barred from state hospitals; virtually every state with a commitment law affecting chronic substance abusers in the early 1960s had repealed it by the mid-1970s. See Jim Baumohl and Robert B. Huebner, "Alcohol and Other Drug Problems Among the Homeless: Research, Practice, and Future Directions," *Housing Policy Debate* 2, 3 (1991): 837–866.

10. Other forms of temporary work—in clerical services, for instance—have also become dominated by the temp industry, but historically these have been less important to poor or homeless people living from day to day. On trends in the temporary help industry, see Robert E. Parker, *Flesh Peddlers and Warm Bodies* (Brunswick, NJ: Rutgers University Press, 1994).

11. 'Shelter poverty,' as defined by Michael Stone in *Shelter Poverty: New Ideas on Housing Affordability* (Washington, DC: Economic Policy Institute, 1990), refers to the inability of households, regardless of income, to meet essential needs because of the burden of housing costs. For many purposes, it is a more sensitive measure of 'affordability' (conventionally set at 'thirty percent of gross income,' based upon the standard of 'what most households pay'). (The shelter poverty index is more sensitive to household size, for example.) This approach suggests strongly that any program of housing

support can only be designed or evaluated with reference to parallel programs for meeting other essentials at some minimal level of decency. A 'shelter poor' household may have its housing costs reduced to zero through subsidy and still not be able to meet other necessities.

12. See discussions in *Over the Edge* and *Malign Neglect.*

13. Rosenheck, Robert A. and Alan F. Fontana. "A Model of Homelessness among Male Veterans of the Vietnam War Generation," *American Journal of Psychiatry* 151 (1994): 427.

# 5

## SLAVERY IN THE FIELDS

*Daniel Rothenberg*

It is common knowledge among African-American farmworkers that there are places throughout the rural South where you can be taken, forced to work in the fields, and paid no wages for your labor. The crewleaders who run these labor camps typically send family members or trusted henchmen to homeless shelters, soup kitchens, and poor neighborhoods to find new workers. Recruiters strike up conversations with men and women who have fallen on hard times, promising good jobs with free housing, cheap food, and high wages. For those seeking a break from the day-to-day struggles of life on the streets, the offer seems almost too good to be true. Some workers are drawn in by the possibility of a decent place to live, the opportunity to save a little money, and the dream of starting life anew. Others are won over by the promise of easy access to wine, beer, and crack cocaine. For alcoholics and drug users, labor camp life provides a chance to slip anonymously into the numbing comfort of addiction, safe from the violence and uncertainty of the street.

Workers who accept the recruiters' offers are loaded into a van or an old school bus and driven to the crewleader's labor camp, which is usually located in a remote, rural area, sometimes hundreds of miles away. Upon arrival, it becomes clear that each of the recruiters' promises was either a gross exaggeration or an outright lie. Instead of a clean bed in a newly furnished house, prospective workers discover that they must sleep on dirty mattresses in crowded barracks with holes in the floor, leaking roofs, and filthy outhouses. Instead of home-cooked meals, workers find themselves eating endless meals of bologna sandwiches, rice and beans, and turkey necks.

New recruits quickly learn that labor camp life revolves around 'the line,' where workers can purchase wine, beer, cigarettes, or drugs from either the crewleader or an assistant. Even those without money can go through the line, since virtually everything at the camp is sold on credit at highly inflated prices. In some cases, crewleaders also lend money to workers, typically charging one hundred percent interest.

On the first payday, workers unfamiliar with labor camp life begin to understand the nature of the world they've entered. At the end of the week, the cost of food, rent, loan payments, and credit purchases of wine, beer, liquor, and drugs are deducted from each worker's wages. As a result, migrants living on these camps rarely earn more than a few dollars a week for their labor. In fact, many workers end each week owing money to the crewleader. Since what was owed from the previous week is carried over to the following week and then added to that week's purchases, few workers can pull themselves out of debt.

Those unfamiliar with this system are outraged at what they find. Workers find themselves stranded in labor camps, which are often located far from town, surrounded by fences, and watched by guards. Some workers try to pay off their debts in order to leave as quickly as possible. This is difficult, since the crewleader controls the books, marking down all credit purchases, real or invented. Crewleaders are generally armed and often rely on groups of thugs, known as henchmen, who police crews, threaten workers, and assault those who refuse to cooperate. Workers who want to leave a labor camp while still in debt to the crewleader must deal with the henchmen. Occasionally workers are beaten as an example to other members of the crew, and there are cases where farmworkers have died at the hands of crewleaders and their henchmen. To leave this type of labor camp, it is usually necessary to escape, to slip away in the middle of the night, winding one's way along rivers, railroad tracks, and back-country roads.

FRED SAMPSON *AUGUSTA, GEORGIA*

Fred Sampson sits on a bench at the Greyhound bus station. He is on his way to Atlanta to see his family for the first time in years. Two nights ago, he escaped from a labor camp in the ridge country of South Carolina, the heart of the state's peach industry.

Sampson is forty-five years old. Until a few years ago, he was building houses outside of Atlanta and earning over $400 a week. When the project was finished, he lost his job. At first, he lived on his savings, but he was unable to find another job and couldn't collect unemployment since he had been working off the books. After a few months, he had spent all his money. He lost his apartment, became homeless, and spent nearly a year living on the streets.

*I am not going to tell no lies because lies come back to haunt you. I don't have to lie about what happened to me.*

*I was smoking. I was getting high. But I took care of myself. I paid my rent, never got evicted, never sold anything out of my house. It's just a weak person that uses crack as an excuse for crime and violence.*

*After I lost my job, things fell apart. I ended up homeless. I spent a year on the street, I was about to give up. I was looking for anything to get me off the streets, to get me some money and a place where I could sleep.*

*I was on a soup line in Atlanta. The crewleader's son recruited me. He looked like a regular guy. He wore a T-shirt, jeans, and sneakers. He talked real good.*

*"Any of you guys want to go to work?"*

*Someone asked, "What are you doing?"*

*"We're going to South Carolina to pick peaches."*

*A lot of people shied away from him, but no one tried to tell me what was up. So he started talking to me and a few other guys, and we started listening. One of the guys asked him, "Hey man, y'all run rocks?"*

*He said, "Yeah, but you have to talk to my mama about all that. You know you can get you some beer, some wine, cigarettes, run that line."*

*At the time, I didn't know what a line was, but I knew what rocks were, so when he said, "run that line," I just put two and two together. I figured that the line was where you could go to get you a little something to smoke. Then he told us that just for coming, his mama would give us a rock for free, to recruit you. He said anything after that comes out of your pay.*

*I figured making minimum wage for forty hours a week, that's roughly a hundred and sixty dollars. He said my food bill would be about forty-five dollars a week; I figured that would leave me with over a hundred dollars. I'd spend a little and have some money left over each week. So I went with him to Johnston, South Carolina, to do peaches.*

*The first week they didn't let us work too much. They put us out in the field, but they wouldn't let us pick for more than two or three hours each day. At the time, I didn't know what they were doing, but now I understand. See, when you first get to the camp, the crewleader won't let you make enough money to clear that first week. That way, you go into debt. Even before you get a chance to put your own self in debt, she gets you in the hole, and she won't let you out. I felt used, but, shoot, I couldn't turn around and go back to the streets. That's what I was running from. Man, I needed money. I needed a place to stay.*

*We left Johnston around August to go to Benson, North Carolina, to pick sweet potatoes. You'd fill up a bucket of sweet potatoes, put it on your shoulder, and walk across the rows to the truck. You'd lift the bucket up to the guy in the truck and he'd give you back your bucket with a ticket. That's your count. That's to show that you dropped. Then you go back to your row. They paid us thirty-five cents a bucket.*

*After sweet potatoes, we left North Carolina and went to Glennville, Georgia, to plant onions. We were sticking little Vidalia onion plants in small holes. It was getting cold. Man, there were times it was so cold that the ground froze hard as a rock. You'd make a fire and they'd come and put the fire out. They'd say, "Get your ass back to work. You keep warm by working."*

*What can you do, man? You're out there. You're alone. You're somewhere way out in the fields. You can't buck the man. You ain't gonna fight him.*

*Man, the camps was really bad. In Glennville, we lived in a chicken coop. It was a big place with wood boards for the walls and tin for the roof. Everybody lived in there together. The roof leaked and there were rats everywhere. Mice used to get up and watch television with me. The bathroom and the showers were in the same place with the sinks. Sometimes it would all back up and the human waste would come out through the shower. You couldn't stand on the shower floor because of all the mess that was there. If you wanted to keep clean, you had to go outside and bathe with a bucket.*

*We spent the winter in Georgia, and then in the spring we picked and cut onions. It would take two big buckets to fill up a sack that weighed sixty to seventy pounds. You'd get seventy cents for a sack. It was hard work but if the onions were good, I could fill about eight sacks an hour. Still, I never made minimum wage. Never. One week, I earned ten dollars. Other weeks, I was paid two dollars, three dollars, four dollars. Some weeks, I got nothing.*

*Saturday was payday. The crewleader would call your name: "Send Fred in." I'd go in and she'd say, "Well, Fred, you have so many dumps and this is what you made. Sign this." That was the check. Sometimes it was the right number of dumps and sometimes it wasn't. I kept a record mentally. At one time I kept it on paper, but it didn't do no good. I heard guys sit and argue with her saying they had more dumps, but what could they do about it? Ain't nothing they could do.*

*Once I signed the check, she'd say, "What you want?"*

*"The usual." On Saturday, it was a pack of cigarettes, a beer, a pint of wine, a rock, and a few dollars. There were times when I got no dollars.*

*It was a mean life with those people. I can't say about other camps, 'cause I never went to but one camp. For thirteen months and two days I stayed with that crew. I was there so long because I didn't have nowhere else to go. A lot of times, I wanted to leave, but then I'd look at the television news and see that the economy was bad. I figured there were no jobs. So I hung on in there and took it.*

*A lot of times I was so far from everything that I didn't know how to get away. Then, when we were in Trenton, South Carolina, I found out that I could go to Augusta and get some assistance. The night before I left, I asked the crewleader about taking me back to Atlanta. That night in the wee hours of the morning I was awake and I saw her husband standing in his trailer watching my room.*

*I left the night before last and made sure the crewleader didn't see me. I left between midnight and one o'clock. I wasn't scared when I left the camp. Once I made up my mind to leave, I wasn't going to work for them again. I didn't run. I walked. I walked away and didn't stop. I walked all the way from Trenton, South Carolina, to Augusta, Georgia. It took twelve hours. My back hurts. The instep of my feet hurts. Last night, I had to sleep on tile floor at the Salvation Army.*

*It's been an experience, I'll tell you that. I'll never forget it. Never. It's nothing that you'd put your worst enemy through. I mean, they work you to death. They just don't care. Man, the way they treat people? It's miserable. That ain't even living. You're just existing. A lot of times I kept going by telling myself, "I ain't going to let it beat me. I'm going to find a way out."*

*For a person to be a migrant worker and continue to be a migrant worker, his mentality has got to be low. Either that or he just done gave up. So this is where I am today. It makes me feel mean and bitter. Mean and bitter. Right now, I got two quarters in my pocket. I don't feel sorry for myself because this experience is going to make me stronger. I hope it makes me strive to get something and then keep it. Before, I took everything for granted. Now I'll be more aware because I could fall again.*

*I've been thinking of telling everybody that I've been in jail, but I can't do that. I'm going to tell my children the truth. I hope it don't make them feel that I was weak. I'm going to tell them everything because it might happen to them. I am going to tell the truth.*

In 1992, a federal task force was formed to investigate abusive contractors working in the South Carolina peach harvest. About a year after Sampson fled the labor camp, his crewleader, her husband, and their son were arrested for peonage, criminal violations of the Migrant and Seasonal Agricultural Worker Protection Act (MSAWPA), and drug-related charges. All three plea-bargained, the crewleader pleading to MSAWPA violations and the son to conspiracy to hold workers in peonage. Only the son received a jail sentence.

Over the last three decades, a number of courts have established that the conditions of debt peonage under which thousands of farmworkers live and work violate federal antislavery statutes. Farmworkers living in camps where they are held in debt peonage are forced to labor against their will and subject to threats and acts of extreme violence.

Since the mid-1970s, the federal government has periodically organized task forces to investigate allegations of debt peonage among farmworkers. Between 1977 and 1990, the Justice Department filed twenty cases charging seventy-one defendants with holding workers in involuntary servitude. Eighty-five percent of these defendants either pleaded guilty or were convicted of enslaving migrant farmworkers. Nevertheless, most crewleaders convicted of holding farmworkers in involuntary servitude serve limited sentences, often leaving jail to continue operating labor camps.

Debt peonage represents the most extreme form of farmworker abuse. Although it is increasingly uncommon, until quite recently, large numbers of African-American farmworkers labored under conditions of debt peonage throughout the South. There are also isolated cases of immigrant farmworkers who are forced into debt and held against their will. Most of these situations involve recently arrived undocumented immigrants who have no knowledge of their legal rights and limited contacts with established migrant communities. In some cases, Latino immigrants fall into debt to coyotes who then pass workers on to contractors. These contractors hold crews in labor camps where they are forced to pay off their smuggling fees as well at additional debts for transportation, housing, food, and liquor. In several cases, contractors have been found guilty of holding immigrant farmworkers in involuntary servitude.

While the Civil Rights Movement transformed many aspects of racial inequality in the South, rendering segregation illegal, providing remedies for employment discrimination, and allowing blacks to vote, these changes by no means signaled the end of debt peonage for African-American farmworkers. Debt peonage remained one of the central elements of the black farmworker experience up through the 1970s, gradually diminishing in the 1980s, and to some degree continuing up until the present.

Improved opportunities, continued migration from rural communities to urban areas, regional economic shifts, and the institution of a variety of social benefits have steadily drawn African-American workers away from farm labor. By the 1970s, the black farm labor force was growing older and fewer young African-Americans were willing to work in the fields. Increasingly, the most abusive African-American crewleaders were forced to recruit workers out of urban missions and homeless shelters, often hiring men and women with no previous farm labor experience. Most recently, crewleaders have moved away from the traditional alcoholic workforce and have begun employing crack addicts recruited off the streets in large cities.

Crewleaders sometimes justify their actions by arguing that no one else is willing to provide these workers with housing, food, and employment. In fact, many homeless workers stay in abusive labor camps not only out of fear, but because they have few options other than returning to the harsh reality of life on the streets. Some of the worst abuses of farm laborers continue in part because these workers have been abandoned by society. Workers who escape from one violent labor camp often find themselves back in skid row neighborhoods, sleeping in missions or in parks, sometimes biding time until another recruiter comes along, offering them work in the fields.

Over the last several decades, the number of black crewleaders has steadily diminished as African-American farmworkers are being replaced by Latino immigrants. Currently, over eighty percent of migrant farmworkers in the South are Latinos, most of whom are recent immigrants—young, experienced farm laborers who are preferred by agricultural employers. Recent Latino immigrants are generally willing to work for low wages and accept difficult living conditions without having to be coerced through systems of debt peonage, intimidation, and violence. Consequently, the most abusive African-American crewleaders are disappearing, not because of a concerted law enforcement campaign to eliminate debt peonage, but as the inevitable result of the arrival of large numbers of vulnerable immigrant workers.

It is an extraordinary experience to enter a labor camp where workers are held in debt peonage. Some camps are unassuming, small clusters of wooden shacks or rows of rusting trailers, while others are long barracks-style buildings surrounded by chain link fences and signs warning visitors to keep out. There are often piles of garbage everywhere, broken bottles, and crushed beer cans. Old school buses and rusting vans used to transport workers are parked to one side, and beside them, the crewleader's car—often a white Cadillac or a newly purchased four-wheel-drive truck. When workers are not in the fields, they have little to do. They hang around in groups talking, watching television, or standing around a fire drinking. Some listen to portable radios, while others are passed out in their rooms or sleeping under the trees. Many workers look beaten down, their eyes glazed over. There are often several old men wandering around, their hair gray and clothes tattered.

Few outsiders enter these labor camps, and visitors quickly draw the attention of crewleaders and their henchmen. People stare.

Conversations die down. At the toughest camps, the crewleader and his henchmen arrive almost immediately, eager to find out who you are and what you want, since visitors usually mean trouble. Henchmen often dress like urban gangsters, flaunting gold jewelry and baggy clothes, alternately threatening and evasive. If you are well dressed or white, you're likely to be treated with deference, though it's always clear that the crewleader wants you to leave as soon as possible.

What is most memorable about a visit to one of these camps is the visceral sense of workers' fear. When the crewleader is nearby or the henchmen are listening, workers nervously tell you that the work is good, the housing fine, and the wages fair. Left alone for a moment, workers will draw you aside and whisper stories of abuse or slip notes into your hand pleading for help. Legal advocates, church groups, and others who visit these camps grow accustomed to the fear and hopelessness of these migrants. They often receive midnight telephone calls from workers who have managed to escape and are hiding in the woods, desperate for assistance.

Farmworker advocates estimate that there are currently between fifty and a hundred crewleaders who rely on debt peonage still operating in and around the rural South. These crewleaders provide employment to several thousand workers each year and represent a small percentage of the total number of farmworkers in the United States. Consequently, growers often claim that focusing attention on cases of debt peonage unfairly brands the agricultural industry as corrupt, criminal, and anachronistic. While it is true these situations are now the exception rather than the rule, the fact that involuntary servitude and debt peonage remain serious issues among America's farmworkers in the 1990s is extraordinary, raising deeply troubling questions about both the history and structure of our nation's farm labor system.

# 6

## THE STATE OF AMERICA'S CHILDREN
### *Children's Defense Fund*

America appears to be riding high on the cusp of the twenty-first century and third millennium. Wall Street is booming. Excess, Russell Baker says, has become a way of life for the very rich. In what may be the ultimate in corporate hubris, Miller Brewing Company has applied for a trademark or been recently registered as the "official sponsor of the Millennium," according to *Harper's* magazine. Corporate CEOs, who earned forty-one times what their workers made in 1960, made 185 times as much as their workers in 1995. The average CEO in 1995 earned more every two days than the average worker earned in a whole year. Fortune 500 CEOs averaged $7.8 million each in total compensation. This exceeds the average salaries of 226 school teachers a year.

The rosy view of American prosperity at the top hides deep and dangerous moral, economic, age, and racial fault lines lurking beneath the surface. Unless we heed and correct them, they will destroy America's fundamental ideals of justice and equal opportunity, family and community stability, economic productivity, and moral legitimacy as the democratic standard bearer in the next era.

In the last twenty-five years great progress has been made in improving children's lives in many areas. Millions of children with disabilities have a right to education; millions of poor children have received a Head Start, health care, immunizations, better child care, and permanent adoptive homes. But shamefully high child poverty rates persist, and children are the poorest group of Americans. The gap between America's poor and rich has grown into a chasm, the wages of young families with children have eroded, and many middle class families are treading economic water.

Since 1989 the poorest fifth of families have lost $587 each and the richest five percent have gained $29,533 each. We have five times more billionaires, but four million more poor children. While millions of stock options helped quintuple the earnings of corporate CEOs between 1980 and 1995, those same employers threw millions of children out of health insurance plans at their parents' workplaces, and parental wages stagnated.

More than eleven million children are uninsured, ninety percent of whom have working parents. More parents worked longer hours and more families sent a second or only parent into the labor force to meet family necessities. But for millions of families, work did not pay a family-supporting wage, and a minimum wage no longer prevents poverty. Sixty-nine percent of poor children live in working families. Ending welfare as we know it will not help them. Ending poverty as we know it will. Sustained economic investment in rebuilding our communities and in stable jobs with decent wages, quality affordable child care, and health insurance must become top American priorities.

Six years of economic expansion with low inflation and a soaring stock market have not filtered down to 36.5 million poor people, including 14.5 million children. In 1996 the number of very poor people who live below half the poverty line (a mere $8,018 for a family of four) increased, while the current income of households in the top five percent increased by $12,500. Today more than one in five children is growing up poor and one in eleven is growing up extremely poor. This is shameful and unnecessary.

If we are truly concerned about preventing welfare, teen pregnancy, youth violence, school dropouts, and crime, then we need to start first by preventing child poverty and ensuring every child a fair start in life. The moral, human, and economic costs of permitting 14.5 million children to be poor are too high.

- A baby born poor is less likely to survive to its first birthday than a baby born to an unwed mother, a high school dropout, or a mother who smoked during pregnancy.

- Poverty is a greater risk to children's overall health status than is living in a single-parent family.

- Poor children face greater risk of stunted growth, anemia, repeated years of schooling, lower test scores, and less education, as well as lower wages and lower earnings in their adult years.

• Poverty puts children at a greater risk of falling behind in school than does living in a single-parent home or being born to teenage parents.

Dr. Laura D'Andrea Tyson, former chair of the President's Council of Economic Advisors, says, "Policies to reduce the poverty rate among children–which typically remains higher in the United States than in any other advanced industrial countries—must be a fundamental part of our efforts to build a healthy economy for the twenty-first century." Nobel laureate in economics Robert M. Solow of the Massachusetts Institute of Technology states, "In optimistic moments, I like to believe that most Americans would want to lift children out of poverty even if it costs something. It is hard to blame little children for the problems that surround them now and will damage their future health, ability, and learning capacity. Doing nothing about it seems both immoral and unintelligent."

All segments of society pay the costs of child poverty and would share the gains if child poverty were eliminated. America's labor force is projected to lose as much as $130 billion in future productive capacity for every year 14.5 million American children continue to live in poverty. These costs will spill over to employers and consumers, making it harder for businesses to expand technology, train workers, or produce a full range of high quality products. Additional costs will be borne by schools, hospitals, and taxpayers and by our criminal justice system. Poor children held back in school require special education and tutoring, experience a lifetime of heightened medical problems and reliance on social service, and fail to earn and contribute as much in taxes.[1]

When legitimate avenues of employment are closed, poor youths and adults turn to illegitimate ones, especially the lethal underground economy of drugs and crime fueled by out-of-control gun trafficking. Since 1970 America's prison population has increased more than fivefold at an annual taxpayer tab exceeding $20 billion. Almost one in three young black, and one in fifteen young white males between the ages of 20 and 29 are under some type of correctional control (incarceration, probation, or parole). Two-thirds of state prison inmates in 1991 had not completed high school and one-third had annual incomes under $5,000. Joseph Califano, head of Columbia University's

National Center on Addiction and Substance Abuse, reports that if present trends persist, one of every twenty Americans born in 1997 will spend some time in jail, including one of every four black men.

Is this America's dream for its children and itself? Can an $8.7 trillion American economy not afford decent jobs, quality child care, education, and health care for all its children?

---

### KEY FACTS ABOUT AMERICAN CHILDREN

| | |
|---|---|
| 1 in 2 | *preschoolers has a mother in the labor force.* |
| 1 in 2 | *will live in a single-parent family at some point in childhood.* |
| 1 in 2 | *never completes a single year in college.* |
| 1 in 3 | *will be poor at some point in childhood.* |
| 1 in 3 | *is a year or more behind in school.* |
| 1 in 4 | *is born poor.* |
| 1 in 4 | *is born to a mother who did not graduate from high school.* |
| 1 in 4 | *lives with only one parent.* |
| 1 in 5 | *is poor now.* |
| 1 in 5 | *is born to a mother who received no prenatal care in the first three months of pregnancy.* |
| 1 in 7 | *has no health insurance.* |
| 1 in 7 | *lives with a working relative but is poor nonetheless.* |
| 1 in 8 | *never graduates from high school.* |
| 1 in 11 | *lives at less than half the poverty level.* |
| 1 in 12 | *has a disability.* |
| 1 in 13 | *is born at low birthweight.* |
| 1 in 24 | *is born to a mother who received late or no prenatal care.* |
| 1 in 25 | *lives with neither parent.* |
| 1 in 132 | *dies before the age of 1.* |
| 1 in 680 | *is killed by gunfire before age 20.* |

THREE QUESTIONS ALL AMERICAN CITIZENS
SHOULD ASK OURSELVES AND OUR POLITICAL LEADERS
ABOUT NATIONAL PRIORITIES

*1. Why is our nation continuing to spend $265 billion a year, $5.1 billion a week, $727 million a day, and $30 million an hour on "National Defense" in a post-Cold War era with no towering external enemies?*

Our military budget exceeds the total military expenditures of the twelve next-largest spenders—including Russia, France, Great Britain, Germany, and China—combined. Congress gave the Pentagon $9 billion more than it requested in 1996, while cutting $54 billion from child nutrition programs for poor and legal immigrant children and families. The military plans to purchase three new tactical fighter systems that will cost $355 billion—systems the U.S. General Accounting Office says we don't need and can't afford—at a time when millions of struggling parents left behind in the global economy need better paying jobs and millions of children need health care, quality child care, education, and housing.

As President Dwight Eisenhower reminded us in 1953, "Every gun that is made, every warship launched, every rocket fired signifies... a theft from those who hunger and are not fed, those who are cold and not clothed. This world in arms is not spending money alone. It is spending the sweat of its laborers, the genius of its scientists, and the hopes of its children."

- Every fourteen hours we spend more on the military than we do annually on programs to prevent and treat child abuse.

- Every twenty-nine hours we spend more on the military than we do annually on summer jobs for unemployed youths.

- Every six days we spend more on the military than we do annually on the Child Care and Development Block Grant for child care for low income working parents.

- Every six days we spend more on the military than we do annually on Head Start, which still serves only one in three eligible children.

• Every eleven days we spend more on the military than we do annually on Title I compensatory education for disadvantaged children.

It takes only a few nuclear weapons to blow up humankind. America spends tens of billions of dollars to maintain a nuclear overkill 'advantage' at a time when irresponsible leaders and gangsters seek access to inadequately secured nuclear weapon stockpiles and a cheap computer chip can accidentally launch a nuclear war. "Can't we do better than condone a world in which nuclear weapons are accepted as commonplace?" asks retired General George Lee Butler, former head of the Strategic Air Command. "The elimination of nuclear weapons," Butler states, "is called utopia by people who forget that for so many decades the end of the Cold War was considered utopia."

As we near the close of a twentieth century marked by dazzling scientific and technological progress, but also the bloodiest century in history, we all need to reassess the meaning of power and of life. More than 109 million human beings lost their lives in wars during this century, and far more civilians than soldiers died due to military conflicts. We must heed General Omar Bradley's warning on Armistice Day in 1948:

> We have grasped the mystery of the atom and rejected the Sermon on the Mount...
>
> Ours is a world of nuclear giants and ethical infants. We know more about war than we know about peace, more about killing than we know about living. The way to win an atomic war is to make certain it never starts. And the way to make sure it never starts is to abolish the dangerous costly nuclear stockpiles which imprison humankind.

*2. How much do we truly value children and families when we don't put our money and our respect behind our words?*

Is a child care worker who earns $6.12 an hour, $12,058 a year, and receives no benefits 182 times less valuable to America's future than the average professional basketball player who earns $2.2 million a year, or

162 times less valuable than the average HMO head who made $1.95 million in 1996? Is she only one-fourth as important to America's well-being as an advertising manager for a tobacco brand who makes $23.32 an hour? Most states require 1,500 hours of training to become a manicurist or hair stylist, but more than thirty states do not require a single hour of training for child care workers.

What family values dictate a public policy in many states that pays more to nonrelatives than to relatives to care for children whose parents cannot nurture and protect them? Why are we willing to spend $10,000 a year to place a child in a foster home and much more to place a child in an institution after the family fails, but refuse to invest $4,500 in job creation, child care, and income supplements for poor parents? Why does an average welfare payment of $365 a month to a poor family undermine personal responsibility when billions in 'subsidies and incentives'—euphemisms for government welfare for the non-poor and powerful—do not?

*3. Why is the United States, save Somalia (which lacks a legally constituted government to act), alone among nations in failing to ratify the Convention on the Rights of the Child?*

All the other nations of the world are willing to commit to the convention's goals of ending illegal child labor, sexual exploitation, violent abuse of, and capital punishment for children. Why do we refuse to pledge to make reasonable efforts to give all of our nation's children the adequate health care, food, shelter, and education that should be every child's birthright?

Reprinted from "A Child Shall Lead Us" in *The State of America's Children Yearbook 1998* (Washington, DC: Children's Defense Fund, 1998). Copyright ©1998 Children's Defense Fund. Used with permission of the publisher.

NOTE

1. These and other findings are detailed in a Children's Defense Fund report by Arloc Sherman, *Poverty Matters: The Cost of Child Poverty in America* (Washington, DC: Children's Defense Fund, 1998).

## PART TWO

# Root Causes

Carmen Cabrera is a cashier at a fast food chain in downtown Washington, DC. She works eight hours a day and earns $5.25 an hour. She had been out of work for a month before finding this job. With what she's making, she can't really support her four children. Unable to find a job that paid a livable wage and provided health benefits, she had to settle for this option.

In the twenty years that John Folk labored at the Huffy Bicycle plant in Celina, Ohio, he worked as a welder, machine operator, and material handler. Today, as president of his union local (USWA Local 5369), John is trying to relocate 1,000 of his fellow steelworkers. Despite nine consecutive profitable quarters, the 43 year-old bicycle plant closed its Celina facility and moved to Mexico in search of cheaper labor.

The experiences of Carmen and John take us to the heart of much of the anger and anxiety in America. People feel their lives becoming increasingly insecure, the ground beginning to shift under their feet. Part Two examines the root causes of that insecurity. There is no single 'smoking gun' responsible for the "New American Crisis" described in Part One. Rather there are a series of policies—like placing trade agreements before jobs, and the failure to assure that the minimum wage kept pace with inflation—that have worked together to generate the worst inequality seen in America since the Depression.

In the first chapter of Part Two, "Who's Poor in America," Randy Albelda and Chris Tilly take a look at how we measure poverty, finding that official statistics tend to undercount poor people. They then show how women, children and people of color are the groups most at risk of being poor, although by dint of sheer numbers, the typical poor person is actually European-American.

In Chapter Eight, "How the U.S. Economy Creates Poverty and Inequality," the authors plot the post-World War II transformation of our economy into one incapable of providing decent jobs for far too many Americans. Harry Browne and Beth Sims tell us why in Chapter

Nine, "Globalization and Runaway Jobs." They show how the move toward free trade and corporate globalization, which began well before the controversy over the North American Free Trade Agreement (NAFTA) brought it to the attention of most people, is driving wages downward around the world. Workers and communities everywhere are forced to compete for jobs in the global economy on the basis of who will work for less, while the profits of U.S.-based transnational corporations skyrocket.

The final piece of the puzzle is the gutting of anti-poverty social programs in the United States. In the final chapter of Part Two, Jim Hug shows us how the 'War on Poverty' has been transformed in "The War on the Poor." While our elected officials were telling us that our social programs were ineffective and discouraged 'hard work,' the facts actually indicate otherwise. Imperfect programs like Medicaid, food stamps and Aid to Families with Dependent Children (AFDC) helped millions to improve their lives, but most have been drastically cut back. He closes with the spiritual crisis facing America: that those who have more than they need rest comfortably, while those who lack basics struggle and suffer.

If we pay attention only to the corporate media, we might believe in the sparkling, computer-driven, global marketplace, a new economy where everyone is better off. As we now know, the reality is otherwise for millions of Americans. We call for a national debate that addresses the root cause of the crisis that we face, and places them in the context of basic human rights for all.

# 7

## WHO'S POOR IN AMERICA

### *Randy Albelda and Chris Tilly*

The United States—far more than other countries—worships the 'individual.' People admire and promote the ability of individuals to rise above adversity and take control of their environment through self-initiative. Stories of the 'self-made man' abound, and a whole folklore glorifies the 'rugged individual,' underscoring the notion that people's fortunes (or misfortunes) are largely of their own making.

While it is clear that individuals need to take responsibility for themselves, there are two problems with blaming those who don't seem to be pulling themselves up by their own bootstraps. First, the playing field is not level. Deeply embedded attitudes about race, gender, and class color our economic and social institutions and limit access and opportunity, keeping many from succeeding despite their persever-ance. With an officially acceptable six percent level of unemployment (the rate the Federal Reserve Bank argues is consistent with low levels of inflation) and a minimum wage far below its level of twenty or thirty years ago (after adjusting for inflation), 'losers' are built-in—almost inevitable—in our economic system. Second, no one is truly self-made. We all grow up in families, and we all need the support and care of communities. Behind every successful person is a network of people who have provided him or her with much of the necessary confidence, care, family resources, and inspiration. And lack of economic success often has more to do with shortcomings in these areas than with any lack of gumption. This chapter places individual wealth and poverty in a family context, examining who is most likely to be poor in the United States.

## WHO'S POOR AND HOW DO YOU KNOW?
## MEASURING POVERTY IN THE UNITED STATES

The Census Bureau of the Department of Commerce officially collects and publishes poverty data in the United States. The origins of these poverty statistics lie in the early 1960s, when Molly Orshansky, a staff economist for the Social Security Administration, developed the concept of a poverty threshold for different types of families, that was adopted by the Office of Economic Opportunity (OEO) in 1965.

Based on consumer household expenditure data from the 1950s, she determined the cost of a minimum adequate diet for different family types. At the time of the surveys, food accounted for about one-third of low-income families' total budget, so she multiplied the different food budgets by three to arrive at the poverty income thresholds. Those thresholds, indexed for inflation, are still used today. So the present poverty threshold for a family of four is the 1963 poverty threshold income for that family type ($3,100), adjusted for changes in consumer prices.

The way in which poverty is measured is of far more importance than just research. As economist James Tobin remarked in the late 1960s, "Adoption of a specific quantitative measure, no matter how arbitrary and debatable, will have durable and far-reaching consequences. Administrations will be judged by their success or failure at reducing the officially measured prevalence of poverty."[1] In addition, the poverty line's definition matters in a very practical way, since so many of the government programs base eligibility on the poverty level. Twenty-seven of the seventy federal and federal-state programs that provide either cash or in-kind aid to low-income persons are directly linked to established official poverty guidelines.

The advantages of the current measurement of poverty are that it remains consistent over time, it adjusts for need, and, at least initially, it was based on some real measure of adequate income level for basic survival. Still, many argue that the measure is deeply flawed and underestimates poverty. Probably the biggest problem with the U.S. poverty income thresholds is that they have not been adjusted for changes in consumption patterns since they were established. Today, food represents less than one-third of total family expenditures—housing, childcare, and medical costs have become larger components of people's budgets. Orshansky herself has said that the poverty measure should be periodically adjusted to reflect expenditure changes.

Still another problem with the current measure is that it does not account for wide variations in the cost of living across states and regions, and sometime even within states. Most notably, heating and housing costs are dramatically higher in the Northeast than they are in the South. Using one standard income threshold for all families, regardless of where they live, does not really project a consistent measure.

Some argue instead that the present measure overestimates poverty. In the 1980s, conservatives in the Reagan administration attacked the poverty threshold as being too high, claiming that the annual adjustment index overestimated inflation. In its place, they established an alternative index that estimated a lower rate of inflation, and as a result, lowered the poverty income threshold. With the mere stroke of a pen, the Reagan administration reduced the poverty rate!

Others argue that in estimating poverty, non-cash income, like food stamps, should be included as income. Poverty rates would then be lower for those who receive such benefits. This is absolutely true, but poverty calculations also do not exempt income that goes toward taxes, health care costs, or costs of working, such as transportation or child-care. Payroll taxes, state sales taxes, and local property taxes take a large percentage of low income people's budgets. If after-tax income (including food stamps) were measured and then adjusted for costs, the poverty rate would be considerably higher.

In a recent report, a panel of poverty experts assembled by the Committee on National Statistics at the National Research Council, published their findings on measuring poverty in the United States.[2] They found the current measurement inadequate for all the reasons mentioned above, and they recommended a new measure that takes into account in-kind benefits (like food stamps and housing subsidies) and out-of-pocket expenses (like taxes and childcare), and is based on recently collected data on the costs of food, clothing, and housing (adjusted for differences among geographic areas). Even using a low estimate of the income level necessary to fulfill a family's basic needs, the panel found that once income is adjusted for in-kind benefits and certain costs, poverty rates in the United States are currently being underestimated. Using 1992 data, the panel estimated that the poverty rate for all persons would have been 18.1 percent using their proposed measure, instead of the official 14.5 percent.

In short, the definition of poverty is a subjective choice on the part of policymakers and researchers, only loosely based on a measure of an income that meets basic family needs.

## WOMEN, CHILDREN, AND PEOPLE OF COLOR FIRST

Any way you slice the data, however, the poor are disproportionately comprised of people of color, children, and women. While only one out of six Americans is nonwhite, people of color represent one-third of the poor. Only twenty-seven percent of the U.S. population is under eighteen, yet children comprise forty percent of all poor people. Similarly, women account for fifty-one percent of all people aged eighteen and over, but make up sixty-two percent of those adults who live in poverty.

For close to one hundred years, social scientists have documented the extremely uneven distribution of poverty. In recent decades, many researchers have noted that the most common face of poverty in the United States among adults is a woman's. Sociologist Diana Pearce dubbed this phenomenon the "feminization of poverty." Economist Nancy Folbre added that the highest risk of poverty comes from being female and having children—which helps explain the high rates of both female and child poverty in the United States. Folbre called this trend the "pauperization of motherhood."[3]

The financial disadvantages of being female—and especially of being a mother—are clear and consistent. But it's not just gender that matters. Race, ethnicity, education, age, and family type all greatly affect the probability of being poor as well.

Let's start with race and ethnicity. Compared to whites, African-Americans and Latinos are three times as likely to be poor, Native Americans are more than twice as likely to be poor, and Asian-Americans' odds of poverty are one and a half times as great. Black and Latina women fare the worst, with poverty rates around thirty percent.

City dwellers are more often poor than suburbanites or residents of rural areas—or, to put it another way, poor people are most likely to live in the city. Almost one in seven residents of what the Census

Bureau calls "central cities" (the one hundred or so largest hub cities, such as New York, Cleveland, Houston, or San Francisco) is poor, compared to one in fifteen residents in smaller cities and suburbs. Poverty rates in rural areas fall between these two groups.

Education helps lift people out of poverty; conversely, the poor are less likely to finish high school or gain access to higher education. The poverty rate among high school dropouts is nearly two and a half times that of high school graduates and six times that of four-year college graduates. For women, education is particularly important in staving off poverty. Four years of college sharply reduce their chances of being poor: from fourteen percent to under five percent. But the gender gap persists: women with a high school diploma face poverty one and a half times more than male high school graduates.

Another pattern that applies most strongly for women is the connection between having children and poverty. For women, having at least one child under eighteen increases the chance of being poor from twelve percent to nineteen percent; having a child under six boosts that probability up to twenty-three percent. For women, then, there is quite an economic penalty for raising a family! For men, on the other hand, the penalty is much smaller—though still present.

Single mothers are more than four times as likely to be poor as other women. Women who are not single mothers fall into poverty at a rate only slightly higher than that of men. The poverty problem for women is, above all, a problem suffered by single mothers.

This quick tour through the poverty statistics reveals disproportionate poverty over and over again. Children under 18 are heavily overrepresented among the poor. Non-Latino whites, almost three-quarters of the U.S. population, account for less than half of the poor, though they are still of the largest group of poor people. African-Americans, Latinos, and Native Americans make up proportions of the poor population that are double their proportions of the overall population. Despite these disproportional odds, it is important to point out that—counter to stereotypes—the typical poor person is white, and that blacks make up only one-quarter of the poor population.

Finally, let's return to the predicament of single mothers. Though they account for a slim four percent of all U.S. adults, single moms living without other adults represent over fifteen percent of poor adults.

Other women constitute a slightly less than proportional fraction of poor adults. It is important to note that although single mothers are at much higher risk for falling below the poverty line than other adults, they still make up only a small fraction of all poor adults.

In short, the odds of ending up poor fall disproportionately on certain groups in the U.S. population. At the same time, many stereotypes of 'the typical poor person' are misleading. African-Americans, central-city dwellers, and single mothers each make up only a minority of poor people. A black single mother living in a central city is five times as likely as the average adult to be poor—but only one poor adult in sixteen is a black, central-city single mother.

Reprinted from "Who's Poor? Patterns of Poverty" in *Glass Ceilings and Bottomless Pits: Women's Work, Women's Poverty* by Randy Albelda and Chris Tilly (Boston, MA: South End Press, 1997). Copyright ©1997 Randy Albelda and Chris Tilly. Used with permission of the publisher and authors.

NOTES

1. Ruggles, Patricia. *Drawing the Line: Alternative Poverty Measures and Their Implications for Public Policy* (Washington, DC: Urban Institute, 1990), pg. 4.

2. The committee's report was published by Constance F. Citro and Robert T. Michael, eds., *Measuring Poverty: A New Approach* (Washington, DC: National Academy Press, 1995).

3. Pearce, Diana. "The Feminization of Poverty: Women, Work, and Welfare," *Urban and Social Change Review* (February 1978); and Nancy Folbre, "The Pauperization of Motherhood: Patriarchy and Social Policy in the U.S.," *Review of Radical Political Economics*, vol. 16, no. 4 (1985).

# 8

## HOW THE U.S. ECONOMY CREATES POVERTY AND INEQUALITY

*Mary Huff Stevenson and Elaine Donovan*

Any capitalist economy creates winners and losers, and the United States is no exception. What is noteworthy about the U.S. economy in the 1990s is that the gap between the winners and the losers is larger than it has been in the past fifty years, and that the United States is now generating more inequality than any other advanced capitalist nation.[1] These features of the contemporary U.S. economy have undermined the standard of living for many U.S. households, and are particularly threatening to households that depend heavily on women's earnings.

At the end of World War II, the U.S. economy was about to start on an expansion that brought higher living standards and greater economic security to a wide range of families. From 1945 until the early 1970s, most households could expect that their purchasing power would grow from one year to the next. In heavy industries such as automobiles or steel, a male wage earner without a high school degree could support a family with an income not only above the poverty line, but high enough to purchase a single-family home and still have enough left over to save for retirement or for the kids' college education.

Even in those expansionary times, however, not all households shared in the general prosperity. Observers spoke of the "paradox of poverty amid plenty." In 1960, Michael Harrington described "the other America," the people the expansion left behind.[2] They included the elderly, families in economically deserted areas such as Appalachia, minority households that faced economic discrimination, and families without access to a working man's wages. Much of the optimism with which the 'War on Poverty' was launched in the mid-1960s was based on the notion that poverty and economic insecurity were aberrant, and could be fixed with the proper combination of income security for the elderly, economic development for depressed areas, job training for those lacking skills, and anti-discrimination legislation to overcome a legacy of prejudice.

From the vantage point of the mid-1990s, that optimism seems sadly unfounded. Economic insecurity is rapidly becoming the norm, not the exception, for many U.S. households. Real wages (that is, the actual purchasing power of a worker's paycheck—the amount of goods and services it will buy) have been declining since the early 1970s. Like the gerbil inside the running wheel, who has to run faster just to stay in place, many households have responded to the decline in real wages by increasing the amount of time their members spend working, just to be able to afford the same standard of living. This also means that compared to a generation ago, many households need to have more members who are working for wages, and/or members who are working more hours, to avoid falling below the poverty line.

What has happened over the last twenty-odd years to change the course of the post-World War II expansion that improved living standards for many (but not all) U.S. households? What accounts for the phenomenon that Harry Bluestone and Bennett Harrison have called "the great U-turn?" Experts cite a number of factors, but chief among them is a change in the structure of the U.S. economy.3 This change is the product of several forces, including technological innovations that have reduced transportation and communication costs, and have given many companies much wider latitude (literally, and longitude as well) in deciding where to locate their production facilities. While the story of mobility of capital is an old one in regions such as New England, which saw its shoe and textile industries move south in the 1920s in search of cheaper and more pliable workers, the freeing of economic constraints that formerly tied companies to a specific location has occurred at a dizzying pace in recent years. As companies find it easier to make their location decisions on a worldwide basis, workers (organized, if at all, on a local or national level) find it harder to protect their economic position from erosion. Some observers worry that jobs providing decent wages and steady work for workers with no more than a high school diploma will soon be scarce as the proverbial hen's teeth. As these jobs flow from central city to suburb, from Rustbelt to Sunbelt, from the United States to other nations, or as they simply evaporate—made obsolete by new technology—they leave behind a group of workers with grim prospects. Moreover, as companies restructure internally, even those employers who stay put are less likely to offer a lifetime employment commitment, as they come to rely more heavily on 'contingent' (that is, part-time, part-year, temporary, or independent contractor) workers.[4]

While the expansion of the global economy and its attendant mobility of capital and internal workplace restructuring has accounted for much of the change that has contributed to the growing economic insecurity facing many U.S. households, public policy decisions of the last twenty years have exacerbated the problem. Sins of commission, such as the 'supply side' economics of the Reagan years (deliberately reducing the tax burdens of corporations and wealthy individuals, and increasing payroll taxes that fall most heavily on the working poor) and sins of omission, such as failure to pass labor law reform or meaningful increases in the minimum wage, are public sector problems that have aggravated the inequalities produced by the private sector.

These economic realities of the late twentieth century cut a wide gap through many U.S. households, including those with male wage earners, female wage earners, and no wage earners. They affect older workers whose post-layoff prospects are grim, and younger workers who face far more limited opportunities than their counterparts of the previous generation. Though higher education is not an iron-clad guarantee, they fall harder on those without college degrees and affect people of color disproportionately. It is against this backdrop of growing economic insecurity that we must examine the way the U.S. economy produces poverty and economic insecurity for many.

If we take the weekly earnings data provided by the Bureau of Labor Statistics and extrapolate from it yearly earnings (by assuming that workers receive these wages continually for fifty-two weeks without any spells of unemployment), a grim picture emerges for full-time wage and salary workers with no more than a high school diploma. Among full-time workers without a high school diploma, women, both black and white, earned below the poverty line for a family of four ($14,800 in 1994).

Moreover, if we look at the bottom twenty-five percent of the earnings distribution for high school dropouts, we find that while none of these workers, male or female, could support a four-person family above the poverty line, the women workers would not even be able to support a three-person family above poverty. Even among high school graduates, neither black men, white women, nor black women could bring a four-person family above the poverty line.

A final reality check: a full-time year-round minimum wage worker would not earn enough to bring even a two-person family above the poverty line. Nearly two-thirds of the minimum wage workforce is female, the vast majority of whom are adults, not teenagers.[5]

It is these realities of the U.S. labor market that must be kept in mind during debates about welfare reform. At the low end of the earnings distribution, the prospects are already quite bleak. Forcing mothers off Aid to Families with Dependent Children and swelling the ranks of job seekers will only make things even bleaker.

Within the economics profession, there are many economists who would not agree with the foregoing assessment. By and large, it is not the data itself that would be disputed, but the interpretation of that data. Conservative, liberal, and radical economists start from very different assumptions about the nature of the U.S. economy, and therefore reach very different conclusions.

Conservative economists emphasize the importance of individual choice, and the desirability of a competitive market economy, with its own self-correcting mechanisms. In this neoclassical framework, government intervention is not only unnecessary, but undesirable.[6] Liberal economists admire the workings of a competitive economy under ideal circumstances, but argue that the operation of markets is far from ideal. These economists point to constraints, barriers, and noncompetitive elements in the real world that prevent the market from functioning the way an economics textbook might describe it. The implication is that government intervention is necessary to correct the abuses of a private market mechanism that is malfunctioning.[7] The radical approach shares with the liberal approach a rejection of the neoclassical framework, but is much more explicitly concerned with understanding the dynamics of a capitalist system as it changes over time. Radicals also examine the confluence of economic and political power in a society divided along lines of class, race, and gender.[8] Although they share the liberals' disaffection with private markets, radicals are less optimistic about government intervention in a system where the elite have undue control of the reigns of government. True progress for ordinary people would depend on their ability to exert economic and/or political power.

NOTES

1. Bradsher, Keith. "Gap in Wealth in U.S. Called Widest in West," *The New York Times,* April 17, 1995.

2. Harrington, Michael. *The Other America: Poverty in the United States* (New York: MacMillan, 1962).

3. See Barry Bluestone and Bennett Harrison, *The Great U-Turn: Corporate Restructuring and the Polarization of America* (New York: Basic Books, 1988) or Robert B. Reich, *The Work of Nations* (New York: Alfred A. Knopf, 1991).

4. duRivage, Virginia. "Flexibility Trap: The Proliferation of Marginal Jobs," *The American Prospect,* Spring 1992.

5. "Women and the Minimum Wage," briefing paper, Institute for Women's Policy Research, Washington, DC, 1995.

6. Milton Friedman and Gary Becker are examples of economists who write from a conservative prospective.

7. John Kenneth Galbraith and Lester Thurow are examples of economists who write from a liberal perspective.

8. David M. Gordon and Samuel Bowles are examples of economists who write from a radical perspective.

# 9

## GLOBALIZATION AND RUNAWAY JOBS

*Harry Browne and Beth Sims*

Understanding the scope of the runaway jobs problem means understanding globalization. Since the end of World War II, national economies around the world have become increasingly integrated into a global economy. A profound shift in the organization of manufacturing is to a large degree behind this integration. Advances in telecommunications, information processing, and transportation technology have made it possible to coordinate extremely complex manufacturing processes—from product design and investment financing to inventory management and marketing—in several countries simultaneously. In an attempt to make their companies more efficient, corporations have 'rationalized' their operations by splitting up portions of their production chains and relocating the various links to countries with lower labor costs, more competitive suppliers, cheaper natural resources, or more favorable government policies. Separated by international borders, language, and culture, groups of workers around the world who work for the same company function as employees in a global factory. They produce for the same markets with largely the same technology, answer to the same executives, and generate dividends for the same shareholders.

Besides revolutionary changes in technology, the international economy is made possible by financial and banking networks that span the globe and facilitate trade, investment, and other economic relationships, Also important is an increasingly centralized international economic system, with an overarching economic regime that sets the rules for international economic relations. Formalized in a variety of economic agreements and institutions constructed by the postwar capitalist powers, but dominated by the United States, this economic regime is designed to give businesses as much freedom as possible to move money, jobs, and other resources to seek the most profit.

## GROWTH OF RUNAWAYS

One of the worst byproducts of the global factory and the global harmonization of trade and investment rules is the runaway plant. Runaways are a relatively new phenomenon. In the 1950s a number of visionary corporate managers saw that freer trade flows and the revolutions in communications and transportation meant access not just to foreign consumer markets but also to vast low paid labor markets. Led by the electronics and apparel industries, these managers set up labor-intensive facilities in Asia, the Caribbean, and Mexico. Opening new investment sites abroad would simply be corporate expansion if existing enterprises in the United States were kept running at normal capacity. Instead, by the mid-1960s, transnational corporations (TNCs) began cutting back on personnel or closing down operations at U.S. plants in order to set up shop where costs were lower for one aspect or another of the production process.

Over the years the number of U.S. plants that have headed abroad has ballooned. Mexico is only one of their destinations. The country's proximity and the amount of U.S. investment there make it a prime example for study, but U.S. corporations have shipped jobs to countries around the globe. From El Salvador to Malaysia, the world has become a global factory for U.S. transnational corporations.

The growth of runaways as a major problem in the United States has been closely associated with the decline of industrial production, a process known as de-industrialization.[1] Instead of plowing profits back into existing plants or investing in new U.S. manufacturing operations to spur innovation, upgrade equipment and worker skills, and thus boost productivity, many corporations since the 1960s have chosen instead to maximize profit rates by other means. Sometimes they have moved production to sites where operating costs would be lower, thus becoming runaways.[2] Speculative investments and acquisitions also contribute to de-industrialization by diverting funds that might otherwise be used to upgrade and modernize current plants.

For whatever reason dis-investment and de-industrialization occur, they erode the competitiveness of U.S. industries and have profoundly negative effects on the economic security of workers and communities. Major sectors of the U.S. economy are closing down. The structure of the economy is changing from one that used to support a range of decent-paying jobs with reasonable benefits to one that offers mostly low wage, no-benefits employment in the service sector. During the 1950s, nearly a third of all U.S. workers were employed in manufacturing. By the 1980s only twenty percent had such jobs. In the early 1990s the figure had slipped to seventeen percent and was still falling.[3] In addition, the share of the gross domestic product provided by manufacturing has also declined, especially since 1979.[4]

Labor-intensive industries like electronics assembly and apparel were the first to experience the shift of jobs abroad. Increasingly, however, runaways are likely to be capital-intensive operations, or even firms in the service sector. This change in the composition of industries that are moving abroad is especially clear in Mexico, where the sector known as the *maquiladoras* has expanded to include a wider range of high-value production.

The decline in U.S. manufacturing jobs, with all its ill consequences for U.S. workers, has not meant a crisis for many of the U.S. corporations involved in such manufacturing. Statistics show that U.S. manufacturers capable of transnationalizing have adapted to global competition by doing so. Although the share of world manufactured exports produced in the United States dropped from 17.1 percent in 1966 to 13.4 percent in 1985, the share of global production held by U.S.-owned corporations actually increased from 17.3 percent to 18.3 percent. The corporations had not lost business or gone under. They had simply shifted much of their production to foreign subsidiaries.[5]

THE HUMAN DIMENSION

The logic of the globalization process puts the workers, communities, and governments of the world in direct competition for a limited pool of capital and technology. The rivalries that are stimulated—in tandem with national policies and international agreements that are biased against workers, the environment, and public health and safety—exert a downward tug on living and working conditions around the world.

As cash-starved governments fight to offer the lowest paid and most compliant work forces, for instance, they often resort to repressing labor and ignoring national laws on minimum wages and working conditions. A. Sivanandan, the director of London's Institute of Race Relations, offered a grim description of the process:

> *The governments of the [underdeveloped countries], desperate not for development as such but the end to unemployment that threatens their regimes, enter into a Dutch auction with each other, offering the multinational corporations cheaper labor, de-unionized labor, captive labor, female labor, and child labor—by removing whatever labor laws, whatever trade union rights have been gained in the past from at least that part of the country...which foreign capital chooses for its own.*[6]

In most cases the shift to new, globally oriented plants enabled corporations to weaken the grip of labor unions and increase managerial control over the organization of work. Threats of relocation aimed at unionists and other workers in the United States are frequently used to extract concessions in terms of wage and benefits packages, work conditions, hours of work, job classifications, and organizing efforts.[7] In addition to eroding standards for worker protection, unions themselves have been discredited, dismantled, and destroyed both in the United States and abroad.[8]

Negative spinoffs of de-industrialization and the runaway phenomenon (such as the decline of unionism, eroding standards for environmental and consumer protections, and decay of infrastructure) result only in part from the impersonal actions of international economic forces. In fact, even seemingly 'natural' forces like international economics are shaped by the political choices of governments and influential private actors. But problems like these also stem from the domestic policies of national governments. When the administration of President Ronald Reagan moved to crush the air traffic controllers union in the early 1980s, the move was not aimed at transforming the global economy or the position of the United States in it. Instead the U.S. president acted as the leader of a coalition of conservative politicians, economists, and interest groups who were employing the 'discipline of the whip' against U.S. labor.[9] From trickle-down economics to the deregulation frenzy of the 1980s, U.S. domestic politics savaged labor, the working poor, the middle class, and the environment. In interaction with the forces of globalization, such policies contribute to the runaway phenomenon and to its negative impacts on U.S. workers.[10]

## PRESSURE ON WORKERS AND COMMUNITIES

The price tag attached to de-industrialization and the runaway phenomenon is an expensive one. Although corporations that 'run away' may find their own profits climbing, the communities and workers they leave behind are often tossed into economic catastrophe. When the factory gates are padlocked, the economic and social repercussions ripple throughout affected communities. The loss of wages and benefits is traumatic enough, but displaced workers often also lose their homes, cars, and savings. Social problems like alcoholism, domestic violence, divorce, and crime increase. Other local and regional businesses feel the pinch, too, and may even go under themselves if enough of their customers lose significant buying power.[11] Although demands on social services rise due to increased unemployment, local governments suffer lost revenue from plant closures, both from corporate taxes and from taxes formerly paid by plant employees.

## DYING FOR A JOB

Plant closures and layoffs carry a prohibitive cost for many of the workers who lose their jobs, as well as the communities in which they live. From substance abuse to domestic violence, from heart disease to suicide, the toll is severe.

Each one percent increase in the unemployment rate that is sustained over a period of six years is associated with:

- 37,000 total deaths
- 920 suicides

- 650 homicides
- 500 deaths from cirrhosis of the liver
- 4,000 admissions to state mental health hospitals
- 3,300 admissions to state prisons[12]

The most profound evidence of de-industrialization and decline in the United States is seen in the slide in middle class living standards and the climb in the poverty rate. These problems are not only the result of globalization, of course. Through tax policies, cutbacks in social programs, deregulation, union-busting efforts, inadequate funding for watchdog agencies, and similar initiatives, the Reagan and Bush administrations undermined the poor and the middle class, while shifting income upward to the wealthy.[13] In addition, corporate raiding, leveraged buyouts, corporate restructuring, and other get-rich-and-get-out schemes have led to plant closures and layoffs across the country, in part because government policies reward such adventurism. Globalization itself—both because it has led to a restructuring of the U.S., economy and because it poses the threat of plant relocation and job loss—also eats away at income levels for the majority of workers in the economy. Whether through concessions on wages and benefits or through outright job loss due to plant relocation, the downward pressure on living conditions is severe.

NOTES

1. Comprehensive descriptions of the changing U.S. economy can be found in Donald Barlett and James Steele, *America: What Went Wrong?* (Kansas City: Andrews and McMeel, 1992); Bennett Harrison and Barry Bluestone, *The Great U-Turn: Corporate Restructuring and the Polarizing of America* (New York: Basic Books, 1991): and Juliet Schor, *The Overworked American: The Unexpected Decline of Leisure* (New York: Basic Books, 1991). See also the Economic Policy Institute's voluminous collection of employment and wage data for the decade: Lawrence Mishel and Jared Bernstein,

*Declining Wages for High School and College Graduates: Pay and Benefits Trends by Education, Gender. Occupation, and State, 1979–1991* (Washington, DC: Economic Policy Institute, 1992), and Lawrence Mishel and David M. Frankel, *The State of Working America 1990–1991* (Armonk, NY: M.E. Sharpe Inc., 1991).

2. With after-tax profits falling fairly steadily since the mid-1960s, slashing labor costs has proven to be the quickest way to hike profits. For information on the decline of the after-tax profit rate of U.S. corporations since the 1960s, see Samuel Bowles, David M. Gordon, and Thomas E. Weisskopf, *After the Waste Land: A Democratic Economics for the Year 2000* (Armonk, NY: M.E. Sharpe Inc., 1990), pp. 43–45, 77–79, 157–161; Barry Bluestone and Bennett Harrlson, *The Deindustrialization of America: Plant Closings, Community Abandonment and the Dismantling of Basic Industry* (New York: Basic Books, 1982), pp. 147–149; and Robert B. Reich, *The Work of Nations: Preparing Ourselves for 21st-Century Capitalism* (New York: Alfred A. Knopf, 1991), pg. 75–76.

3. *America: What Went Wrong?*, pg. 18.

4. Lawrence Mishel has determined that manufacturing's share of the gross domestic product declined sharply after 1973. According to Mishel's calculations. the share of GDP held by manufacturing fell from twenty-four percent in 1973 to 22.5 percent in 1979 and to 20.8 percent in 1985, where it held steady at least until the date of his study. Lawrence R. Mishel, "The Late Great Debate on De-industrialization," *Challenge*, January–February 1989.

5. Kwan, Ronald. "Footloose and Country Free: Mobility Key to Capitalists' Power," *Dollars & Sense*, March 1991, pg. 7.

6. Sivanandan, A. "The Global Market Place," *International Labor Reports* 36, November–December 1989.

7. See the case study of relocation and corporate 'blackmail' of workers to obtain concessions in John Gaventa, "Capital Flight and Workers," in John Cavanagh et al., *Trading Freedom: How Free Trade Affects Our Lives, Work, and Environment* (San Francisco: Food First Books, 1992), pp. 19–23.

8. See Kimm Moody, *An Injury to All: The Decline of American Unionism* (London, UK: Verso, 1988); Harrison and Bluestone, *The Great U-Turn* , especially the chapter on "Zapping Labor," pp. 21–52; Bowles et al., *After the Waste Land*, pp. 85–88: and Bluestone and Harrison, *The Deindustrialization of America*, pp. 164–170, 178–180. Organized labor in the United States has suffered in part because of its own failures, including flawed organizing strategies, the leadership's disengagement from the rank and file, excessive bureaucratization, corruption, encrusted ideological stands, undemocratic decision-making processes, and lack of militancy. For a close look at U.S. labor's own political, strategic, and organizing failures, see *An Injury to All*; Staughton Lynd, *The Fight Against Shutdowns: Youngstown's Steel Mill Closings* (San Pedro, CA: Singlejack Books, 1982); and Beth Sims, *Workers of the World Undermined: American Labor's Role in U.S. Foreign Policy* (Boston: South End Press. 1992).

9. The term comes from Bowles, *After the Waste Land*, pg. 133.

10. Focusing on the role that domestic politics plays in undermining U.S. living conditions is not meant to suggest that concerns about international competitiveness are irrelevant to union-busting efforts. Competitiveness issues—such as the increasing share of the U.S. market captured by imports—feed the attack against labor and are used to justify it. Domestic policy choices, however, are extremely important in their own right and have served to undermine, rather than to shore up, the position of workers and their communities in the interests of bolstering the position of large corporations and the wealthy. For close examinations of this transfer of wealth and power over the decade of the 1980s and the domestic political motivations behind it, see *After the Waste Land; America: What Went Wrong?; The State of Working America.*

11. Estimates of the total number of jobs lost in a community and in supplier industries as a result of cutbacks or a shutdown by a given employer vary depending on the industry in question and its linkages to other industries in the production chain. Looking at the auto industry, U.S. government studies in the early 1980s found that one to two jobs were lost in supplier industries (steel, rubber, glass, and textiles, for example) for every job lost in the motor vehicle industry itself. See summaries in *The De-industrialization of America,* pp. 71–72. Another factor that influences the size of the 'ripple effect' following a shutdown is the size and diversity of the community's economic base and the level of its dependence on the plant in question. A study of the 1987 closing of the GM plants in Norwood and Fairfield, Ohio, found that at least three jobs were lost throughout the region for every one job lost at the plants. At the time of the closing, the GM plant in Norwood accounted for more than forty percent of the city's jobs, and the two plants bought services and materials from nearly 1,400 suppliers in the region. Cited in Michael Wallace and Joyce Rothschild, "Plant Closings, Capital Flight, and Worker Dislocation: The Long Shadow of De-industrialization," in Michael Wallace and Joyce Rothschild, eds., *De-industrialization and the Restructuring of American Industry.* vol. 3 of *Research in Politics and Society* (Greenwich, CT: JAI Press, 1988).

12. Brenner, Harvey. *Estimating the Social Costs of Rational Economic Policy: Implications for Mental and Physical Health and Clinical Aggression*, Report prepared for the Joint Economic Committee, U.S. Congress, (Washington, DC: Government Printing Office, 1976), cited in Barry Bluestone and Bennett Harrison, *The Deindustrization of America: Plant Closings, Community Abandonment, and the Dismantling of Basic Industry* (New York: Basic Books, 1982), pg. 65.

13. See *America: What Went Wrong?*

# I O

## THE WAR ON THE POOR

### *Jim Hug*

The 'War on Poverty' has been transformed into a 'War on the Poor.' The reality is that blunt and outrageous. Under the cover of official responsibility and balancing the budget, the U.S. Congress is shedding its social responsibility and further destroying the already tenuous and faltering balance in and among our communities. The fundamental national guarantee that people of the wealthiest nation on the planet will have at least the minimal basic necessities for survival, is being eliminated. Federal funding for social needs is being cut back seriously and sent as block grants to the states with few, if any, strings attached to prevent the extensive abuses at the state level that led to federal programs in the first place.

'Compassion' has been slandered as a tragically naive attitude. As embodied in federal programs, the argument goes, it has created welfare dependency. It is the "enabling behavior of a well-meaning but co-dependent" society.[1]

Private charities are being asked to replace impersonal government bureaucracies with the kind of personal involvement that changes people's lives. That seemingly idealistic challenge begs two important questions. How realistic is it to expect private charities, which now, all together, provide $8 billion annually to the poor, to make up for a projected federal cutback of $57 billion in its services to those same poor? And what is the appropriate responsibility of a government as the final guarantor of the well-being of all its people?

### POVERTY'S CAUSES AND CURES

Historically there is a link between the public analysis of the causes of poverty and the types of anti-poverty programs embraced.[2] With the discovery of the depressing environment of ghettoes and slums, the nation set about building more humane housing environments. When unemployment was discovered to be a structural problem, public works and other government programs mushroomed.

Now the reigning political 'wisdom' proclaims these programs failures, identifying the real cause of poverty as spiritual and moral. Poor people are trapped in a 'culture of poverty,' a culture of dependency fostered by those who tried to help them through government programs. Poverty will never be overcome, the argument goes, until the poor themselves assume responsibility for their own lives. Morality and spirituality are equated with personal responsibility.

FALSE AND SIMPLISTIC

This position reflects several false assumptions that undermine constructive public dialogue on these issues.

Have both the 'War on Poverty' and the government social programs of the last sixty years *really* failed? Susan Mayer, professor of public policy at the University of Chicago, and Christopher Jencks, professor of sociology at Northwestern University, argue that the government's own data show that the major anti-poverty programs have basically done what they were meant to do:[3]

- Before 1965, the poor made 20 percent fewer doctor visits a year than the wealthy despite being sicker. By 1980 Medicaid closed that gap.

- Within seven years in the 1970s, the food stamp program cut in half the negative effects of family income on food consumption and made hunger and malnutrition much harder to find.

- The proportion of seventeen-year-olds with very low math and reading scores has dropped substantially in the last twenty-five years, suggesting the success of programs like Head Start for low income populations.

- The poverty rate among the elderly has fallen since the early 1970s— which was the goal of Supplemental Security Income and Social Security.

- Aid to Families with Dependent Children (AFDC) benefits have never been adequate to raise people out of poverty. Does it foster illegitimacy as claimed? The birth rate among teenagers fell in the years when anti-poverty spending rose the fastest and rose when AFDC benefits fell.

None of these programs was perfect. Poverty still exists and is growing. But that is not so simply or clearly due to the 'failure' of these programs. Secondly, to argue that the cause of poverty is spiritual rather than structural is simplistic. The causes of poverty are complex. They are indeed spiritual; they are also structural.

Every day newspapers and business journals are full of discussions of the structural changes sweeping the planet. New technologies and globalization processes are restructuring the work place. Unskilled manufacturing jobs have been lost to machines and/or cheap labor in other parts of the world. Corporations, claiming pressure from international competition, have downsized their operations, laying off full-time workers with benefits and rehiring them as part-time or contingent workers at greatly reduced pay and without benefits. Approximately forty percent of the U.S. work force is now 'contingent' in this way. And forty-six percent of U.S. companies are using or studying 'variable pay plans,' which would further endanger employee pay. Under these schemes, company profits are made more secure, skilled specialists improve their income and lower-income households find themselves more insecure.[4]

Structural changes require programmatic responses. We must not force poor people off welfare rolls, demanding that they "become responsible and get jobs," if there are no jobs produced for which they qualify. Maryland has reported that the average number of families on AFDC in the state in 1994 was 79,317. That same year the private sector added only 5,690 jobs for which those families could compete—and these were principally minimum wage jobs currently incapable of raising a family out of poverty. The 38,725 other jobs created in the state required college or advanced degrees.

A SPIRITUAL PROBLEM

Structural problems are not the only ones that plague us, however. There *is* a spiritual problem at the heart of our current economic situation. It is more serious and corrosive than the irresponsibility of the relatively small percentage of poor people succumbing to welfare dependency. It is the social irresponsibility of those responsible for structuring the economy so that people are squeezed out and communities devastated in the pursuit of greater profits for a few or 'economic efficiency' in the system.

The current public debate reflects a simplistic identification of 'spiritual' and 'moral' with an individualistic emphasis on 'personal responsibility.' The profound social dimension of every major world religion is being shrouded in silence. In the light of that mission, it is truly a major spiritual crisis when those who have more than they need rest comfortably while those who lack basics struggle and suffer: the spiritual crisis of the comfortable.

Reprinted from "From the War on Poverty to the War on the Poor" in *What Governments Can Do: Hunger 1997* (Silver Spring, MD: Bread for the World Institute, 1996). Copyright ©1996 by Bread for the World Institute. Used with permission of the publisher.

NOTES

1. This is Marvin Olasky's argument in *The Tragedy of American Compassion* (Washington, DC: Regnery/Gateway, 1992), reportedly given to each member of the U.S. House of Representatives by Speaker Newt Gingrich.

2. Gladwell, Malcolm. "The Failure of Our Best Intentions," *Washington Post*, Outlook Section, December 3, 1995.

3. Mayer, Susan and Christopher Jencks. "War on Poverty: No Apologies, Please," *The New York Times*, November 9, 1995.

4. "Unstable Pay Becomes Ever More Common," *Wall Street Journal*, December 4, 1995.

## PART THREE

# What's Wrong with Welfare

"Ending welfare as we know it" was a campaign slogan for Bill Clinton in 1992. Today we can measure its impact on people's lives. Consider Heather McKelvey, a single mother of two in Philadelphia. Under the old welfare law, Heather was attending school almost full time, trying to get a B.A., and getting by on welfare and food stamps. But in November 1997, after welfare reform, Heather had to quit school or risk being sanctioned. She started working from nine to five as a receptionist at a hair salon, bringing in $218 a week, of which she had to pay out $105 in child care. When she asked the welfare officer for child care, she was turned down and told that if she quit her job, then she would not be eligible for any benefits at all. Unable to cover child care costs, she quit her job in May 1998 and her food stamps were cut from $300 to $136 a month, leaving her in a worse situation than ever.

John Robinson Jr., single parent of two children, has held a series of security jobs in Washington, DC. He works really hard to make ends meet but still has nothing left at the end of the month. Child care poses a big problem for John as well. In the District, welfare benefits have been reduced significantly. According to John, "in the United States, which is the richest country in the world, a person who is willing to work should be able to get a job at a living wage. What I need to get off welfare is a decent paying job with medical benefits and reliable child care."[1]

More than sixty years ago the government created a public assistance program, which came to be known as Aid for Families with Dependent Children (AFDC). It implicitly acknowledged a minimum degree of economic stability as a human right. On August 22, 1996 President Bill Clinton eliminated programs like AFDC with the stroke of a pen, when he signed the welfare reform bill.

By 1999, the U.S. Conference of Mayors reported, welfare reform has had a broad, negative impact on hunger and homelessness in U.S. cities. In 1998, ninety-two percent of cities reported that many families and individuals were relying on emergency food assistance facilities as a steady source of food over long periods of time, not just for emergencies. Ninety-three percent of cities expected requests for emergency shelter to increase; 88 percent expected such requests by homeless families to increase as well. In nearly half of the cities reporting, people had been turned away due to lack of resources.[2] While federal officials celebrated the dramatic shrinkage in public assistance rolls, some acknowledged that they do not know what has happened to families who have lost assistance.[3]

In Part Three we take a look at anti-poverty policies and welfare in America. In Chapter Eleven, "Why American Poverty Policies Don't Work," Randy Albelda and Chris Tilly trace the history of anti-poverty policies beyond the colonial era, all the way back to poor laws in England. They find disconcerting consistencies throughout American history: blaming the victim, scapegoating, and ill-conceived 'welfare to work' programs. Seen in this historical light, the recent move toward 'welfare reform' is but more of the same, and no more likely to end hunger and poverty than were earlier incarnations.

In "Women, Welfare and Work," Mimi Abramowitz takes a close look at present day generalizations—she calls them 'myths'— about women, welfare, and childbearing. She shows how arguments which suggest that poor women have kids for welfare money, that welfare encourages bad parenting, etc., have no evidence to support them. Nevertheless this contemporary scapegoating of poor women has provided the emotional arguments behind welfare reform.

It is the impact of the 1996 welfare reform law that we take on directly in Chapter Thirteen, "Welfare Reform Violates Human Rights." The $54 billion in cuts from America's social programs have led to devastating upswings in hunger, as poor people have been thrust into a job market that offers few options adequate for raising a family. We show how fundamental human rights enshrined in the Universal Declaration of Human Rights (UDHR) are being systematically violated under new welfare policies. These include the right to an adequate standard of living, the right to food, the right to special care and assistance for mothers and children, the right to education, and the right to adequate employment, and we issue a call to join our *Economic Human Rights: The Time Has Come* campaign.

With a human rights framework, it is the government's obligation to respect, protect, facilitate, and fulfill people's basic human rights. Using that approach, policies such as welfare reform only serve to undercut the U.S. commitment to international standards as set forth under the UDHR.

NOTES

1. John Robinson, Jr. testimony given at Congressional Hearing, September 1998, Washington, DC.
2. Report from the U.S. Conference of Mayors, January 1999.
3. Pear, Robert. "Welfare Rolls Sink to the Lowest Level Since 1971," *The New York Times*, January 21, 1998.

# I I

## WHY AMERICAN POVERTY POLICIES
## DON'T WORK

*Randy Albelda and Chris Tilly*

The anti-poverty policies of the United States do not work very well. The clearest evidence of their ineffectiveness is that poverty has persisted at relatively high levels and has even grown during some periods over the last couple of decades. Does this mean that government action cannot end economic deprivation, or that anti-poverty policies have actually contributed to the growth of poverty? Not at all. But our efforts have been incomplete and halfhearted, guided by flawed theories. So it should not surprise us that we have failed to tackle poverty.

### FLAWED POLICIES, FLAWED THEORIES OF POVERTY

Why does the United States have such a bad track record on alleviating poverty? And why has anti-poverty policy shortchanged mothers in particular? Dating back to their origins, U.S. poverty policies have always been limited in scope, stigmatized the poor, and incorporated gender and race biases. Over the last thirty years, the political pendulum has swung from liberal to conservative, and the theories guiding anti-poverty policy have changed. Yet consistent flaws in these theories have always hobbled the government's effectiveness in lifting families up and out of poverty.

### A LONG HISTORY OF STINGINESS

British settlers in what became the United States began institutionalizing relief programs shortly after their arrival in North America, establishing the first such program in the Plymouth Colony in 1642.[1] Relief programs modeled on the British poor laws were in effect through the nineteenth century. They rested on local funding and administration, and distinguished sharply between the 'deserving' and 'undeserving' poor. Importantly, local governments sought to make welfare undesirable by providing benefits well below prevailing wage levels, attaching degrading conditions, and requiring work in many cases. The overseers of the poor in Beverly, Massachusetts, expressed a typical view in the early 1800s: they worried that the "industrious poor" would be "discouraged by observing that bounty bestowed upon the idle, which they can only obtain by the sweat of their brow."[2]

The outright degradation of relief recipients was greatest during the colonial era. Some colonies required recipients to wear a badge bearing the letter 'P' for 'pauper;' others denied recipients the right to marry or made them subject to jail, slavery, or indenture. Some restrictions persisted for decades. In the 1930s, for instance, fourteen states still banned welfare recipients from voting or holding political office.

Beginning in the 1700s, relief authorities often imposed work requirements, setting up workhouses or, in some cases, 'houses of industry' that provided private sector jobs at rock-bottom wages. In the 1800s, the authorities gravitated toward more punitive work regimes, requiring hard physical labor that sometimes amounted to make-work.

While stigmas and restrictions were the norm for white, native-born poor people, in many instances people of color and immigrants were excluded from assistance altogether. African-American slaves, of course, were at the mercy of their masters. For decades after emancipation, local welfare authorities simply classified blacks and other people of color as 'undeserving,' forestalling any welfare assistance. Even the welfare rights movement of the late 1960s discovered continuing barriers to the eligibility of women of color. Native Americans have had a particularly bitter history. After hundreds of years of being forcibly pushed from their lands and livelihoods, they were repeatedly promised federal assistance in nineteenth-century treaties, only to have these promises, like many others, broken. Though federal assistance reaches Native American reservations today, they remain the poorest areas in the country; in some, such as the Winemucca Colony in Nevada, *all* members are poor.[3]

In addition to racial distinctions, welfare policies from early on embodied what sociologist Mimi Abramovitz calls the "work ethic" and the "family ethic."[4] The work ethic insists that relief must pay less than wage labor, in order to avoid disrupting low wage labor markets. The family ethic holds that a woman should marry a man capable of supporting her, and that assistance should reward women who conform to this ethic (such as widows) and punish those who do not (such as divorced or never-married mothers). Based on the family ethic, relief for men and women typically differed. At the turn of the twentieth century, progressive era welfare programs built in gender distinctions, offering workmen's compensation for industrial working class men and mother's aid for impoverished widows with children. Both programs were limited primarily to whites.

## THE FEDS STEP IN

The watershed 1935 Social Security Act created a national system of relief. What made this effort different from previous ones was the full recognition that the capitalist system couldn't always provide a job for male breadwinners or assure economic viability for families without a man. But, as with the state and local efforts that preceded it, the work and family ethics lay at the core of the legislation. For 'deserving' workers unemployed through no fault of their own, the act offered Unemployment Insurance. For those families without a viable male breadwinner, two distinct programs were established. The first, Old Age, Survivor, and Disability Insurance (OASDI, Social Security's official name), gave support to the elderly according to their lifetime earnings, and in 1939, also supported the widows and children of men who had logged substantial earnings. The second, Aid to Dependent Families (later to become Aid to Families with Dependent Children), was a residual program, offering low levels of aid to those mothers (mainly widows, initially) for whom OASDI did not adequately provide. The law locked in strict distinctions between "men's" and "women's" welfare programs, and between "deserving" and "undeserving" recipients.

The color line also persisted. Due to the influence of Southern congressmen, the Social Security Act perpetuated a racial double standard. The Act's core programs, unemployment compensation and old age assistance, excluded agricultural workers and domestic servants, and thus the majority of black workers in the South. Blacks were left to less generous social assistance programs. Moreover, Southerners purged from the legislation any hint of uniform national standards. In practice, the state and local authorities who administered social welfare programs gave African-Americans second-class treatment.[5]

In some form, all of these double standards remain with us to this day. In the United States, anti-poverty policies continue to revolve around the firm belief that hard work pays off, traditional 'family values' should be rewarded, and people of color relying on welfare are less deserving than other recipients. Nonetheless, policy emphases have shifted over time. Policymakers in the 1960s stressed the need to assure economic growth in order to reduce poverty. A robust economy, they argued, would reduce unemployment; as more people had jobs, poverty would decline.[6] These liberal policies are often called Keynesian, in honor of British economist John Maynard Keynes, who in the 1930s developed theories about how governments could stimulate economic expansion. The Keynesian approach focused not on the characteristics of individuals and families who were poor, but rather on the economic environment conditioning poor people's opportunities.

In the late 1970s, a much more conservative theory rapidly supplanted Keynesian economics. The emphasis on jobs still held sway—but instead of focusing on the structural problems of the economy, policymakers insisted that structural problems of individuals and families caused poverty. Human capital—such individual characteristics as education level and job experience—and motivation, rather than the unemployment rate, were seen as the determining factors in one's ability to get and keep a job.[7] Since the early 1980s, changes in anti-poverty programs have put the spotlight on single mothers, and the main thrust of the programs has been toward job training and placement plus behavioral restrictions, attempts to bolster the same old work and family ethics.

Despite their contrasting perspectives, both the economic growth-based and behavior-based approaches to alleviating poverty are flawed and fail to address widespread poverty among single mother families. Let's take a closer look at each approach.

## THE GROWTH THEORY: A RISING TIDE LIFTS ALL BOATS

When the Johnson administration began its 'War on Poverty' in the mid-1960s, the conventional wisdom held that policies promoting economic growth were the most effective way to combat poverty. Further economic growth was also assumed to be the best way to promote a higher standard of living for all and bring about greater economic equality.

During the 1960s and 1970s, the emphasis on growth played out both in attempts to stimulate the national economy and in targeted aid to depressed regions (such as Appalachia) and localities. The geography-based regional and local job creation programs included rural literacy and development projects, job training, urban development, and education grants. To some extent, the notion that a rising tide lifts all boats persists among many policymakers at the state and national levels, but it has more recently been translated into new policy prescriptions. The 'trickle down' economic policies of eliminating

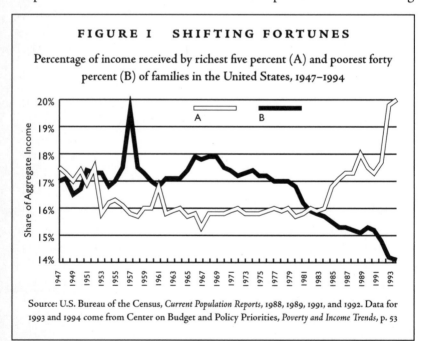

**FIGURE I    SHIFTING FORTUNES**

Percentage of income received by richest five percent (A) and poorest forty percent (B) of families in the United States, 1947–1994

Source: U.S. Bureau of the Census, *Current Population Reports*, 1988, 1989, 1991, and 1992. Data for 1993 and 1994 come from Center on Budget and Policy Priorities, *Poverty and Income Trends*, p. 53

regulations on businesses while decreasing taxation on corporations and wealthy individuals represent a conservative variation on the 'rising tide' approach.

The central proposition of the rising tide approach is that a growing economy will mean more jobs and more income for all. And indeed, in the 1960s and the early 1970s, nationwide growth did lessen poverty and increase equality. Since the early 1970s, however, the links between economic growth, reduced poverty, and greater equality have become much weaker. Despite economic growth, inequality among families in the United States has increased considerably, and growth has done little to reduce poverty. Figure 1 depicts the shifting distribution of income by comparing the richest five percent of the population to the poorest forty percent: while the bottom forty percent made gains during the 1960s, the top five percent pulled ahead once more over the 1970s and 1980s. Figure 2 shows the poverty rate from 1959 to 1995 in the United States for three age groups: people under eighteen, people eighteen to sixty-four, and people sixty-five years and older. Despite

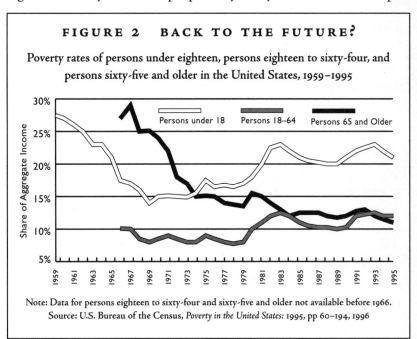

**FIGURE 2    BACK TO THE FUTURE?**

Poverty rates of persons under eighteen, persons eighteen to sixty-four, and persons sixty-five and older in the United States, 1959–1995

Persons under 18    Persons 18–64    Persons 65 and Older

Share of Aggregate Income

Note: Data for persons eighteen to sixty-four and sixty-five and older not available before 1966.
Source: U.S. Bureau of the Census, *Poverty in the United States: 1995*, pp 60–194, 1996

ups and downs reflecting short term booms and busts in the economy, the long term downward trend in poverty rates ended in the 1970s, and poverty rates among children have risen markedly since that time. This reversal took place even though long term economic growth continued (with occasional setbacks when recessions hit).

There are several reasons for this seeming paradox of economic growth accompanied by increased inequality and persistent poverty. First, the fruits of that growth have not been equally shared. Between 1983 and 1989, close to forty percent of the increase in income and sixty-six percent of the increase in financial wealth went to the richest one percent of the population.[8] Further, income growth in the 1980s was due, in large part, to property income gains, not increases in wage income. The high interest rates of the 1980s, the fortunes made in leveraged buyouts and corporate mergers, and the real estate speculation bonanza all largely benefited those with lots of money to begin with. Meanwhile, the decline in manufacturing jobs in the United States lowered the standard of living for many workers—especially men without college degrees. Average wages for non-supervisory workers fell (after adjusting for inflation), meaning that for a growing number of families, jobs do not provide an escape from poverty. The growth-based approach of poverty policy in the post-World War II period assumed growing industrial employment for breadwinners. That assumption no longer holds.

Massachusetts provides a good case study of the changing relationship among growth, poverty, and inequality. The rising tide of wage growth in Massachusetts in the 1980s—the 'Massachusetts miracle'— was among the most spectacular of all the states. Yet the 'miracle' was not enough to lift many families out of poverty. Massachusetts saw average incomes rise rapidly from 1979 to 1987, with a 16.5 percent increase in the average inflation-adjusted family income (compared to 4.2 percent for the whole United States). But not all families 'cashed in.' While two-adult families without children saw their incomes rise by thirty-six percent, two-adult families with children only experienced a fourteen percent increase—less than the state average. Faring the worst of all, however, were single-mother families—the family type most likely to be poor at the onset of the miraculous economic performance. Single mother families' incomes grew by a puny two percent, while their poverty rate went from forty-eight percent in 1979 to forty-seven percent in 1987.[9] In the United States as a whole, the income rise was not as dramatic, but the same pattern prevailed: single mothers got almost no advantage from economic growth.

In short, an economic recovery *on its own* offers little hope of economic relief for single mother families. Even before the Massachusetts experience, conservatives seized on this fact and drew a simple conclusion: it must be the fault of the single mothers themselves.

## BLAMING THE VICTIM: SINGLE MOTHER BASHING

Government-sponsored poverty programs of the 1980s focused on regulating the behavior of single mothers. This represented a shift away from the earlier model that used government spending to propel national growth while assisting rural and urban areas with high levels of poverty. Beginning in the late 1970s, these programs were sharply curtailed as federal, state, and local government deficits put increased pressure on officials to reduce social welfare spending. In 1981, the Reagan administration turned fifty programs into nine block grants, reducing their funding by twelve percent.[10]

At the same time, the Reagan administration severely tightened eligibility requirements for non-elder individuals receiving income transfers, specifically AFDC and disability-based SSI payments. And for those still receiving welfare, the 1988 Family Support Act made job placement a paramount goal. Reagan administration spokespeople claimed that welfare created dependency and that government did more harm than good by offering 'handouts.' Despite the fact that the government offers all sorts of 'handouts' to disabled veterans, unemployed people, and elders, welfare recipients were painted with a broad brushstroke as weak and dependent for having to rely on government income as a main source of support. Racial stereotyping helped fuel this assault, despite the fact that most welfare recipients are white and non-Latino (other government assistance programs go even more overwhelmingly to whites).

The demonizing of the poor, especially welfare recipients, has reached new heights in the 1990s. Political candidates (Democrat and Republican alike), talk show hosts, and conservative journalists use welfare as a political football. The range of rhetoric spans from President Clinton's popular 1992 campaign promise to "end welfare as we know it" to Rush Limbaugh's blast, "The poor in this country are the biggest piglets at the mother pig and her nipples."[11] A heightened frequency of racist salvos directed at immigrants and people of color has fed these attacks on welfare. In a short period of time, we have seen the 1960s 'War on Poverty' evolve into a war on the poor.

Conservatives have particularly focused on out-of-wedlock births in an attempt to pump up the family ethic in welfare reform at a time when family structure is in tremendous flux. The two pillars that have allowed for an extremely limited social safety net in the United States are crumbling: plentiful industrial-based jobs for male breadwinners and the traditional married-couple family. The increasing diversity of families, along with the inability of the growing economy to alleviate the pangs of poverty, has created a new conundrum for policymakers. Unfortunately, far too many have responded by lashing out at the victims of economic inequality.

### THE SELF-STYLED BAD BOYS OF POVERTY RESEARCH: CHARLES MURRAY AND ROBERT RECTOR

Well-funded conservative think tanks have played a major role in fueling the poverty policy shifts of the 1980s and 1990s. True, the 'single mother bashing' approach to poverty policy is driven primarily by ideology, not by logical arguments. But there are researchers who devote themselves to providing a 'scientific' gloss to this punitive philosophy. Foremost among them are sociologist Charles Murray of the American Enterprise Institute (AEI) and Robert Rector of the Heritage Foundation. The clout wielded by AEI and Heritage, two of the leading Washington-based right wing think tanks, can hardly be overstated. These two conservative brain trusts, along with others, have saturated the media and Congress for years with their calls for dismantling AFDC and adopting what they call a "tough love" approach to poor people.[12] In the first 100 days of the 1995 Congress, staff members from the Heritage Foundation testified before lawmakers forty times.[13]

Lurking behind the soundbites is the dubious scholarship of Murray and Rector. These two delight in appearing controversial and present themselves as courageous scholars who dare to say what others won't. But in reality, how much courage is involved in riding a swelling conservative tide? Murray and Rector are simply providing intellectual cover for views that blame poor people and 'big government' for perpetuating poverty, and they have become wealthy right wing celebrities as a result.

Murray's notoriety began with the publication of his book *Losing Ground* in 1984.[14] The centerpiece of the book was a chart that showed U.S. poverty rates rising through the 1970s and early 1980s, at a time when government spending on poverty was also rising. Murray glibly concluded that government anti-poverty programs were contributing to poverty by making it easier to survive without working for pay. He argued that government policies should instead make poverty as uncomfortable as possible—in his view, the squalid workhouses of old were a reasonable solution.

Critics pointed out that Murray had overlooked some of the obvious explanations for the increases on his chart. First, Murray chose to ignore the fact that long struggles to distribute benefits to those who were legally entitled but effectively excluded from receiving welfare were finally being won. Some of the spending expansion in the late 1960s and 1970s was directly attributable to successful lawsuits challenging restrictive eligibility rules, along with the organizing done by those in the civil rights and welfare rights movements. These efforts transformed what had been a small program largely restricted to white widows into a welfare program increasingly available to single and nonwhite parents as well. Second, through the 1970s and early 1980s, a harsher economic climate pushed more people into poverty, which in turn led to more spending on the entitlement programs available to poor people. Economists have demonstrated that the poverty rate closely tracks overall economic well-being and rose consistently in step with economic deterioration over the 1970s and 1980s.[15] In fact, although after-inflation AFDC benefit levels and coverage rates (AFDC recipiency as a percentage of the poor) rose in the late 1960s and early 1970s, benefits and coverage fell from the mid-1970s onward—so Murray's claim of growing government generosity rings hollow.

But Murray brushed these objections aside, and was off and running. In 1994 he made headlines again, along with co-author Richard Herrnstein, with the publication of *The Bell Curve*.[16] Herrnstein and Murray declared that income differences—including those of race—are primarily and increasingly a result or genetically determined intelligence. Again, the evidence for this far-reaching claim is flimsy indeed, as numerous critics have pointed out.[17] Leaving aside problems of sloppy statistical methods (which are rife in *The Bell Curve*), there are several reasons for rejecting this claim. First, many differences in intelligence test scores are due to systematic differences in home, school and neighborhood environments—differences that, like genes, tend to be passed down from parent to child in our stratified society.

Second, performance on standardized tests is affected by the expectations of oneself and others. For example, in a study on black and white Stanford University undergraduates, psychologists Claude Steele and Joshua Aronson found that blacks performed worse than whites when required to identify their race at the start of the test, but performed better than whites when this requirement was removed.[18]

Third, race and gender discrimination in employment are alive and well. Recent 'audit' studies that sent black and white applicants with identical résumés to apply for jobs found that, on average, whites were more likely than blacks to get called in for an interview and more likely to be offered a job if interviewed.[19] Direct interviews with employers reveal that many of them freely voice crude racial stereotypes.[20] And sex segregation in jobs, along with the accompanying gender stereotypes, persists despite women's limited inroads into "men's" work.[21]

In other recent broadsides, Murray has argued that rising welfare benefits have driven increases in single motherhood.[22] Again, this position is difficult to maintain, since even his own charts show that the most dramatic rises in single motherhood have taken place during times when inflation-adjusted AFDC benefits decreased. But as always, the facts have not slowed Murray down.

Rector echoes Murray's views, contending that "welfare is an insidious system in which the more you spend, the more clientele for the programs you create…. The more you spend, the more you erode the work ethic, the more out-of-wedlock births you have." Unlike Murray, Rector doesn't write books and has stayed out of academic debates. But his impact on policy is even greater than Murray's. As a policy analyst for the Heritage Foundation, he has been directly involved in lobbying Congress, providing intellectual fodder for conservative groups, and drafting legislation. "He's the think-tanker for a large network of people," comments Stuart Butler, Heritage's director of domestic policy studies.[23] Rector is pushing a harsh welfare reform agenda that has increasingly found a home in state and federal legislation: cuts in benefit levels, strict work requirements, and making benefits contingent upon 'responsible behavior' (for example, requiring teen mothers to live with their parents).[24]

## SPENDING ON WELFARE: NOT TOO MUCH, BUT TOO LITTLE

> *In 1992, federal, state, and local governments spent $305 billion on means-tested welfare programs for low income Americans. Welfare now absorbs five percent of the Gross National Product, up from 1.5 percent in 1965 when the War on Poverty began.*
> —Heritage Foundation[25]

This soundbite exemplifies the Heritage Foundation's mythmaking machine at work. But a closer look at Heritage's numbers is instructive. There has been an enormous amount of media attention devoted to AFDC and its successor program, Temporary Assistance to Needy Families (TANF). Both programs, however, have represented a tiny— and recently shrinking—portion of the government budget.

As a percent of both the Gross Domestic Product (GDP) and the federal budget, combined federal spending on AFDC and food stamps has declined. In 1980, the two programs accounted for 0.8 percent of the GDP and 3.2 percent of the federal budget. By 1993, the two programs made up 0.7 percent of the GDP and 2.4 percent of the federal budget.[26] With federal spending on TANF now capped at $16.4 billion per year, these percentages stand to diminish still further. State spending on AFDC has also remained low. In 1970, states spent three percent of their budgets on AFDC benefits; by 1993, that percentage dropped to just under two percent.[27] And TANF frees states to spend still less on welfare.

Because of rising health care costs, a much larger percentage of state and federal budgets goes toward Medicaid. In 1992, Medicaid took up five percent of the federal budget, up from 2.5 percent in 1980.[28] It is only by including Medicaid as 'welfare spending' that the figures used by the Heritage Foundation resemble reality. But less than thirty percent of total Medicaid spending is for welfare recipients.[29] The lion's share of Medicaid goes to elders and others who need long term care; middle class families rely on Medicaid to pay for their ailing parents in nursing homes. The rapidly rising cost of health care—whether publicly or privately financed—cannot and should not be blamed on the health care demands of poor children and their mothers.

And what about the $305 billion figure? Government spending on poor women and their children is one-quarter of the Heritage Foundation's purported figure. In 1992, federal and state governments spent a combined total of $43 billion on AFDC and food stamps. Total Medicaid spending for families receiving AFDC was $27.5 billion. So an accurate estimate of the costs of welfare spending in that year is $70.5 billion. By way of comparison, federal spending on two common middle class tax exemptions came in at just under $100 billion: the value of the tax exemption for employer-sponsored health insurance was $47 billion and the mortgage deduction from income taxes was $49 billion.[30]

The Heritage Foundation's depiction of a bloated welfare state is a myth, yet the crisis of U.S. anti-poverty policy is a real one. The move away from economic development strategies to an individually based anti-poverty program focused on pushing poor people into jobs has not worked for single mothers and their children. It has failed to reduce poverty among single mother families, and it has failed to make women less 'dependent.' Poverty rates among children and single mother families have steadily risen, and the rates at which low income single mothers return to welfare after getting off have not improved. The failure to reduce poverty among single mother families, however, is not due to the failures of the recipients or the excessive generosity of the welfare payments. Rather, this failure results from the inadequacy of poverty programs, the inability of the labor market to adequately absorb and compensate women workers with limited education, and the fragility of traditional family relations.

Specifically, welfare grants pay not too much, but too little. Since AFDC payments did not automatically rise with inflation and states have been reluctant to increase payments, welfare has taken fewer and fewer single mothers out of poverty. In 1973, twenty-two percent of all single mother families were lifted out of poverty by government assistance, but only eleven percent were in 1993.[31] AFDC benefits for a family of three in a typical state fell from $690 in 1970 to $366 in 1994 (using 1994 dollars).[32] Nationwide, *fewer* poor children receive AFDC today than in past decades. The percentage of poor children receiving AFDC peaked in 1973 at eighty percent, but had dropped to fifty-nine percent by 1990.[33]

Eligibility requirements restrict welfare to a small number of very needy families. To be eligible to receive cash assistance, one must be extremely poor and have children (or be pregnant). Income eligibility varies from state to state and by length of time on welfare. Federal requirements stipulated that individuals might only own a car with a net market value of $1,500 or less, and might have no more than $1,000 in cash, checking, and savings accounts, or other assets. Once on welfare, families were legally allowed to keep $50 of any child support payments per month, remitting the rest to the state. Under new federal legislation, states have complete discretion over these requirements, for good or ill.

Welfare is funded jointly by the federal government and states. The total amount of money, adjusted for inflation, spent by states and the federal government on AFDC in the mid-1990s was no higher than it was in the early 1970s. And while total spending for the food stamp program has increased over the same period, it has not been able to keep up with the increase in the numbers of poor women and children. Between 1971 and 1993, the number of poor people in female-headed families increased by one hundred percent, but the number of AFDC recipients only increased by fifty percent.[34]

The notion that the United States spends too much on welfare is strained indeed. U.S. relief programs started out stingy and, for the most part, have remained so for over 300 years. Guided by the 'work ethic,' the 'family ethic,' and durable racial stereotypes, the federal, state, and local governments have kept benefits low, tied them to work and family structure requirements, and excluded whole groups as 'undeserving.' While the 'rising tide' strategy targeting economic growth and regionally based assistance did little to raise the boats of single mother families, subsequent policies have made the situation worse by blaming the victims of poverty.

NOTES

1. This historical discussion is based on Nancy Rose, *Workfare or Fair Work? Women, Welfare, and Government Work Programs* (New Brunswick, NJ: Rutgers University Press, 1995), particularly chapter 1, and Nancy Rose, "Gender, Race, and the Welfare State: Government Work Programs From the 1930s to the Present," *Feminist Studies*, vol. 19, no. 7 (1993). Other useful historical sources include Mimi Abramovitz, *Regulating the Lives of Women: Social Welfare Policy from Colonial Times to the Present* (Boston: South End Press, 1988), and Linda Gordon, *Pitied But Not Entitled: Single Mothers and the History of Welfare, 1830–1335* (New York: Free Press, 1994).

2. *Workfare or Fair Work?*, op. cit., pg. 19.

3. Amort, Teresa L. and Julie A. Matthaei. *Race, Gender, and Work: A Multicultural Economic History of Women in the United States* (Boston: South End Press, 1996).

4. *Regulating the Lives of Women*, op. cit.

5. Quadagno, Jill. *The Color of Welfare: How Racism Undermined the War on Poverty* (New York: Oxford University Press, 1994), chapter 1.

6. For a review of some of this literature, see Isabel Sawhill, "Poverty in the U.S.: Why Is It So Persistent?" *Journal of Economic Literature*, vol. 26, no. 3 (September 1988).

7. For a comprehensive view of human capital theory, see Gary Becker, *Human Capital: A Theoretical and Empirical Analysis* (New York: Columbia University Press, 1964).

8. Wolff, Edward N. *Top Heavy: A Study of the Increasing Inequality of Wealth in America* (New York: Twentieth Century Fund, 1995).

9. Tilly, Chris and Randy Albelda. "It'll Take More Than a Miracle: Income in Single Mother Families in Massachusetts, 1979–87," occasional paper, University of Massachusetts-Boston, John W. McCormack Institute for Public Affairs, 1992.

10. Gold, Steve. "The ABCs of Block Grants," *State Fiscal Brief, Center for the Study of the States* (Albany, NY: Nelson A. Rockefeller Institute of Government), no. 28 (March 1992).

11. Limbaugh, Rush. *The Way Things Ought to Be* (New York: Pocket Books, 1993), pg. 41.

12. The Heritage Foundation materials are quite misleading, if not inaccurate. See Randy Albelda, Nancy Folbre, and the Center for Popular Economics, *The War on the Poor: A Defense Manual* (New York: The New Press, 1996).

13. Georges, Christopher. "Conservative Heritage Foundation Finds Recipe for Influence: Ideas and Marketing Clout," *Wall Street Journal*, August 8, 1995, pg. A10.

14. Muray, Charles A. *Losing Ground: American Social Policy, 1950–1980* (New York: Basic Books, 1994).

15. Ellwood, David. *Poor Support: Poverty in the American Family* (New York: Basic Books, 1988); Peter Gottschalk and Sheldon Danziger, "Macroeconomic Conditions, Income Transfers, and Poverty," in *The Social Contract Revisited*, ed. D. Lee Bawden (Washington, DC: Urban Institute Press, 1984).

16. Herrnstein, Richard and Charles A. Murray. *The Bell Curve: Intelligence and Class Structure in American Life* (New York: Free Press, 1994).

17. For a sampling of commentary on *The Bell Curve*, see Steven Fraser, ed., *The Bell Curve Wars* (New York: Basic Books, 1995), and Russell Jacoby and Naomi Glauberman, *The Bell Curve Debate* (New York: Times Books, 1995).

18. Steele, Claude M. and Joshua Aronson. "Stereotype Threat and the Intellectual Test Performance of African-Americans," *Journal of Personality and Social Psychology*, vol. 69, no. 5, 1995.

19. Turner, Margery A., Michael Fix, and Raymond J. Struyk. *Opportunities Denied, Opportunities Diminished: Racial Discrimination in Hiring*, Urban Institute report 91-9 (Washington, DC: Urban Institute, 1991); Marc Bendick Jr., Charles W. Jackson, and Victor A. Reinoso, "Measuring Employment Discrimination through Controlled Experiments," *Review of Black Political Economy* (Summer 1994).

20. Kirshenman, Joleen and Katherine Neckerman. " 'We'd Love to Hire Them, But....': The Meaning of Race for Employers," in *The Urban Underclass*, eds. Christopher Jencks and Paul E. Peterson (Washington, DC: Brookings Institution, 1991). Philip Moss and Chris Tilly, "'Soft' Skills and Race: An Investigation of Black Men's Employment Problems," *Work and Occupations*, vol. 23, no. 3, 1996.

21. Reskin, Barbara F. and Heidi I. Hartmann. *Women's Work, Men's Work: Sex Segregation on the Job* (Washington, DC: National Academy Press, 1986).

22. Murray, Charles. "Does Welfare Bring More Babies?" *The American Enterprise Institute* (January/February 1994).

23. Quotes are from Hilary Stout, "GOP's Welfare Stance Owes a Lot to Prodding from Robert Rector," *Wall Street Journal*, January 23, 1995, pg. A1.

24. Rector, Robert. "Requiem for the War on Poverty: Rethinking Welfare After the L.A. Riots," *Policy Review Magazine* (Summer 1992).

25. Heritage Foundation. *Combating Family Disintegration, Crime, and Dependence: Welfare Reform and Beyond* (Washington, DC: Heritage Foundation, 1994), pg. 1.

26. *The War on the Poor*, op. cit.

27. AFDC expenditures are from *U.S. House Committee on Ways and Means, Overview of Entitlement Programs, 1994* Green Book (Washington, DC: Government Printing Office, 1994), pg. 389; state expenditures for 1970 are from *Advisory Committee on Intergovernmental Relations, Significant Features of Fiscal Federalism*, 1989 Edition, vol. II; state expenditures for 1992 are from *Statistical Abstract of the United States, 1994* (Washington, DC: Government Printing Office, 1995).

28. U.S. Bureau of the Census. *Statistical Abstract of the United States* (Washington, DC: Government Printing Office, 1995).

29. Ibid., table 162.

30. *The War on the Poor*, op. cit. Figure for mortgage interest deduction is for 1993.

31. Calculated by authors from U.S. Bureau of the Census, *Current Population Survey*, March 1974 and 1994.

32. Parrott, Sharon and Robert Greenstein. *Welfare, Out-of-Wedlock Childbearing, and Poverty: What is the Connection?* (Washington, DC: Center on Budget and Policy Priorities, 1995).

33. *Overview of Entitlement Programs*, op. cit.

34. Ibid.

# 12

## WOMEN, WELFARE, AND WORK

*Mimi Abramovitz*

The United States is proud of its work ethic—Americans believe that people who can find work ought to—and as a result, welfare and work have always been linked. We can see how the link is a particularly capitalist one, however, when we realize that calls for welfare reform crop up at times when women are using the welfare system as an alternative to dirty, dangerous, and low-paying jobs. Thus it is at those moments when wages fall below the welfare grant or when employers want to increase the supply of low-paid workers that policymakers try to reform welfare to make sure that only the most desperate choose it over employment.

In the current debate, welfare critics have focussed on women's work behavior and justified their assault by invoking negative, unfounded, and often racialized stereotypes of poor women. For instance, they have claimed that welfare recipients do not want to work for wages, that they are lazy and need the strong arm of the government to make them change their ways. As one example, Governor Kirk Fordice of Mississippi was reported to have declared that "the only job training that welfare recipients need is a good alarm clock." Lawrence Mead, a conservative political scientist, concluded that "the poor remain economically passive in a society where other low-skilled people find abundant opportunity." Robert Rector, a policy analyst with the Heritage Foundation, told Congress that if everyone would simply "finish high school, get a job, any job, and stick with it and not have children outside of marriage, no one would be poor."[1]

Despite evidence that the labor market can neither absorb all those willing and able to work nor pay a living wage to everyone who needs one, these welfare opponents insist that work empowers poor women, raises their self-esteem, and provides them with a sense of control over their lives. However, if they had been asked, the women on welfare would have told the reformers that the reality is far more complex.

Until the mid-1970s, a full-time, full-year job paying the federal mini-mum wage could lift a worker out of poverty, but that has not been the case in any year since. As one thirty-seven-year-old New Jersey JOBS participant put it, "How are you supposed to survive on the minimum wage—feed the kids, pay the rent, utilities?"[2]

Take the example of April. She comes from a middle class family. After her boyfriend left her to raise their two children alone, she took a job working the swing shift in a nursing home. After three months she was forced to leave because the job "wasn't even paying my bills. At the end of the week I'd get a check for less than $100. Daycare cost $75. I'd have $10 to eat and $10 to put gas in the car so I could get back and forth to this useless job." Another woman agreed: "It's like a roller coaster. Once you get up there, you realize you can't pay for medical, you can't pay for childcare, you can't pay for your transportation, and then you wonder why you are working. It doesn't make sense why you're putting in all these hours of work and you're not getting any-where. It's like a vicious cycle that everyone gets caught up in."[3]

Years of academic research confirm what these women are saying—that women on welfare desperately want to work or are *already* working—and puts the situation in a larger perspective. Using longi-tudinal data, LaDonna Pavetti, a researcher at the John F. Kennedy School of Government, found that seventy percent of women who receive AFDC leave the rolls within two years, either to work or to marry, and that only seven percent stay for more than eight years. She also reported that while unstable jobs, lack of childcare and health benefits, and failed relationships sent a significant number of women back onto AFDC within five years, most of the returnees only used wel-fare as a short-term economic backup during a crisis. A small number did need assistance for longer than eight years, but these tended to be single mothers of young children who were school drop-outs with lit-tle work experience, or women who were too ill or disabled to work at all.[4]

A study by the Washington, DC-based Institute for Women's Policy Research (IWPR) found that the average AFDC mother works about 950 hours a year, approximately the same as all mothers in the work-force; that over forty percent of women on welfare 'package' AFDC with wages, either simultaneously or sequentially; and that an additional thirty percent spend substantial time looking for work but cannot find it. The IWPR also reported that the state of the local labor market made a big difference: welfare mothers living in states with unemployment rates of ten percent or more had only a thirteen percent chance of finding jobs, while those in states where unemployment was 3.5 percent or less had a twenty-nine percent chance. In addition, many working welfare mothers hold sporadic full-time jobs rather than steady part-time ones, and the majority are in low-wage 'women's occupations.'[5]

Even those women who found jobs did not earn enough to make ends meet. Although three-quarters of the single mothers who received AFDC during the two-year period studied by the IWPR were in the paid labor force, few worked enough hours or earned enough to lift their families out of poverty. These women earned an average of $4.29 an hour (in 1990 dollars) on their primary job, compared to $10.03 for non-farm private sector employees in 1990. The IWPR researchers concluded that "recipients use AFDC for many reasons, including to supplement their low-wage work effort and to provide a safety net during periods of unemployment, disability, and family crises." While AFDC may need to be reformed because of its inadequacies, it "cannot be eliminated without causing great harm to already impoverished families."[6] These findings have been confirmed by other well-known studies of welfare-to-work programs, which conclude that most recipients would readily leave welfare if they could—in other words, if there were enough jobs with decent wages and such benefits as childcare and healthcare.[7]

The welfare critics also downplay the difficulties women have balancing work and family. Indeed, only half of all mothers with young children—even those with husbands—work at all, and many only work part time. Work does indeed provide important personal and social benefits, but working in a dirty, dangerous, demeaning, and low-paid job does not guarantee a positive outcome. Yet reforms that will require that a certain percent of a state's caseload be off welfare and at work will throw millions of women into the labor force. According to the Economic Policy Institute, swelling the labor pool in this way could lead to a more than ten percent decline in the wages of low-paid workers—more in states with larger welfare populations, such as New York (an estimated 17.1 percent decline) and California (an estimated 17.8 percent decline). In five states, wages could end up below the federal minimum.[8] Unions, especially those representing public employees, have been especially concerned about this, but effective guarantees against their members being displaced in this way do not appear in the reform bills.

Some reformers do recognize that welfare alone is not enough, but it is doubtful that the few supplements they favor will help welfare mothers unless they are modified to take women's work and family life into account. Neither the Earned Income Tax Credit (EITC—a tax rebate for the working poor) nor Unemployment Insurance supports people who are not in the labor force or who stay home to raise children. A woman who packaged EITC and part-time or temporary work would be less well off financially than if she combined AFDC and the same job.[9] Furthermore, Congress, in its rush to weaken all federal programs, has put even the highly touted EITC on the chopping block. In today's economy, Clinton's promise "to make work pay for those who try hard and play by the rules" rings hollow for women on welfare. One New York AFDC recipient explained, "You need real jobs for people...throwing people off welfare won't work, how are they going to get jobs if they are in the streets?" Testifying at a Connecticut hearing, a thirty-two-year-old woman who has had to alternate between menial jobs and welfare said, "I have no problem working, but the skills I have are not enough." A welfare mother in Oregon focused on the larger picture: "Women are supposed to fill all the minimum wage jobs in this country," she declared. Like other women on welfare, she realized that pushing mothers off AFDC into low-paid jobs benefits businesses and politicians, but keeps women in 'their place.'[10]

## UPHOLDING THE FAMILY ETHIC

Another assault has been on women's marital, childbearing, and parenting behavior. Indeed, welfare reform has been governed by a 'family ethic' as well as a work ethic. According to the American 'family ethic,' or set of beliefs about how families should operate, people should marry and live in two-parent households, preferably with one wage earner and one homemaker. All other family types are considered deviant. Realizing that this is a patriarchal concept of the family will help us understand why calls for welfare reform often arise alongside public concerns about changes in women's roles and in the structure of the family. For instance, in recent years conservative social scientists have associated rising rates of nonmarital births with the 'breakdown' of the family and have deplored the 'reproductive deviance' of poor women.[11] They charge that AFDC finances "a subculture of people" who want children but not marriage, who disdain family commitments, and "who downplay the importance of male figures." The typical AFDC parent today, they say, is not the worthy widow envisaged in the original legislation but a divorced, deserted, or never-married woman.

Beneath all this rhetoric lies the patriarchal premise that any family without a father is defective. As one expert who testified a few years ago about the impact of welfare on families concluded, "Raised in an environment in which fathers don't provide for the young and dependency on government is assumed, few children will develop the skills of self-sufficiency, or even the concept of personal responsibility. Young men will not strive to be good providers, and young women will not expect it of their men."[12]

Many politicians from both political parties agree that all kinds of social problems—from poverty to crime to the deficit—stem from this decline in 'family values.' To underscore this point, they have resurrected such long-discredited terms as 'unfit' mothers and 'illegitimate' children, and have associated single parenthood with a decline in morality. For instance, both the Democratic and Republican welfare plans link eligibility for AFDC to compliance with certain standards of marital, childbearing, and parenting behavior, penalizing women who depart from certain prescribed wife and mother roles.

Single mothers are punished in at least three ways. First, there is the highly controversial child exclusion, also called the family cap because it denies AFDC to children who are born while their mothers are receiving AFDC and to unmarried teen mothers and their children. If a woman insists on becoming pregnant, the lawmakers tell her that she should turn to relatives, apply for charity, or place her child in an orphanage—ignoring the fact that these cost an average of $36,500 per child per year. Second, paternity penalties are stiffened. States are required to withhold some benefits from mothers who refuse to help identify the child's father, as well as from mothers who cooperate with the authorities but fail to establish paternity due to bureaucratic red tape or the father's ability to conceal his whereabouts. While establishing paternity can help children to gain access to child support and Social Security survivor's benefits, these unduly restrictive procedures penalize women for not having men in the home and at the same time place their children in harm's way. In fact, one estimate suggests that enforcement of the paternity rule would throw nearly thirty percent of children off the AFDC rolls.[13] Third, there is an 'illegitimacy' bonus—extra federal money for states that lower their nonmarital birth *and* abortion rates.[14]

These efforts to regulate marriage, childbearing, and parenting began in the states. As he did with time limits, President Clinton encouraged the states to develop their own child exclusion and 'parenting' programs by waiving federal rules that prevented such actions.

When such measures are imposed as a *condition* of aid, they take advantage of a woman's dire financial situation, leaving her with little choice but to trade her health, as well as her contraceptive, religious, and parenting preferences, for an AFDC check. This type of economic coercion presumes that poor women are unable to make their own reproductive decisions and therefore must be subjected to the strong arm of the government.

MYTHS ABOUT WOMEN, WELFARE, AND CHILDBEARING

Like the welfare reforms that target women's work behavior these efforts to control their reproductive behavior have been fueled by numerous myths and stereotypes, all of which have repeatedly been proved wrong by researchers. It has been suggested, for example, that AFDC is responsible for changes in family structure—not only the declining rate of marriage and the rise of single mother households, but also the increase in the nonmarital birth rate. In fact, neither poor women nor welfare can be held responsible for changes in family patterns that have spread throughout society and affected women in all walks of life.

*Marriage:* One myth is that AFDC breaks up families. Even though AFDC rules disqualify most two-parent families, the program does not create single parent households. Welfare critics say AFDC causes marriages to break up because the program for single parents sometimes leads men to move out so their families can survive. But research, psychological knowledge, and plain commonsense suggest that even poor people marry and divorce for a host of reasons that have nothing whatsoever to do with the availability of an AFDC check. Indeed, in 1993 half of all women in the United States between the ages of fifteen and forty-four were not married; compared to earlier periods, people are getting married later, divorcing and separating more, and are less likely to remarry and more likely to cohabit. Moreover, the number of one parent families with children more than doubled between 1970 and 1993, while those with two parents fell, from 87.1 percent to 73 percent. As a result, single parents headed twenty-seven percent of all families with children in 1993, up from only 12.8 percent in 1970. More than half of all children born today will be raised by only one parent during a part of their lifetimes. And while single motherhood is more prevalent in the black community than in the white, those who hold welfare responsible rarely note that two-thirds of all single parents are white.[15]

Fears about women and marriage have been projected onto AFDC as fewer and fewer mother-only families, both on AFDC and throughout society, are headed by widows—still the most socially acceptable basis for a mother-only family—while more and more are headed by never-married women.[16] As for the racial breakdown, from 1976 to 1992 blacks comprised the majority of never-married recipients, although the proportion declined (from seventy-one to fifty-one percent), while the proportion of white families in this category rose (from nineteen to twenty-seven percent). As a result, the racial composition of never-married women on welfare increasingly resembles that of all never-married women.[17]

*Childbearing:* Another myth about the effect of AFDC on family life is that poor women have kids for money. In fact, women on AFDC have lower fertility rates than women in the general population. Further, the average family on welfare includes a mother and two children, which is also the average for the nation. Forty-three percent of today's AFDC households have only one child and thirty percent have two.[18] Since a women must have at least one child to qualify for AFDC in the first place, and since most women have only one more child while on the rolls, welfare can hardly be considered to cause large families. In any case, many women at all income levels have unintended pregnancies, suggesting the futility of bonuses and penalties.[19] Moreover, the states only provide an average of about $60 a month for each additional child, barely enough to pay for milk and diapers. A more efficient and humane way to lower the nonmarital birth rate than shrinking the already skimpy AFDC grant would be to focus on pregnancy prevention, sex education in the schools, and providing access to family planning and abortion services.

In 1994, seventy-nine social scientists issued a press release to refute the notion that the availability of welfare determined a women's childbearing decisions.[20] These scholars pointed out, for instance, that states with more stringent welfare rules do *not* have fewer nonmarital pregnancies. On the contrary, some states with low benefits have very high nonmarital birth rates. Those few studies that have reported an association between higher benefits and nonmarital births found only a slight connection, and that was only for whites. Moreover, the nonmarital birth rate for all women rose from 26 per 1,000 live births in 1970 to 44 per 1,000 in 1990, while the value of the AFDC grant plummeted by thirty-six percent in the same period.[21] And while child exclusion advocates argue that workers' wages do not automatically rise when they have children, in fact workers receive an additional tax exemption for each new dependent, and many can still count on an annual pay raise when they plan to expand their families. Child exclusion supporters who fear that AFDC payments invite women to have children do not worry that the income tax exemption for dependents, the famed Income Tax Credit for families with children, and the proposed $500 tax credit per child will lead other working and middle class families to have kids 'for money.'

As for the controversial teen mother group, in 1992, five percent of single women receiving AFDC were teen mothers, up from two percent in 1976. Women who gave birth as teenagers made up forty-two percent of the AFDC caseload—but this proportion has remained roughly the same throughout the seventeen-year period, even though the nonmarital birth rate among *all* teenagers has increased steadily.[22] Not only are nonmarital births more common for women in their twenties, but teenage girls often become pregnant by men age twenty or older.[23]

*Parenting:* A third myth about AFDC's impact on family life is that it undermines effective parenting. The view of single parent families as 'broken' or 'deviant' reflects the long-standing distrust of women who raise children without men as heads of the household, especially if the women are poor, non-white, or foreign born. The same negative thinking fuels today's proposals to place children in foster care or orphanages if their mothers cannot find work. In 1994, Myron Magnet of the conservative Manhattan Institute declared, "Anyone who looks at underclass children—neglected, abused, unimmunized, deprived of the moral and cognitive nurturing that families provide—has to ask whose welfare is advanced by a system that consigns so many children to emotional and intellectual stunting and to likely failure in school and later life." From the child's point of view, he added, "an incompetent mother on crack is not better than a Dickensian orphanage." Magnet then recommended that poor children and their mothers be placed in community hostels that would provide them with "the whole array of cognitive and moral categories that one is supposed to learn at home."[24] The effects of this argument, which generalizes from individual instances of self-destructive behavior to all poor women on welfare, can be seen in the current welfare reform bills, which preserve unlimited federal support for children who have been removed from their homes to shelters, foster homes, or institutions. Based on what is happening in states (such as Wisconsin) that have already made drastic AFDC cuts, child protection officials predict that even before the federal reforms are in place, changes at the state level will flood the child welfare system.[25]

Distrust of the ability of poor women to socialize their children (which must sound odd to the women hired to take care of children in middle and upper class homes) clearly underlies such state and federal programs as Learnfare and Healthfare, which use threats to reduce AFDC checks as a way to teach recipients how to parent 'responsibly.' The value of attending school and visiting the doctor goes without saying, yet Learnfare's own evaluators concluded that "a troubling large number of teens described their schools as dangerous and frightening places where learning was difficult and recommended both educational and welfare reform."[26] Improving the public schools and increasing access to healthcare would help poor parents far more than any get-tough 'personal responsibility bill.' And where parental guidance is needed—as it may be in some cases—positive outreach works better than threats of punishment by the state.

The campaign to wring child support from 'deadbeat dads' targets the parenting behavior of poor men. Child support advocates argue that revoking the driving (or professional) licenses of absent fathers who do not pay up will turn them into responsible providers and reduce welfare costs. Critics contend that overly strenuous child support efforts could jeopardize the relationships that many AFDC fathers are able, sometimes with difficulty, to maintain with their children. They also warn that the aggressive pursuit of child support may expose women to male violence. Child support enforcement will in any case produce only minimal funds because poor women partner with poor men and because most of the funds collected go directly to the state.

The truth is that, in the name of increasing parental responsibility, most of the current welfare reform proposals will make it harder for poor women to parent. For one thing, reducing benefits and increasing poverty only adds to family stress. Time limits and mandatory work programs not only devalue a woman's caretaking work, but leave children unsupervised in neighborhoods that have inadequate schools, substandard housing, lack of medical services, and may be plagued by drugs, crime, and violence. A Wisconsin welfare mother avoided attending a job search program while she was going to school so that she could have time to spend with her kids. While her caseworker believed that she could do both, she said, "I know I can, but who would my kids be eating dinner with? Who would put them to bed if I were to work nights and go to school during the day? Even AFDC kids need their moms." Speaking about her efforts to cope after her brother was killed by a stray bullet, a Massachusetts woman explained, "I would walk the girls to the bus, then I would walk to the train and go to work. I would call home about 3:00 PM; my mother was supposed to be home when the girls came home. And if they were not home, I would be frantic. It was so hard, I was going nuts."[27]

If the welfare reformers had bothered to ask the women who receive AFDC, they would have found that they turn to welfare in order to better care for their children. Many years after leaving AFDC, Lynn Woolsey (D-CA), the only former welfare mother ever to serve in Congress, told *The New York Times,* "I know what it is like to lie awake at night and worry about not having any health insurance. I know how hard it is to find good childcare. I had thirteen different baby sitters in one year. I know what it is like to choose between paying the rent and buying new shoes. Like so many American families, we turned to AFDC."[28]

The idea that a female-dominated welfare culture keeps families trapped on welfare from generation to generation is another myth about AFDC that is unsupported by the research. Longitudinal studies indicate that while women from welfare families are more likely than women from non-welfare families to receive AFDC as adults, most women who receive welfare as children do not turn to the program when they grow up.[29] Those studies that found links between welfare and 'intergenerational dependency' did not control for income—leaving it unclear whether daughters of welfare mothers turn to AFDC because they received public assistance as children or because they never escaped poverty.

The evidence suggests that it is *living in poverty,* not welfare, that can lead to families to break up and can bring harm to children, and most women on AFDC were poor before they became recipients. When low wages and high unemployment prevent men from carrying out their breadwinner roles, fewer men and women want to, or can, marry. This is especially true in the African-American community, where racism takes a heavy economic toll. Economic insecurity can also lead marriages to dissolve. In any case, marriage is not every woman's preference; nor is it necessarily an effective anti-poverty strategy. While two incomes are usually better than one, the sad truth is that many women remain poor even if they tie the knot: two-earner households are one of the nation's fastest growing poverty groups.

Poverty, rather than a welfare check, can also harm children.[30] Poverty reduces the chance of getting an education and a job, limits economic mobility, and negatively affects health and self-esteem. The pressure placed on adults who have to juggle employment and childcare, find adequate housing, and manage small incomes can place children at risk of parental abuse. Those who link welfare to negative behavior often fail to take the role of poverty into account—even though everyone on welfare is poor. Since social problems do appear more frequently among poor families and since single mothers (whether never-married or divorced) do tend to be poor, blaming poverty on welfare conveniently deflects attention from its roots in the economy.

## THE WAR ON WELFARE CONCERNS ALL WOMEN

Welfare reform harms women on AFDC for being poor and raising children on their own. But the proposed reforms threaten the rights of *all* women to decent pay, to control over their own sexuality, to a life free of abusive relationships, and to a choice of families that do not fit the two-parent model. They do this by weakening women's caretaking supports, threatening their reproductive rights, and undercutting their independence.

*Caretaking supports:* Welfare reform has become a launching pad for a wider attack on all of the nation's social welfare programs. Yet many health, education, childcare, social service, and social security programs, as well as tax expenditures (mortgage interest deductions, childcare credits, etc.), help all but the most affluent families by reducing the cost of basic consumption items, helping pay health and education bills, and providing for those who cannot support themselves. Yet the attack on welfare legitimizes both cutting all social programs and shifting the cost of caretaking from the government to women at a time when they need more, not fewer, family supports.

*Reproductive rights:* The attack on poor women's reproductive choices undermines the reproductive rights of all women. Shortly after 1973, when the Supreme Count (in Roe versus Wade) granted women the right to an abortion, the right-to-life forces won passage of the Hyde Amendment, which forbids the use of Medicaid dollars for abortions. Today, poor women in two-thirds of the states lack access to this service except in cases of rape or incest, and even this exception is under attack. The current use of economic coercion to control the childbearing decisions of poor women on welfare broadens the attempt by government to control women's reproductive lives; it also implicitly endorses efforts by abortion foes to deny more women access to abortion, either by introducing piecemeal restrictions (such as the called-for ban on abortions for military wives, women prisoners, and federal employee insurance beneficiaries) or by passing a constitutional amendment.

*Economic independence:* The attack on welfare threatens the economic independence of all women by making it harder to earn an adequate living. For one, a smaller welfare state means fewer of the public sector jobs that enabled many women—both white women and women of color—to enter the middle class. Second, low benefits ensure that only the most desperate women will choose welfare over work, while time limits and workfare channel large numbers of low-paid female workers into the labor market; both will increase the competition for jobs and depress women's wages. Third, the reform proposals virtually eliminate all support for high school and college education, two widely accepted routes off welfare and out of poverty. And finally, the reforms undercut the role of AFDC as an economic back-up, making it easier for employers to keep women in line by evoking fears of unemployment. The economic security provided by AFDC also permits women to take the risks associated with resisting male domination in the home.

WHY NOW?

We have seen how the drive to undermine welfare has relied on myths about the relationship between welfare and women's work, marital, childbearing, and parenting behavior to build support for reforms that contradict research findings, labor market realities, and the dynamics of family life. But why is welfare being attacked right now? What purpose does demonizing poor women and impugning welfare serve?

Simply put, attacking welfare and the women who receive it eases the economic, moral, and racial panics provoked by economic insecurity, changing family structures, and racial progress. It diverts attention from the underlying causes of the nation's problems and focuses instead on the values and behavior of the poor. Bashing welfare also protects politicians and employers from angry protests by a middle class that is worried about its deteriorating economic situation.

The attack on welfare is also aimed at calming the nation's 'moral panic' by projecting fears about society-wide changes in family structures and women's roles onto the poor. Punishing women who do not live in traditional families is a way to ward off challenges to male control posed by single motherhood, as well as by the increased economic independence of women and the expansion of gay and lesbian rights in all income and race groups. The hidden secret about welfare is that *many* women—perhaps even half—turn to AFDC to escape male violence. Indeed, battered women's shelters report that three-quarters of the women they serve use AFDC to establish lives away from batterers.[31] Although social circumstances have changed, patriarchal concepts remain at the center of how families are defined and understood in our culture and penalizing single mothers sends a message to all women about what happens to those who do not marry, who raise kids on their own, and who otherwise do not 'play by the rules.'

Finally, the welfare reformers have turned welfare into a code word for race in order to ease the 'racial panic' among white Americans that has arisen as people of color have institutionalized their political and economic gains. Wooing support by pandering to racial fear is not a new phenomenon in U.S. history, but it has certainly had an upsurge since the 1980s. For instance, to incite public hostility to welfare, President Reagan evoked racial stereotypes when he told fictional stories about 'welfare queens' who defrauded AFDC and used the money to buy pink Cadillacs. During his 1988 campaign, George Bush splashed pictures of Willie Horton onto televisions across the country in order to indict liberal social programs and tarnish the Democratic candidate for the White House, Michael Dukakis. Horton was an African-American who had committed rape and murder while participating in a prison furlough program run by Massachusetts, Dukakis' home state; the presumption was that all prisoners on furlough would act as Willie Horton had. Most recently, Bill Clinton, Newt Gingrich, and many other politicians have tried to enhance their conservative credentials by encouraging the public misperception that almost all women on welfare are black or Latina—when in fact, forty percent of the AFDC caseload is white. Unable to see past the next election, these officials use racial and ethnic stereotypes to win votes, to protect the wealthy, and to divide people who might join forces and mount a serious challenge to 'the system.'

Reprinted from "Under Attack: Women and Welfare Reform Today" in *Under Attack, Fighting Back: Women and Welfare in the United States* (NY: Monthly Review Press, 1996) by Mimi Abramovitz. Copyright ©1996 Mimi Abramovitz. Used by permission of Monthly Review Foundation.

NOTES

1. Governor Kirk Fordice quoted in Kevin Sack, "In Mississippi, Will Poor Grow Poorer with State Welfare Plan?," *The New York Times*, October 23, 1995, pg. A1; Lawrence M. Mead, *The New Politics of Poverty* (New York: Basic Books, 1992), pg. 12; Rector quoted in Center on Social Welfare Policy and Law, "Welfare Reform Hearings: January 1995" February 8, 1995, short brief, pg. 1.

2. Skricki, Irene. "Unheard Voices: Participants Evaluate the JOBS Program," January 1993 report (Washington, DC: Coalition on Human Needs, 1993), pg. 13.

3. April quoted in Jane Collins and Donna Southwell, *Life on the Edge: The Stories of Seven Massachusetts Women on Welfare* (Boston: Massachusetts Human Service Coalition, 1994), pg. 13.

4. Pavetti, LaDonna. "The Dynamics of Welfare and Work: Exploring the Process by Which Young Women Work Their Way Off Welfare," cited in House Committee on Ways and Means, *Overview of Entitlement Programs, 1994 Green Book* (Washington, DC: Government Printing Office, 1994), pp. 441–442.

5. Spalter-Roth, Roberta and Beverly Bun, Heidi Hartmann, and Lois Shaw. "Welfare That Works: The Working Lives of AFDC Recipients," March 20, 1995 report (Washington, DC: Institute For Women's Policy Research, 1995), pp. 40, 43–44.

6. Ibid., pp. 1, 43.

7. Hagen, Jan and Irene Lurie. *Implementing JOBS: Progress and Promise* (Albany, NY: Nelson A. Rockefeller Institute of Government, 1994), pg. 230; Robert Moffitt, "Incentive Effects of the U.S. Welfare System: A Review," *Institute for Research on Poverty Special Report*, no. 48 (Madison, WI: Institute for Research on Poverty, University of Wisconsin-Madison, 1991); James Riccio and Daniel Friedlander, *GAIN: Program Strategies, Participation, Patterns, and First-Year Impact in Six Counties* (New York: Manpower Demonstration Research Corporation, 1992); Government Accounting Office, *Welfare to Work: States Begin JOBS, but Fiscal and Other Problems May Impede Their Progress* (Washington, DC: Government Printing Office, 1992), pg. 43.

8. Mishel, Lawrence and John Schmitt. "Cutting Wages by Cutting Welfare: The Impact of Reform on the Low-Wage Labor Market," report (Washington, DC: Economic Policy Institute, 1995).

9. "Welfare That Works," pg. 59.

10. *Hunger Action Network of New York State Newsletter,* February 15, 1995, pg. 8; Jonathan Rabinowitz, "Welfare Fallout Traps Mothers: Plan Threatens Education," *The New York Times,* May 19, 1995, pg. B1; "Unheard Voices," pg. 13.

11. Jencks, Christopher. "What Is the Underclass—and Is It Growing?" *Focus* 12, no. 1 (Spring/Summer 1989), pg. 21.

12. White House Working Group on the Family. "The Family: Preserving America's Future," Department of Education, Office of the Under Secretary, November 13, 1986. Press release and report, pg. 33.

13. Department of Health and Human Services. *Characteristics and Financial Circumstances of AFDC Recipients* (Washington, DC: Government Printing Office, 1992), table 16.

14. Because anti-abortion groups feared that the child exclusion provision would lead pregnant women to seek abortions, they insisted that the bonus be based on non-marital births and abortions as a percentage of births to all women in the state, instead of just within the AFDC caseload, thus linking control of reproduction among AFDC women to control of all women in the state.

15. *Incentive Effects of the U.S. Welfare System: A Review*; U.S. Department of Health and Human Services, *Report to Congress on Out-of-Wedlock Childbearing*, executive summary, monograph (West Hyattsville, MD: Department of Health and Human Services, 1995), pp. 2–3; *Overview of Entitlement Programs*, pg. 1111; Bureau of the Census, *Studies in Marriage and the Family, "Singleness in America," Current Population Reports*, Ser. P23, no. 162 (Washington, DC: Government Printing Office, 1990), pg. 6.

16. *Overview of Entitlement Programs*, pg. 401; Government Accounting Office, *Families on Welfare: Teenage Mothers Least Likely to Become Self-Sufficient* (Washington, DC: Government Printing Office, 1994), pp. 16–17. In 1992 divorced women headed thirty-seven percent of mother-only families, up somewhat from thirty-two percent

in 1970. During the same period, however, the percentage of never-married single mothers surged from seven percent to thirty-six percent of all single mothers.

17. Government Accounting Office. *Families on Welfare: Sharp Rise in Never-Married Women Reflects Societal Trends* (Washington, DC: Government Printing Office, 1994), pp. 16–17, 46–48; Bureau of the Census, *Martial Status and Living Arrangements*, March 1993 (Washington, DC: Government Printing Office, 1994), pg. xiii; *Overview of Entitlement Programs*, pg. IIII.

18. Rank, Mark. "Fertility Among Women on Welfare: Incidence and Determinants," *American Sociological Review* 54 (April 1989): pp. 296–304; *Overview of Entitlement Programs, 1994* Green Book, pg. 409.

19. Data from the 1988 National Survey of Family Growth indicate that eighty-eight percent of the pregnancies experienced by never-married women, sixty-nine percent of the pregnancies experienced by previously married women, and forty percent of the pregnancies experienced by married women were unintended; *Report to Congress on Out-of-Wedlock Childbearing*, pg. 8.

20. "Researchers Dispute Contention That Welfare Is a Major Cause of Out-of-Wedlock Births," Press release issued by Sheldon Danziger, Director, Research and Training Programs on Poverty, the Underclass, and Public Policy, School of Social Work, University of Michigan, Ann Arbor, MI, June 23, 1994.

21. Center on Hunger, Poverty, and Nutrition Policy. "Statement on Key Welfare Reform Issues: The Empirical Evidence," short brief, Medford, MA, 1995, pg. 3.

22. *Families on Welfare: Teenage Mothers Least Likely To Become Self Sufficient*, pg. 3; *Report to Congress on Out-of-Wedlock Childbearing*, pp. 2–4.

23. The Alan Gutmacher Institute reports that half the babies born to mothers aged fifteen to seventeen were fathered by men twenty years of age or older; twenty percent of the fathers were six or more years older than the teen mother. See Jennifer Steinhauer, "Study Cites Adult Males for Most Teenage Births," *The New York Times*, August 2, 1995, pg. A10.

24. Magnet, Myron. "Problem No. 1: The Children," *The New York Times*, November 25, 1994, pg. A37.

25. Bernstein, Nina. "Foster Care System Wary of Welfare Cuts," *The New York Times*, November 19, 1995, pp. 1, 26.

26. Lend, David, and Robert Wood, and Hilary Kopp. "The Effects of LEAP and Enhanced Services in Cleveland, Ohio's, Learning, Earning, and Parenting Programs for Teenage Parents on Welfare," report (New York: Manpower Demonstration Research Corporation, 1994, ), pg. vi.

27. Quoted in Ruth Coniff, "Big Bad Welfare," *The Progressive* (August 1994): pg. 21; and *Life on the Edge*, pg. 11.

28. Woolsey, Lynn. "Reinvent Welfare, Humanely," *The New York Times*, January 22, 1994, pg. 21.

29. Duncan, Greg and Martha Hill and Saul Hoffman. "Welfare Dependence Within and Across Generations," *Science* 239, January 29, 1988.

30. Levin-Epstein, Jodie. "Rising Poverty Rates: Changes in Families and a Changing Economy," *Family Matters* 7, nos. 1–2 (Spring/Summer 1995): pp. 3–4; "Researchers Dispute Contention That Welfare Is a Major Cause of Out-of-Wedlock Births."

31. *Life on the Edge*, pg. 2.

# 13

## WELFARE REFORM VIOLATES HUMAN RIGHTS

*Anuradha Mittal, Peter Rosset, and Marilyn Borchardt*

*"It's time to honor and reward people who work hard and play by the rules. That means ending welfare as we know it—not by punishing the poor or preaching to them, but by empowering Americans to take care of their children and improve their lives."*[1]
—Bill Clinton, 1992

*"At Colonel Sanders they used to put out leftovers in the garbage bin. There used to be ten or fifteen people every night looking for food in the garbage, including myself—just looking for something to eat. I know it's hard on them. It was hard on me."*
—Rufus Herold, formerly homeless senior,
now on staff at St. Mary's Center, Oakland

Rufus Herold may not be an expert on welfare reform, but he does know about hunger. Herold could write a book on his experiences while looking for something to eat. Today, he helps seniors find their way out of dehumanizing hunger, poverty, and homelessness.

While Herold ladles out soup, our government leaders tell us that the economy is booming with low employment, rising incomes, and shrinking welfare rolls. But more and more people are sliding through the cracks. Herold wishes that policymakers, who have never known hunger, could get a closer look at the people waiting in food lines. Then maybe they would understand, and maybe they would change things.

On August 22, 1996 in the Rose Garden of the White House, President Clinton signed into law the Orwellian-sounding Personal Responsibility and Work Opportunity Reconciliation Act, better known as Welfare Reform, the most sweeping change in our welfare system in sixty years. With his signature, Clinton's talk of "not punishing or preaching" became indistinguishable from the Republican

Party's poor-bashing 'Contract with America.' How Mr. Clinton slid from a welfare plan that would have added about $10 billion more in spending to embracing one that would cut $54 billion is a sad tale of American politics. Furthermore, it raises the specter of systematic violations of basic human rights here in the United States of America, if we are judged by the international standards of the Universal Declaration of Human Rights, adopted fifty years ago by the United Nations General Assembly.

In this report, we tally the impact of welfare reform, expose seldom reported corporate profit-taking and conflict of interest in privatizing parts of the system, and examine the human rights implications of current policies. We end with a call to join our *Economic Human Rights: The Time Has Come!* campaign.

## CHANGES IN THE WELFARE SYSTEM

Welfare reform couples budget cuts with delegation of responsibility to the states. AFDC has been replaced by Temporary Assistance to Needy Families (TANF) block grants. AFDC provided monthly cash benefits to 12.8 million including more than eight million children; almost as many whites as blacks, with women accounting for nine out of ten adult recipients.[2] AFDC rules were national—under TANF states create and implement their own rules. Now there is no guarantee that all who need help will receive it. A significant problem is that the $16.4 billion provided yearly in block grants contains no additional new funding for job creation, training, or placement. The federal funding level is fixed until the year 2002 with no provision for inflation, population growth, or increased unemployment. Furthermore, states can lose their block grants if they do not remove enough people from the rolls, whether those people find work or not.

Food stamps have been slashed. More than half of the $54 billion in welfare cuts ($27.7 billion) are coming from the food stamps that 25 million poor Americans depend on. Over eighty percent of food stamps go to families with children. Another $3 billion has been cut from child nutrition programs, including child care and summer care programs. Food stamps for adults without dependents have been slashed to three months out of every three years, and anyone convicted of felony drug charges is now denied food stamps and all other benefits.

The new law requires most recipients to find work within two years, and imposes a cumulative lifetime limit of five years on benefits paid with federal money, with states free to impose shorter time limits if they like. Mothers who do not or cannot help establish their children's paternity, have regular welfare payments cut by as much as twenty-five percent.[3] Federal funding for social services has been cut by a six-year total of $2.5 billion.

Welfare reform cut Social Security Income (SSI) for some disabled, food stamps for almost 900,000 legal immigrants who formerly received SSI, and for nearly all future immigrants. SSI benefits were restored later to some 250,000 immigrants who were in the U.S. by August 22, 1996. States still have the option of denying immigrants Medicaid and welfare. New immigrants are excluded from most programs, including Medicaid, for the first five years they are in the U.S. This is a $22 billion cut over the six year period, accounting for about forty percent of the total cuts in the reform bill.

Those completely cut off to date have been mostly immigrants and disabled children. The definition of SSI eligibility for disabled children has been narrowed, denying benefits for 315,000 of the 965,000 low income children previously covered.[4] Others will be cut off when the new time limits go into effect, in a maximum of four years, or less if a state so chooses, or when a recession hits.

## THE FIRST CASUALTIES

By the first anniversary of the law, there were 3.9 million people left on welfare—a drop of more than 2.2 million.[5] This dramatic shrinkage conveys the impression that welfare reform has been a resounding success. While administration officials rush to take credit for the decline in welfare rolls, some acknowledge that they do not know what has happened to families who have lost assistance.[6]

## FOOD BANKS ARE STRAINING

Welfare reform has hit hardest those who cannot afford to buy or grow enough food to feed themselves and their families. The food stamp cuts average $4 billion per year while the total value of all food in all food banks in the country is just $1 billion a year. Second Harvest, the country's largest chain of food banks, reported in 1997 that it provided some food for almost 26 million people—nearly ten percent of America's population. Not all who needed food received it; an estimated 2.3 million hungry people were turned away because of lack of food.7

To compensate fully for the government cuts in food programs, each of the 350,000 churches in the U.S. would have to contribute an average of $150,000. Very few churches have total budgets that large.8 To make up for the shortfall, the non-profit sector would have to distribute a total of 24.5 billion pounds of food over the next six years; four times more than current distribution—and enough to fill five million Army National Guard trucks.9

Total federal spending for food programs before welfare reform was only 2.5 percent of the federal budget.10 Economists expect that cutting these programs is actually going to cost the government more through increased health care and other costs of hunger.11

## STATE CUTS: BALANCING THE BUDGET
## ON THE BACKS OF THE POOR

The promise of welfare reform was to improve the economic well-being of poor families. This goal, however, is not being achieved in most states. Under TANF block grants, forty-two states have adopted policies that are likely to worsen the economic security of poor families, and thirty-five have implemented policies that push many families with children off the rolls. Changes that have reduced economic security for low income families include reducing benefits and restricting eligibility; time limits for benefits; work requirements; restrictions for legal immigrant families; limited assistance in obtaining work; and limited subsidized child care.12

Many states have adopted stricter work requirements and shorter time limits than Congress and the President envisioned, with forty-five states and the District of Columbia either adopting the federal lifetime limit of sixty months, or imposing stricter limits.[13] Texas has the shortest limit of twelve months. Tennessee's is eighteen consecutive months, and Connecticut's is twenty-one months. Ten states have twenty-four month limits.[14] Idaho offers a flat grant of $276 per month, while West Virginia's benefits are capped at $477 per month, and Wisconsin's are $518 or $555 per month, without regard for family size.

Federal law requires adults to work within two years of receiving cash assistance, but several states have adopted stricter work requirements. Florida, Tennessee, and Texas expect adult welfare recipients to go to work immediately. And at least nineteen states do not increase payments for women who have additional children while receiving public assistance.[15]

## CATCH 22: SHORTAGE OF LIVING WAGE JOBS

"Work!" It is an order to recipients, a philosophy for administrators, and a mandate under Federal law. Welfare reform is big on personal responsibility but short on work opportunities. Minimum wage jobs coupled with a severe shortage of subsidized child care make working impossible for many recipients.

Many cities have actually lost jobs over the past five to ten years. Since 1990 New York City, with more than 300,000 adults in the AFDC case load, lost 227,000 jobs. Many remaining jobs do not pay enough to support a family. The odds against a typical welfare recipient finding a job that pays a living wage are about ninety-seven to one in the midwestern states of Illinois, Indiana, Michigan, Minnesota, Ohio, and Wisconsin.[16] The non-partisan California Budget Project calculated that for every available job in California, there are seven welfare recipients and unemployed workers.[17] The odds are even worse in seventeen California counties where unemployment is at recession-level eleven percent or greater.

For most of the population targeted for 'welfare-to-work,' job prospects are about as grim as the average worker faced during the depression. Hard hit are women, especially single mothers with no high school diploma and little work experience. Women with less than a high school education face an unemployment rate of 13.6 percent and an underemployment rate of 24.3 percent. For black women, many of whom live in areas where jobs are particularly scare, the rates are 20.9 percent and 35 percent, respectively.[18] A serious obstacle is the low wage that women leaving welfare can expect to earn. Women leaving welfare usually find low-paid service, administrative, and clerical positions, mostly at minimum wage. This doesn't pay enough to support a family.

## THE CHILD CARE NIGHTMARE

For many welfare recipients, the most serious obstacle to gaining employment is the lack of child care. Almost half the children supported by AFDC were under age six, and in a survey about one-third of unemployed welfare recipients cited lack of child care as reason for their unemployment.[19] Requiring TANF recipients to work for their benefits has greatly increased the need for child care. Of the 6.5 million children under the age of thirteen in welfare households, only nineteen percent receive federally subsidized day care.[20]

## WELFARE CUTS HURT ALL WORKERS

Across the country, thousands of people on welfare are going to work, but generally not at new jobs. Instead many are replacing employees whose salaries were higher. This displacement is falling most heavily on the 38 million working poor holding jobs that pay $7.50 an hour or less.[21] It is projected that the influx of former welfare recipients into the low-wage labor market will lower workers' wages by twelve percent by the year 2000.[22] Workers who make $7 per hour could see their wages fall by roughly 84 cents per hour.

The expected fall in wages is steeper for states that have a larger welfare population: 17.8 percent in California and 17.1 percent in New York.[23] The total income lost by these workers nationwide is projected at $36 billion a year—$8.5 billion more than total federal and state spending on AFDC in 1994.[24] In San Francisco, the city's 'workfare' program requires able-bodied adults who receive general assistance to do 'community service,' a euphemism for clean-up work. Recipients get $5.31 an hour, where unionized janitors would earn about $15 an hour plus benefits.[25] This makes it nearly impossible to unionize janitors, as employers threaten to replace them with workfare recipients.[26] This is actually a more general phenomenon: when wages at the lower end of the economic ladder are depressed, those on all the higher rungs are eventually pulled down as well.[27]

## DOES WELFARE REFORM VIOLATE BASIC HUMAN RIGHTS?

Fifty years ago the United Nations General Assembly adopted the Universal Declaration of Human Rights (UDHR). Inspired by the belief that human dignity requires both freedom from fear and freedom from want, the UDHR proclaimed the interdependence and indivisibility of civil-political and economic-social human rights. It affirmed that all people have a right to an adequate standard of living, special care and assistance for mothers and children, education, and adequate employment.[28]

Imposing time limits in the new welfare system without sufficient living wage jobs and training, clearly denies adequate employment for millions. Low wage employment combined with food stamp cuts, makes it impossible for them to rise above the government's definition of poverty even though they may work full time. This violates the UDHR. Those who are completely excluded—people with drug felony charges, children born after mothers have been on aid for ten consecutive months (the 'family cap'), unwed parents under age eighteen, undocumented immigrants, and others—are guaranteed no economic and social human rights at all. Ending support to children with disabilities is mean spirited and clearly falls outside of the UDHR as well.

The right to education for parents is severely compromised under current policy.[29] TANF recipients are now limited to twelve months of training, and can no longer enroll in four-year college programs. Moreover, stringent work requirements and the severe shortage of child care make the pursuit of any educational program almost impossible.

Coerced workfare recipients are denied their right to even a minimum wage and have no right to unionize. Furthermore, some workfare sites do not provide worker's compensation insurance, placing the health and safety of recipients at risk. In our America of 'personal responsibility' and welfare reform, the basic economic and social human rights guaranteed under the UDHR are being systematically violated.

## ECONOMIC HUMAN RIGHTS: THE TIME HAS COME!

Why should we apply a human rights standard to these issues? Human rights standards take priority over economic efficiency. Economic efficiency dictates that policy makers settle on policies that allow a certain percent of the population to fall through the cracks, a threshold calculated with cost-benefit analysis. For example, the factor of economic efficiency allows policy makers to decide that thirty million hungry people are too many, but fifteen million would be acceptable, or even economically 'optimal.' A human rights standard would change that. Even one family going hungry would constitute a human rights violation, and thus would make such a policy option unacceptable. If we have zero tolerance for torture and political prisoners, why should we accept anything else for hunger?

Mere ratification of an international treaty does not ensure economic human rights for all, any more than the 14th Amendment to the U.S. constitution ended racial discrimination. Human rights may be inalienable, but they are never ensured without a fight.

On the fiftieth anniversary of the Universal Declaration, Food First's national campaign, *Economic Human Rights: The Time Has Come!*, is working with more than 180 groups across the country to recommit our country to the goal of human rights for all.

We have organized Congressional hearings on the human rights implications of increasing hunger and poverty in the United States. At these hearings Rufus Herold, along with single mothers, homeless men and women, low wage workers, seniors, and veterans, courageously told Congressional representatives of their daily struggles against poverty and hunger. The testifiers demanded that Congress apply internationally recognized human rights standards to the U.S. We support them in that goal and invite you to join our campaign.

NOTES

1. Clinton, Bill and Al Gore. *Putting People First: How We Can All Change America* (New York: Times Books, 1992), cited in "Charge to the Working Group on Welfare Reform, Family Support, and Independence." This group was formed by President Clinton in June 1993 to develop his welfare reform plan.

2. Johnson, Dirk. "Uncertain Future, On Their Own, Awaits," *The New York Times,* March 16, 1997.

3. Kilborn, Peter. "Welfare Mothers Losing Bonus They Got to Help Track Fathers," *The New York Times,* November 12, 1996.

4. Kilborn, Peter. "With Welfare Overhaul Now Law, States Grapple With the Consequences," *The New York Times,* August 22, 1996.

5. Pear, Robert. "Welfare Rolls Sink to the Lowest Level Since 1971," *The New York Times,* January 21, 1998.

6. Ibid.

7. Second Harvest. *Hunger 1997: The Faces & Facts,* (Chicago, IL: Second Harvest, 1997).

8. "The Issue is Poverty: A Conversation on Welfare Reform," *Sojourners,* March–April, 1997.

9. Rivera, Elaine. "Hungry at the Feats," *Nation,* July 21, 1997.

10. Bread for the World Institute. *Tell Congress: Hunger Has a Cure* (Washington, DC: Bread for the World Institute, 1997).

11. Ibid.

12. Center on Hunger and Poverty. *Are States Improving the Lives of Poor Families? A Scale Measure of State Welfare Policies* (Medford, MA: Tufts University, 1998).

13. Ibid.

14. DeParle, Jason. "U.S. Welfare System Dies As State Programs Emerge," *The New York Times,* June 30, 1997.

15. "Many States Welfare Changes Stricter Than New Federal Law," *San Francisco Chronicle,* February 1997.

16. Weisbrot, Mark. *Welfare Reform: The Jobs Aren't There* (Washington, DC: Preamble Center for Public Policy, 1997). The report also concluded that since these states compare favorably to the rest of the country, that these odds are not significantly better, on average, in the national economy as a whole.

17. California Budget Project. *Job Seekers Exceed Available Jobs Despite a Strong Economy* (Sacramento, CA: California Budget Project, 1997).

18. Ibid.

19. Burtless, Gary. "Welfare Recipient's Job Skills and Employment Prospects," *Welfare to Work,* vol. 7, no. 1, Spring.

20. Sexton, Joe. "Working and Welfare Parents Compete for Day Care Slots," *The New York Times,* May 27, 1997

21. Uchitelle, Louis. "Welfare Recipients Taking Jobs Often Held by the Working Poor," *The New York Times,* April 1, 1998.

22. Marshall, Jonathan. "Welfare Bill Portends More Widespread Poverty," *San Francisco Chronicle,* July 25, 1996.

23. *Welfare Reform: The Jobs Aren't There,* op.cit.

24. Ibid.

25. Rojas, Aurelio. "Lifeline or Deadline?" *San Francisco Chronicle,* February 16, 1998.

26. Told of the unionization drive, Mayor of San Francisco, Willie Brown, was incredulous. "You never know what you'll find in a democracy," he said. Reported in E. Epstein, "Welfare Union Plan Rebuffed," *San Francisco Chronicle,* June 12, 1997.

27. Lappé, Frances Moore and Joseph Collins, and Peter Rosset, with Luis Esparza. *World Hunger: 12 Myths,* Second Edition (New York: Grove/Atlantic, 1998), chapter 11.

28. Article 23, Universal Declaration of Human Rights, 1948.

29. Schmidt, Peter. "States Discourage Welfare Recipients from Pursuing a Higher Education," *Chronicle of Higher Education,* January 23, 1998.

## PART FOUR

# Human Rights for America

*The destiny of human rights is in the hands of all our citizens in all our communities.*
—Eleanor Roosevelt

In 1966, Rev. Martin Luther King Jr. placed a note outside the door of Chicago City Hall.[1] He wrote that not only basic human rights, but the economic rights of all Americans, would need to be safe-guarded before we could call ourselves a real democracy. He demanded livable wages and affordable housing, among other things, to ensure those human rights.

Demand for human rights is not new. There is evidence of human rights demands in the religious scriptures of Judeo-Christian and Islamic traditions. The British Magna Carta, adopted in 1215; the French Rights of Man and of the Citizen, adopted in 1789; and the American Bill of Rights, adopted in 1791, all played key roles in defining relations between governing authorities and those governed.[2]

In the nineteenth and early twentieth centuries, popular demands for human rights grew in many parts of the world. But it was the devastation of World War II and the horror of the Holocaust that moved the struggle for human rights safeguards to a higher level. In 1941 President Roosevelt linked future peace to respect for human rights in his famous "Four Freedoms" speech to Congress. He identified freedom of speech, freedom of religion, freedom from want, and freedom from fear as absolutely necessary freedoms.[3] With the founding of the United Nations, the drafting of an 'International Bill of Rights' became a top high priority. Eleanor Roosevelt was elected as the chairperson of the new UN Commission on Human Rights, where she applied herself to the task.

With tensions rising between the newly divided Eastern and Western bloc countries, the Commission's task was daunting. For delegates from the Western countries, the priority was protecting individual rights from incursions by state powers. For delegates from the Soviet bloc, the priority was protecting human welfare. Mrs. Roosevelt pushed the Commission along. Over fifty governments took part in the final drafting. Every word, phrase, and punctuation mark—in all five of the official United Nations languages—had to be painstakingly approved. The final version of the Declaration presented to the United Nations General Assembly came to a vote in the early hours of December 10, 1948. At 3:00 AM the General Assembly adopted the Universal Declaration of Human Rights (UDHR). Eight nations abstained from the vote, but none dissented. With that vote, the nations of the world proclaimed the human rights and fundamental freedoms of all humankind.4

Despite the legal clarity of human rights as spelled out in many treaties and conventions, and despite the fact that most governments have agreed to abide by them, human rights continue to be violated. The Declaration, soon after its adoption, became entangled in Cold War politics. More then fifty years later, despite the end of the Cold War, the original commitment seems to exist at a mostly rhetorical level. The United States has been a large part of the problem as it has consistently ignored the economic and social rights portions of the Declaration and subsequent treaties. It is probably not coincidental that the U.S., the only industrialized country to reject economic and social human rights, also boasts the highest disparity between rich and poor and the highest child poverty rate among developed countries.

The severe economic inequalities we face today make the concept of economic human rights more essential than ever. Unemployment, underemployment, the wealth gap, and downsizing have created conditions that foster poverty and economic disparity. Like the earlier and on-going labor, civil rights, women's rights, and environmental justice movements, today economic human rights activists are taking a critical look at American democracy and calling for needed changes.

For all the legal intricacies of human rights, and all the government sparring over their definitions and enforcement, true human rights protection depends on pressure from the populace. Experience shows that human rights guarantees become real when people demand them, and human rights abuses cease only when they are subject to public scrutiny and outcry. Only when people speak out, do governments muster the political will to effect change.

The UDHR provides us with universal standards for human dignity by which to measure the human rights performance of nations. Ultimately, people must decide whether their human rights and those of others in their society are satisfactorily respected. Part Four offers tools to begin answering those questions.

In the first chapter, "Rediscovering America's Values," Food First co-founder Frances Moore Lappé offers a Socratic dialog about the meanings of freedom, rights, and the responsibilities of government versus individuals in America. The two personalities in the dialog tackle the tough philosophical issues about human rights in a style that draws us into the debate. Chapter Fifteen, "What are Human Rights?," provides a succinct overview and brief history of what human rights are and where they come from. In "A More Holistic Understanding of Human Rights?," Chandra Muzaffar makes an impassioned plea to emphasize economic and social rights in the human rights movement, and gives us a vision of a world we may not live to see but that we must nevertheless fight to achieve.

In the Epilogue, "Building a Movement for Human Rights in America," we issue a call to change how we think about poverty in this great and wealthy nation. Taking lessons from the right-wing think tanks, who have used the media to strip public discourse of all ethical content, we lay out a blueprint for re-shifting the center of debate along human rights lines. If grassroots movements can come together to force a new language of basic rights into the debate, then we can change how policies are chosen, and construct a new America from the bottom up.

In the words of Eleanor Roosevelt:

*"Where, after all, do universal rights begin? In small places, close to home—so close and so small that they cannot be seen on any maps of the world. Yet they are the world of the individual person; the neighborhood he [she] lives in; the school or college he [she] attends; the factory, the*

*farm or office where he [she] works. Such are the places where every man, woman and child seeks equal justice, equal opportunity, equal dignity without discrimination. Unless these rights have meaning there, they have little meaning anywhere. Without concerted citizen action to uphold them close to home, we shall look in vain for progress in the larger world...."*

Human rights are in your hands, in our collective hands.

NOTES

1. *Sustainable America's Human Rights Organizer Kit* (New York: Sustainable America, 1998), pg. 3.

2. UDHR 50 National Coordinating Committee. *In Your Hands: A Community Action Guide for Human Rights Year and Beyond* (New York: UDHR 50 National Coordinating Committee, 1998).

3. Roosevelt, Franklin D. "Annual Message to Congress," January 11, 1944, in *The Public Papers and Addresses of Franklin D. Roosevelt 1944–45*, ed. Samuel I. Rosenman (New York: Harper and Brothers, 1950), pp. 32–44.

4. *In Your Hands*, op. cit.

# 14

## REDISCOVERING AMERICA'S VALUES

*Frances Moore Lappé*

Let's talk very personally, not in grand concepts. When do I feel free? When I wake up on a Saturday morning and know I can do anything I want to do. I can lie in bed as long as I please, work in the yard, watch TV. Or, I can leave the house a mess and go to the movies with friends. I'm free because there is no one telling me what to do. I'm left alone— that's the key, isn't it?

The freedom to lie in bed on Saturday morning may sound trivial, but I can apply this same understanding to what matters a great deal more to me—the opportunity to strive for any job I want and to move wherever I please. Freedom means no government official or anyone else interfering, telling me which job to take or where to live.

*Sure, lack of interference from others can enhance my freedom, but not always. If lots of people are out of work and I get laid off, too, no one may be "interfering" with me. And that's my problem. I might be left alone by virtually everyone! But how free am I?*

*If freedom is the opportunity to make something of myself and provide for my kids, then your concept of freedom—freedom from interference— isn't enough.*

Of course it's not enough. It's only the beginning. Aren't there really two basic aspects of freedom—freedom *from* interference and freedom *to* do what we want? The second depends on something quite obvious—income.

The more I earn—and can keep out of the government's hands— the more freedom I have. In our society, money is choice. The more money I make, the less I have to worry about paying bills, so I have more peace of mind. I can buy what I like instead of whatever's cheapest. With the raise I got last year, I was able to get the additional training I needed. More important, a decent income means I can provide the best opportunities for my kids.

But money is only one essential to freedom. Another is effective government. Without government to protect me against foreign enemies and criminals and to enforce the rules—from traffic laws to contracts—I couldn't sleep at night, get to work on time, or count on any business deal I sign. Without government to establish and keep order, we'd have chaos. No one would be free.

But only one type of government is consistent with a free society—one interfering *minimally* in people's lives. Good government functions like a referee keeping us from hurting each other, and that's all.[1] Remember that in every society it's government bureaucrats—and only government bureaucrats—who have the legal authority to coerce people. They must be restrained. That's why our founders agreed that the "best government is that which governs least."

*None of our founders ever said that! Those are the words of a journalist writing in the nineteenth century, well after our nation's founding.*[2]

They nevertheless capture our founders' intent—their wariness of government and desire to keep it strictly limited.

Our founders understood that unlike the society of voluntary associations, which grows up naturally out of people's desire for community, government is—I hate to say it—a necessary evil to be strictly limited.

*How can you disentangle community and government? From where does government arise if not also from the need for a common life and for a structure in which to debate the shape of that common life? From where, if not in the provision of so many things—from roads to schools to libraries—that as individuals we would find it impossible, terribly inconvenient, or just plain lonely, to provide by ourselves?*[3]

*Our founders' concern was not so much with limiting the powers of government as wisely distributing them among its various branches and between the state and federal levels. As to your embrace of society and distaste for government, why can't they be mutually supporting? Our private associations based on tastes and interests naturally tend to be with those with whom we widely agree. But democratic government arises from the need for dialogue beyond these circles in order to pursue the common good.*

No, it's precisely such ideas—pursuing the 'public interest'—that have created so many of our modern problems. Once you begin thinking this way, you can justify any extension of government. In fact, our society's biggest mistake is that we haven't known when to put a brake on government. We've come to expect it to do more and more for us, to provide security for everyone—to cure all the ills of the human condition.4 Not only is that impossible, it's dangerous to try, for every accretion of power by government directly threatens our freedom.

In fact, in yearning to make government do what it can't do, we've made government into the greatest obstacle to our freedom.

*How is government an obstacle?*

I'll be very specific. Every time the government takes part of my paycheck in taxes, I am less free. With less money, I can make fewer choices about what I want; the government makes those choices for me.

*Sure, making my own decisions about how to spend my income is one aspect of freedom. But whether I have a chance to earn that income in the first place is even more important.*

*I want to come back to this point, but for now let's assume you're right—it's taxes that diminish our freedom. What if tomorrow we canceled all taxes, even the biggest single chunk that goes to the military? Individually, we'd each be roughly twenty percent richer. But how much freer? What constrains me and most of my friends is the lack of affordable housing, medical and day care. It's concern about our children because of lousy schools and streets we can't enjoy after dark. The dearth of good jobs is also a big constraint. I don't see how each of us individually becoming twenty percent richer would do much to change any of this.*

*If personal freedom means being able to design a satisfying life for myself and my family, it's impossible to achieve unless there are real opportunities available if I work hard enough for them—satisfying jobs that pay enough to support my family, housing, medical care I can afford, and so on.*

But it's up to the individual to *create* opportunities. They aren't just handed to us on a silver platter. A society is free to the extent that it doesn't actively interfere with a person's choices. And this is true whether or not a person's life circumstances provide many options or only a few. It goes without saying that some people will always have more options than others.[5]

*Individual initiative is crucial, but it doesn't exist in a vacuum. Initiative depends a lot on my assessment of my chances for success, and that depends a lot on how fair my society is.*

*But let me understand more fully your concept of freedom as freedom from interference. Do you mean direct, physical interference?*

In part, yes. Interference is a law telling me I have to wear seat belts or, as I said, tax laws reducing my income so that I have less to spend as I see fit while my earnings go to support things I don't even believe in. It's also government rules and regulations that keep me so tied up in paperwork that it's hard to run my business efficiently.

*But what about the interference in our lives that doesn't result from big or intrusive government but from its failure to protect citizens from harm?*

*One young child in four in America now lives in poverty.[6] A lack of good food interferes with their growth, a lack of good schools stunts their intellects, and a lack of safe streets an parks surely must hurt their social skills. Isn't this interference?*

Government can't possibly protect citizens from all harm!

*Of course. But consider the illogic: Our laws are supposed to protect us from being beaten up on the street. In even the poorest neighborhoods a police force is there to prevent attacks on innocent people. What is the difference between being beaten up and being deprived of good food, good teachers, and a clean bed to sleep in? Both destroy the body and kill the spirit.*

*So the most powerful interference in people's lives can be not what government does, but what it* fails *to do.*

## OF ENTITLEMENTS AND RIGHTS

*To clarify what I think is government's responsibility, could we return to my point about the parallel between protecting physical security and protecting economic security?*

There *is* no parallel, certainly where government responsibility is concerned.

*Now wait a minute…our legal system is supposed to protect our right to physical security in part because no other right can be enjoyed without it. Why doesn't protection of basic economic security—the opportunity to earn a living and access to necessities like health care—warrant the same justification?*

*This view that economic security is essential to freedom isn't new. In this country, it goes back to Thomas Jefferson, who understood that owning a piece of land was critical to freedom because, with a base of economic security, citizens could think independently.*

*Let's bring Jefferson's insight up to the twentieth century. In 1944, Franklin Roosevelt advocated extending democracy to include economic citizenship. He called for a second bill of rights covering economic life, starting with the right to renumerative work.[7] In numerous polls since then, most Americans have endorsed the concept.[8]*

Your call for the guaranteed right to earn a living seriously overstates the jobless problem to begin with: only about a third of the unemployed have been out of work for a significant period, and for many the reason is simply their own unrealistic expectations.[9] They're no longer job-seekers but job-shoppers—not accepting work unless it meets their conditions. Government subsidy now gives them the option, like other 'shoppers,' not to buy at all, to opt out of the labor market altogether.[10]

And once you begin extending entitlements to include the right to a job, you've created a socialist economic nightmare—lots of job padding, lots of goofing off, lots of inefficiency.

*Actually, official unemployment figures seriously underestimate unemployment, because they don't count in those so discouraged they've stopped looking, and they don't measure the underemployment of growing numbers of part-time workers who really want full-time jobs.*

*Anyway, I'm not talking about guaranteeing a person a particular job, but about ensuring job opportunities paying enough to meet personal and family responsibilities.*

But can't you see that our problem now is that one group after another keeps asking for special entitlements—for special help from the government. Farmers demand subsidies; the handicapped demand ramps; working mothers demand child care. With each new entitlement, the freedom of everyone else diminishes because, like it or not, everyone is forced to pay. And with, each new entitlement, people become more dependent on government.

*Let me make a critical distinction. Rights aren't a form of charity, given conditionally and demanding subservience from recipients. Citizens establish rights to meet universal needs for protection. Rights require that needs are met with respect because the users of the rights are the citizen/taxpayers to whom the providers are themselves accountable.*

*Rights are justified both from society's point of view and from the individual's. A fully literate society, for example, is understood to benefit everyone, so education is made a right. Exactly the same reasoning applies to the opportunity to work.*

*So when polls record that Americans want health care made a right protected by the constitution, 'right' is precisely what they mean. Everyone needs health care; it is essential protection in enjoying individual freedom and is equally essential to a well-functioning society.*

You are quibbling over terms. The point is that entitlements shift the burden of responsibility and cost from the individual to government. Every additional entitlement—or right, if you must—requires that someone else pay to ensure that the entitlement is met. By definition, entitlements take away some people's freedom and give it to others. There's no net gain in freedom, and in most cases a net loss.

*To the contrary, protecting basic economic rights expands our freedom.*

Your approach would carry along a lot of people who prefer to live off the work of others—that is, off the public purse.

You also fail to appreciate the longer-term consequences of the direction you're proposing. Sometimes, as individuals and as a society, we have to sacrifice present security for future betterment.[11] Ultimately your ideas would make us into each other's keepers. If everyone is required to take care of everyone else—in your endless growth of entitlements—government becomes so big, demanding taxes so high, that we have few resources left to make choices in the marketplace.

And it's as consumers, more than as citizens, that we're empowered to look out for our own interests. As consumers we can vote directly with our dollars; but as citizens individuals have much more attenuated, indirect influence through representatives. When you vote, you usually don't get what you thought you were voting for. But when your dollar votes in the market you get exactly what you voted for, and so does everybody else.[12] So when any function passes from the marketplace into the political arena, the individual loses power.

*But as consumers our votes are very lopsided—the more money, the more votes. As citizens, our votes are theoretically equal. Sure, the wealthy carry much more weight politically as well, but at least a structure exists through which we can work to achieve more genuinely equal representation.*

Once you enlarge government to solve social problems, there's no turning back. The federal government's role in the economy has multiplied about tenfold during the last half-century.[13] That's an enormous change, and as government grows, not only do you and I have less after-tax income because we have to pay for it, but overall economic growth is stunted so our incomes are threatened. The bigger the government, the more private investment is squeezed out.

The freedom that Americans enjoy depends on a prosperous economy. Most of us would feel robbed of our freedom if government stifled growth and we had to face the scarcity that people in socialist economies suffer under.

*As we jump into the big-government-as-a-drag-on-the-economy debate, let's set the record straight on what is and isn't big about ours. We devote much less of our gross national product to government social programs than virtually any other industrial nation.[14] Government employment as a percentage of the total civilian labor force has fallen since 1970 and, at fourteen percent, is now only a few points higher than in the mid-Fifties.[15]*

But much government employment gets disguised by government contracts with private firms; if all these jobs were included, public employment could be five times the official estimates.[16] And any break in the growth in public jobs is probably due only to the tough stand taken in the Eighties against governmental growth.

*Without Social Security, public spending would be smaller now (in relation to national income) than it was in 1960![17] Almost all of the growth has come from Social Security, Medicare, federal retirement benefits, interest on the national debt, and—especially since the late seventies—the military. Most of it represents income and health protection. Does this enhance government power or citizens' power to live free from fear of catastrophic loss?*

You seem to forget we all have to pay for government's growth with our tax dollars, a burden on the family and the national economy.

*But we Americans are among the least taxed people in the West. If it doesn't feel that way, it's because middle-income earners here carry a bigger share of the tax burden than do their counterparts in many other countries.*[18] *You like to blame 'big government,' but an unfair tax system must take the blame for much of the burden Americans feel. As to the threat that government programs sap economic vigor, during the Sixties when many social programs were launched and grew quickly, average family income improved dramatically.*[19]

*If government's size is your big worry, why haven't you mentioned that fifty percent more tax dollars are going to the military, just since 1980? Setting aside direct payments to individuals (mostly covered by Social Security receipts), almost half of the federal budget goes to the military.*[20] *Since World War II, we've spent $10 trillion on arms buildup. Do you know how much money that is? It's enough to buy every single thing in America, except the land—every safety pin, every light bulb, every factory!*[21] *And since you're worried about too many bureaucrats, why not start with the military? It's the military that employs, directly or indirectly, three-fourths of all federal employees.*[22]

## THE HIGH PRICE OF NEGLECT

*In fact, I'd turn your whole argument about the burden of social spending on its head. Not providing opportunity for everyone and adequately protecting citizens ends up costing government a bundle in what I call damage control—efforts to salvage or warehouse people after the destructive fallout of poverty.*

*Keeping low birth-weight babies alive whose mothers were too poor to get good nutrition costs government three-quarters of a billion dollars each year.*[23] *Supporting just one homeless family in a city shelter can cost over $30,000 a year.*[24] *Billions go to deal with mounting child abuse, spousal abuse, and alcoholism, all problems exacerbated by poverty. Crime costs, too. With already more of our people locked up than in any Western industrial society,*[25] *and one in four urban males now arrested by the age of sixteen, imagine the 'taxpayers' bill!*

Wait; you can't blame poverty for crime when crime rates didn't rise, and might even have fallen, when poverty was much more widespread—during the Great Depression. Rising crime rates reflect a shift in social mores, the breakup of the family, and the decline in the role of religion. They reflect an embrace of self-expression as a value in itself, further eroding self-discipline.[26] And high crime rates also result from a law enforcement pattern that encourages lawbreakers by making penalties so weak that, in effect, crime *does* pay![27]

*But violent crime rates in America are several times higher than in other industrial countries, despite much harsher anti-crime attitudes and more severe punishment here. Crime is linked to the deprivation of poverty.[28]*

*Poverty's cost to society can also be measured in the loss of potential wealth. Each class of high school dropouts represents roughly $240 billion in lost earnings and tax revenues alone.[29] Joblessness is a huge drain: every unemployed person costs the government about $25,000 a year in lost revenue and direct outlays.[30]*

Even if you were right, the solutions are much more complex than anything you've suggested—and much more costly than you would probably admit. The price tag on all the initiatives implied in what you've said would drain our tax dollars. Take the Headstart program for disadvantaged preschoolers. It already costs almost $2 billion a year; if we tried to reach every needy child, it could cost five times that much, and that's just one program.

*Even in a five-fold increase Headstart could be covered by reinstating only a fraction of the $60 billion lost in the 1980s tax cuts for the rich.*

I knew you would answer by increasing our taxes! My point is that these programs add up to billions of dollars and they therefore curtail the freedom of everyone who has to pay for them.

*Okay, let's add up the costs of multiple programs to help a poor child, all the way from prenatal care, through Headstart, special help in school, a summer jobs program, and four years at a public university. The total for one child comes to roughly $39,000. That's about what the public pays now to keep one inmate in prison for just seventeen months![31]*

*I don't deny that ending poverty costs money. But the heavier drag—on our tax dollars and our well-being—is poverty itself. We'll see this once we begin to think of poverty in terms of what is missing. In every poverty statistic are the shadows of millions of doctors, musicians, journalists, construction workers, artists, engineers, bus drivers, and athletes whose talents and energies have been stolen from us by poverty. If we can learn to see our invisible loss, we can appreciate the real burden, not of ending poverty, but of poverty itself!*

## GOVERNMENT AS PROVIDER OR RULE SETTER

*But many of the changes necessary to ensure opportunities for all Americans wouldn't mean more costly government with more employees. Government's job is to set the rules; some new rules opening opportunities for all would mean more government, but some would mean less government. West Germans enjoy many more social benefits than we do with fewer government employees per capita.[32]*

*Would, for example, creating the opportunity for every high school grad to get a college education place more burden on government? All college students could be offered government loans to be paid back as a percentage of their future earnings. Covered by a revolving loan fund and paid back through the tax system, such loans would mean no net loss to the treasury or added government bureaucracy.*

*And what would happen if we extended the rights our society protects so that every high school and college grad got the opportunity to use that education in a decent paying job?*

What would happen? A lot of government make-work custodial and clerical jobs that deaden workers and drain the economy.

*Not necessarily. Jobs in the private sector can be expanded as well, because their numbers aren't set by immutable economic law. Many choices we make as a society determine the number of jobs. Let me list a few.*

- *How much federal money goes to build weapons compared to more job-creating enterprises;*

- *The availability of affordable credit to small businesses—the main source of new jobs;*
- *The length of the work week;*
- *What the tax codes reward—mergers, tax shelters, capital flight—or job creation?*
- *Whether government passively pays out unemployment benefits or actively helps to match workers to jobs, to retrain and relocate workers, and if necessary to subsidize wages.*

Quite a list you've come up with! To implement it would require centralized planning and direction of the first order.

*No, but a commitment to jobs would require changing rules—who makes economic decisions and toward what end. Corporations could no longer be allowed to take wealth generated by workers here and use it to transfer jobs overseas. Corporations would have to answer to the workers and the community, not just to stockholders.*

Corporations *already* answer to the community and to workers. They must not break contracts or disobey the law. You seem ready to strip corporations of the rights on which the very basis of our economy's efficiency rests! It's because firms are able to move to wherever production costs are lowest that we consumers can have ever-cheaper products and corporations can afford to make new investments benefiting everybody.

*Profitable business depends on a lot more than cheap wages and cheap real estate, which will always be lower overseas or in the poorest states here. Modern plants and an educated, satisfied work force lower production costs. And keeping well paid jobs here also means more customers here— essential to every profit line. So, holding corporations responsible for reinvesting in modernizing plants in communities where employees themselves have invested lifetimes makes good economic sense.*

*You've stressed the value of responsibility coupled with rights. That is what I want more of, too—ownership rights linked to responsibility.*

But you want to put all the responsibility on corporate management and none on the poor or workers themselves.

*To the contrary, I want to enhance workers' responsibility. When more workers take part in making economic decisions, less government is needed.*

*If workers are involved in decision making, wouldn't less government inspection be needed to make sure the employer is protecting workers' health and safety? Reducing unemployment itself goes a long way in taking the burden off government for overseeing safety, for the employer knows that if the job is unsafe, workers can just go elsewhere.*

*The dumping of hazardous wastes is another example. The more a community is involved in decision making, the less federal oversight is needed. How many communities would knowingly allow themselves to be used as a dump?*

Aren't you aware that some communities have asked to used as waste sites? It means more resources coming into the community, more jobs and income. In doing so, they are freely exercising their property rights.

*Others have vigorously protested. Surely, if people knowingly expose themselves to risk it is because they are desperate.*

I see now how very different is our understanding of freedom and human choice. Without unacceptable loss of freedom, it's impossible for society to protect people from risk or to guarantee a person any particular number of choices.

*A 'choice' between the economic collapse of my town and its becoming a hazardous dump site is like choosing which road to take to the gallows!*

*But I want to get back to my main point here—government not as provider but as rule maker. I've emphasized those policies that determine the availability of jobs, but other invisible economic rules determine whether doors of opportunity are open or shut. While you imply the poor are poor because they aren't bringing in income—they're not working and saving enough—in fact wealth is flowing out of poor communities every day!*

Unable to finance the purchase of a home, a poor family rents a dilapidated apartment for, say, $400 a month; over thirty years this family pays almost $150,000, but gains no security, no wealth. All of it is lost to that family and to the community, if the landlord invests it elsewhere. In poor communities, income earned by businesses and banks rarely returns to finance housing and new enterprises there; it leaves in search of returns. Plus, the poor, because they are poor, often have to pay more than those who aren't. Just one example: Prices in stores in poor neighborhoods are often higher, not lower, than elsewhere.

So no matter how serious we are about improving job opportunities and education, we can't end poverty unless we alter the credit and investment policies that drain people's earnings out of their communities.

## FREEDOM AND THE RESPONSIBILITIES OF GOVERNMENT

Let's talk about responsibility. Rights without responsibility destroy a free society. But shouldn't we start with an accounting of the gross irresponsibility of our society in violating the most essential rights of its citizens?

For children born into neighborhoods where inadequate medical care leaves babies dying at double the national average, where public schools spend only a fourth for each student what is spent in richer districts, where even substandard housing is out of reach for many fully employed families, where drug pushing and violence rule the streets, you can be sure that citizens' rights have been violated from birth.

What amazes me is that so many people survive such assaults to become responsible adults—as most poor people are.

As long as government is shirking its primary responsibility to protect life and opportunity, it stands on pretty shaky ground in castigating citizens' irresponsibility. To legitimately insist on the duties that come with citizenship—essential in a democracy—government must meet its responsibilities.

And what you see as irresponsible dependency can actually reflect parents' attempt to be responsible: some choose welfare over a low paying job, for example, to keep medical benefits to protect their children.

Why focus on the irresponsibility of the poor? Why not try to root out social irresponsibility among the wealthy? A typical poor family pays more *in taxes than do dozens of major corporations, which, despite millions in profits, pay none at all.[33] This loss to society is greater than any loss from the non-working poor.*

If a corporation's gains and losses mean that it pays no taxes one year, that's not bad for society. It means the corporation retains more of its resources to invest in production, benefiting us all.

In any case, you've sidetracked us. You're not denying, are you, that many poor people have opted out of mainstream society to become part of an underclass that's more or less permanent?[34] A new study shows that a third of people on welfare have been there for eight or more years[35]—they're stuck. Even when they're offered jobs, they don't take them; they can do better hustling.[36]

*Even most of those at the very bottom appear not to have given up. The same study you cite shows that most people are on welfare for a short time.[37] Nor do most seem to have opted out of society: half of all welfare homes also include working adults,[38] and most people who grow up in welfare families don't receive welfare as adults.[39]*

*Perhaps most significant, well-managed, subsidized programs to help people get into the work force have paid off.[40] But the underclass will be permanent and grow if as citizens we do not push for changes in the 'rules' I talked about earlier to ensure that more good jobs and child care are available, as well as new credit and investment policies to retain the wealth needed to improve communities, that poor people are already producing.*

To the contrary, only if we as a society end the permissiveness that characterizes our welfare state and expect the same of the poor that we expect of everyone else is there any hope.

*You're assuming most people prefer dependency?*

I assume that many poor people have learned to prefer dependency. In the name of freedom to make meaningful choices you've actually created dependency, but people who are dependent can never be called free.

*Let's say you're right that many parents have learned dependency and that government should do little or nothing. Where does that leave us? One-fifth of all our children live in poverty—two to three times greater than in Scandinavia and sixty percent higher than in the UK.[41] Can any society afford to write off a fifth of its children?*

Our society goes a long way toward making sure the poor get what they need. We heavily subsidize health care for the poor through Medicaid. And we are putting a record amount into food assistance programs, over $13 billion a year into food stamps alone. That's almost $200 a month for each recipient family—not too bad if you shop carefully.

*Are you kidding? More than half the poor are not covered by Medicaid.[42] Almost half of poor kids get no welfare help.[43] And food stamps provide a measly forty cents a person per meal.[44] I'd like to see you put nutritious meals for your kids on the table for that!*

*The best anti-poverty efforts of the sixties and seventies suggest that our money couldn't be better spent than on our children. Quality preschools are a good example that you already brought up. Children participating in Headstart have had more education and job success later in life and have been less likely to get into crime. Yes, taxpayers have had to pay, but Headstart saves government roughly five times more than it costs.[45]*

*If society doesn't uphold its responsibility to children, their development is blocked; they become impaired parents, and there can be no end to the thwarting of human development.*

But wait. We began talking about freedom, what it means to each of us. Your points about what poor children need are a separate topic. For emotional appeal, you're using a verbal sleight of hand to blur an important distinction—that between the meeting of material needs on the one hand and freedom on the other.[46]

*I'm not blurring a distinction, I'm making concrete this beautiful abstraction we call freedom, specifying just what it would take to free our children from interference in their development.*

But why do you ask *me* to assume responsibility for every child who needs it? Most poor children live in single parent households because their fathers have abandoned them. Why should I, the taxpayer, be made the 'economic parent' for children whose parents are so irresponsible? The government's proper role is to force these parents to support their own children, not take over the job for them. That means garnisheeing wages, or whatever is necessary.

*Of course parents must be held responsible for their children. But don't fool yourself into thinking that deducting child support from fathers' wages is going to solve the problem. Many such fathers, if the government can find them, are probably out of work or get such low wages that no amount of pressure will do much for their kids.*

If much of the poverty we see today is a result of government's trying to solve people's problems for them, demanding no corresponding change of behavior on their part, of course it will take time to work itself out—probably generations. People have to relearn that they alone can make something of their lives.

By intervening in these children's lives with more assistance, they'll come to assume that the government is there to depend on. They'll have even less incentive to work their way out of poverty.

*But all children are dependent! Do all then learn lifetime dependency? As I've said, children helped by enriched preschools became more self-reliant as adults.*

*In truth,* most people want to take care of themselves. *If they can't, something powerful is stopping them. Those obstacles, as I've said, are the assaults of poverty from birth that block both development and confidence in one's capacity to shoulder responsibility; all the mechanisms that drain wealth out of poor communities, leaving no basis for growth; and the closing of escape routes out of poverty, including the diminishing numbers of jobs offering middle class futures.*

## FREEDOM AND ECONOMIC SECURITY

While you talk about opportunity, you are really saying that government should provide economic security. But if government tries to
provide economic security for everyone, it removes responsibility from
the individual. And only as we're required to shoulder responsibility do
any of us develop individual autonomy, which, as I've said, is the basis
of personal freedom.

Many well-meaning people want to 'help' by doing for other people. If they cooled that emotional response with a little common sense,
they could see that 'doing for' someone is really taking away their
power and potential for self-respect.

*Security doesn't undercut my freedom; it is the very basis of it! Without
security what freedom do I have?*

*Take job security. With no national commitment to full employment
and a growing proportion of low wage jobs, even if my job is a dead end
and ruining my health, I'd be afraid to quit. I'd do what I was told.*

*I read about Chrysler plant workers in Newark, Delaware, who know
for a fact that they are being exposed to poisonous lead and arsenic, but they
keep going to work!*[47] *And then there was that piece in* The New York
Times *on John Morrell & Company meatpackers in South Dakota. One
worker said his wrist was so injured by the assembly line that he can't even
carry his kids to bed at night.*[48] *But he keeps going to work.*

*And even workers in less desperate straits know that if the quit, they
may not get other jobs paying enough to support their families. Plus, they'll
lose medical insurance. Unemployment benefits offer little help: only a
quarter of the jobless get them.*

Look, everyone doesn't share your values. People who keep working
at a job they don't like obviously value security more than freedom.
And they value the extra pay they get for risking danger or ill health.
That worker in the meat packing plant could get a cashier's job at the
7-Eleven and save his wrist, but it would pay less. That's his choice to
make.

*If I have to choose between a job that damages my health and another that makes it impossible for me to care for my family, the choice isn't between security and freedom. I have neither.*

And you're still ignoring the obvious truth that some people simply choose not to work. Unemployment benefits high enough to provide real security would invite more people to slough off.

*Then why isn't unemployment higher where benefits are higher? In the United States, laid-off workers get about half their former pay and only for several months. Several countries with much higher benefits have had lower unemployment. In Austria, laid-off workers get eighty percent of their previous pay for at least a year, but the jobless rate there has been half of ours for many years.*[49]

## POVERTY: IT'S ALL RELATIVE

As humane as it sounds, your pursuit of economic security for everyone is ultimately doomed. Why? Because desire for security is insatiable. The biblical insight that 'the poor will always be with us' isn't an easy cop out; it's an inescapable truth because of how poverty is perceived. It's as much a state of mind as a state of income.[50] In large measure it is a relative lack of goods: people will tend to see 'poverty' as roughly half or less of the median income at any given time. So the richer we get, the more anti-poverty programs we'll need.[51] There can be no end.

*My concept of poverty isn't mushy. I don't suddenly become poor when I'm the only one left on my block without a BMW!*

Poverty is not just about money or consumer goods. After all, in some parts of the world people have much less than even poorest Americans, yet they feel they're living all right. A set of attitudes, largely about self-respect, defines poverty.

*You're right. Poverty isn't just about lack of money. It means being shut out—the pain of being excluded as a full member society, and in many ways forgotten.*

But ending poverty is an ever-receding goal as people redefine their needs upward.

*No! Poverty isn't just a relative concept.[52] Poverty is what damages people—stunts growth and it kills. It can be measured: poor children are three times more likely to die in childhood.[53] Poor children are twice as likely to be stunted physically compared to those from better-off families.[54] Minimally, we could celebrate an end to poverty in an end to differences in survival and growth among income groups.*

*But poverty is also about our relationships with others, for there is a point, not too hard to discern, at which a lack of resources makes it impossible for us to participate in the community and to find meaning in our daily lives.[55] If we can't put a wholesome meal on the table, if we don't have appropriate clothes to wear to that all-important interview, if we postpone taking a sick child to the doctor because we don't know how we can pay the bill, that is poverty.*

*Let's get clear on one point. In every society, no matter how prosperous, some people just can't work—because of illness, physical impairment, or because they must stay home to care for someone else. Society's help is their sole hope for escaping poverty. Meeting their needs without destroying their dignity is a primary test of any society's humanity. Because Americans so hold to the notion that here anyone can make it who tries, we even seem to blame the incapacitated. How else can you explain why we're stingier in our help for this group than most other Western societies?[56]*

No, the explanation is that in America we assume that the family, the community, and our religions institutions—not the state—carry much of the responsibility to care for the sick and disabled. These groups are closest to the individual and can better tailor assistance to meet particular needs. Outside government 'experts' could never do as well.[57] History has proven this to be true; all government should do is make sure these voluntary helping structures are strong.

*If private, voluntary initiatives could solve the problem of poverty, why were conditions of the poor even more wretched before New Deal programs established government responsibility? And today in highly mobile America where families are separated by hundreds of miles and many people aren't churchgoers, your ideas are out of touch with reality.*

They only seem that way to you because government has preempted the provision of services and private initiative has atrophied.[58] This private initiative must be allowed to revive.

*Without a government-protected right to assistance, those unable to be self-supporting are reduced to supplicants pleading for help from relatives or a religious body.*

Only in rare circumstances. As you replace caring, voluntary associations based on goodwill with government bureaucrats just doing a job, voluntary ties among people, and even our compassion for each other, begin to wither.

And once such organizations decline, nothing is left between the individual and state power.

*Just because people's basic well-being must not depend on the whims of charity does not mean voluntary organizations are any less essential to a free society. They are the buffer between the individual and government, acting as essential watchdogs and advisors to community-guaranteed services, enhancing and personalizing these services.*

*And, of course, the arts, recreation, conservation, education, and all aspects of political life are inconceivable in a democratic society without a myriad of voluntary associations.*

*So, private associations can be a vehicle for meeting government-protected rights, can complement government functions—but they are no substitute for government responsibility.*

NOTES

1. Friedman, Milton. *Capitalism and Freedom* (Chicago: University of Chicago Press, 1962), pp. 1–6, 25–26.

2. O'Sullivan, John L. "Introduction. The Democratic Principle—The Importance of Its Assertion, and Application to Our Political System and Literature," *United States Magazine and Democratic Review* 1 (October–December, 1837): 6. Such statements are often used by conservatives to represent the founders' view. See, for example, Richard B. McKenzie, *Bound to Be Free* (Stanford, CA: Hoover Institution Press, 1982), pg. 13.

3. Jefferson, Thomas. *Thomas Jefferson, Writings*, ed. Merrill D. Peterson (New York: The Library of America/Liberty Classics, 1984), pg. 529.

4. Kristol, Irving. *Two Cheers for Capitalism* (New York: New American Library, 1978), pg. 15.

5. Sowell, Thomas. *A Conflict of Visions* (New York: William Morrow, 1987), pg. 226.

6. Children's Defense Fund. *A Call for Action to Make Our Nation Safe for Children: A Briefing Book on the Status of American Children in 1988* (Washington DC: Children's Defense Fund, 1988), pg. iii. This estimate refers to children under six years of age.

7. Harris, Louis. *Inside America* (New York: Vintage, 1987), pp. 33–38.

8. Levinson, Andrew. *The Full Employment Economy* (New York: Coward, McCann, Geoghegan, 1980), pp. 194–195. Levinson cites five national polls in which from 59 percent to 93 percent of respondents favored a government-guaranteed right to a job.

9. Freeman, Roger A. *The Wayward Welfare State* (Stanford, CA: Hoover Institute, 1981), pg. 252.

10. Mead, Lawrence M. *Beyond Entitlement: The Social Obligations of Citizenship* (New York: Free Press, 1986), pg. 72.

11. Novak, Michael. *The Spirit of Democratic Capitalism* (New York: American Enterprise Institute/Simon & Schuster, 1982), pg. 48.

12. Friedman, Milton and Rose Friedman. *Free to Choose* (New York: Avon, 1979), pg. 57.

13. Ibid., pg. 83.

14. We devote about fourteen percent to social programs, compared to twenty percent to 34 percent in Western Europe and Scandinavia; Ira C. Magaziner and Robert Reich, *Minding America's Business* (New York: Vintage Books, 1983),pg. 16.

15. Folbre, Nancy and the Center for Popular Economics. *A Field Guide to the U.S. Economy* (New York: Pantheon, 1987), table 6.2. For details on public employment, see Louis Uchitelle, "In the Work Force, A Reagan Evolution," *The New York Times*, December 27, 1987, pg. E5.

16. *Bound to Be Free*, pg. 19.

17. Kuttner, Robert. *The Economic Illusion* (New York: Houghton Mifflin, 1984), pg. 82.

18. Ibid., pg. 190. In the mid-Seventies the U.S. ranked fourteenth out of seventeen in taxes as percent of gross domestic product, but eighth in terms of the burden carried by the average production worker.

19. O'Hare, William. "The Eight Myths of Poverty," *American Demographics* 8 (May 1986): pg. 25.

20. The increase is given in real dollars. See Office of Management and Budget, *The United States Budget in Brief Fiscal Year 1987* (Washington DC: GPO, 1987).

21. Sagan, Carl. Speech delivered at the Rededication on the 50th Anniversary of the Eternal Light Peace Memorial, Gettysburg, Pennsylvania, July 3, 1988.

22. Total federal employment:

    2 million civilians not working for the military

    1 million civilians working directly for the military

    2.5 million working for firms under military contract to the Pentagon

    2 million in the armed forces

23. *The New York Times*, February 13, 982, pg. 18. The exact estimate is $2.1 billion for the next three years.

24. deCourcy Hinds, Michael. "New York Welfare Allowance Rising But Homeless Worries Persist," *The New York Times,* December 28, 1987, pg. 14.

25. Currie, Elliott. "Crime and Ideology," *Working Papers* 9 (May–June 1982): pg. 29.

26. Wilson, James Q. "Crime and American Culture," *Public Interest* 70 (Winter 1983): pp. 36–37. For an in-depth conservative argument about crime and society, see James Q. Wilson and Richard J. Herstein, *Crime and Human Nature* (New York: Simon & Schuster, 1985).

27. For a summary of both sides of the argument that weak punishment causes crime, see Elliott Currie, *Confronting Crime* (New York: Pantheon, 1985), pp. 26–28.

28. Ibid., pg. 6, and chapters 4 and 5.

29. Committee for Economic Development. *Children in Need* (Washington DC: Committee for Economic Development, 1987), chapter 1.

30. Simon, Paul. *Let's Put America Back to Work* (Chicago: Bonus Books, 1987), pg. 21.

31. *A Call for Action to Make Our Nation Safe for Children*, pg. vi.

32. *The Economic Illusion*, pg. 23.

33. McIntyre, Robert S. and David Wilhelm. *Money for Nothing. The Failure of Corporate Tax Incentives 1981–1984* (Washington, DC: Citizens for Tax Justice, 1986), pg. 3.

34. Estimates of the size of the 'underclass' range from less than a million to as many as eleven million. Isabel Wilkerson, "Growth of the Very Poor Is Focus of New Studies," *The New York Times,* December 20, 1987, pg. 15.

35. Duncan, Greg I., Martha S. Hill, and Saul D. Hoffman. "Welfare Dependence Within and Across Generations," *Science* (January 29, 1988): pg. 467.

36. Auletta, Ken. *The Underclass* (New York: Random House, 1982), pg. 275.

37. "Welfare Dependence." The median length of receipt is less than four years.

38. Harrison, Bennett. "Welfare Payments and the Reproduction of Low-Wage Workers and Secondary Jobs," *Review of Radical Political Economics* (Fall 1979), pp. 1–16.

39. "Welfare Dependence." Sixty-four percent of young women studied who had been in welfare families received no AFDC during the three-year period of the study. See also Greg H. Duncan, *Years of Poverty, Years of Plenty: The Changing Economic Fortunes of American Workers and their Families* (Ann Arbor: Institute for Social Research, University of Michigan, 1984).

40. *The Underclass,* pg. 231. A five-year national study in the late Seventies found that ex-addicts and AFDC mothers benefited most from the subsidized work program and that "benefits exceed the costs." Ex-offenders and young people did less well. Overall, about a third continued in paid jobs after the program ended. Much of the outcome depended on how well managed was the particular site taking part in the national experiment.

41. *Business Week,* October 12, 1987, pp. 26–28. Note that one-fifth of all U.S. children are estimated to be poor, but one-fourth of all U.S. children under six.

42. Harrington, Michael. *New American Poverty* (New York: Holt. Rinehart and Winston, 1984), pg. 4.

43. Greenstein, Robert. "Myths and Realities about American Poverty," *Food Monitor* (Fall 1987), pg. 62.

44. *Public Welfare in California,* State of California, Health and Welfare Agency, Department of Social Services, Data Processing and Statistical Services Bureau, Statistical Series PA 3–339, calculated from table 11.

45. The study follows the lives of 123 poor children who participated in Headstart programs in Ypsilanti, Michigan. See John Berrueta-Clement, *Changed Lives: The Effects of the Ferry Preschool on Youth Through Age 19* (Ypsilanti, MI: High Scope Educational C Foundation, 1984). For an excellent evaluation of the impact of the War on Poverty, see Sar A. Levitan and Robert Taggart, *The Promise of Greatness* (Cambridge, MA: Harvard University Press, 1976). For a discussion of social programs that do work, see Lisbeth B. Schorr, *Within Our Reach* (New York: Doubleday, 1988).

46. Sowell, Thomas. *Knowledge and Decisions* (New York: Basic Books, 1980), pp. 117–18.

47. Gruson, Lindsey. "Life versus Livelihood at Chrysler Plant," *The New York Times,* July 8, 1987, pg. 10.

48. Glaberson, William. "Misery on the Meatpacking Line," *The New York Times,* June 14, 1987.

49. Lens, Sidney. "Austria's Quiet Revolution Works," *The Nation* , January 12, 1985, pg. 15.

50. Gilder, George. *Wealth and Poverty* (New York: Basic Books, 1981), pg. 12.

51. Ward, Benjamin. *The Conservative Economic World View* (New York: Basic Books, 1979), pp. 50–51.

52. For a useful discussion of this issue, see *The New American Poverty,* pp. 72–76. If poverty were simply defined as the lowest fifth of the population in income, of course it would always exist; but if it is defined in very real measures such as higher death

rates, cross-country comparisons are possible. They demonstrate that it is possible to reduce poverty. The Organization for Economic Cooperation and Development in the early Seventies found that thirteen percent of Americans were poor compared to 3.5 percent of Swedes.

53. Nersesian, William S., M.D., et al. "Childhood Death and Poverty. A Study of All Childhood Deaths in Maine, 1976 to 1980," *Pediatrics*, January 1985, pp. 41–49.

54. Brown, J. Larry. "Hunger in the U.S.," *Scientific American* (February 1987), pg. 41.

55. For a discussion in a similar vein, see Peter Townsend, *Poverty in the United Kingdom* (Berkeley: University of California Press, 1979).

56. Haveman, Robert H., Victor Halberstadt, and Richard V. Burkhauser. *Public Policy Toward Disabled Workers* (Ithaca, NY: Cornell University Press, 1984), pg. 48. Among eight industrial countries, the U.S. ranked among the lowest in medical care, housing, and other programs for the disabled.

57. Woodson, Robert L. "The Importance of Neighborhood Organizations in Meeting Human Needs," in *Meeting Human Needs: Toward a New Public Philosophy*, ed. Jack A. Meyer (Washington, DC: American Enterprise Institute for Public Policy Research, 1982), pg. 140.

58. Meyer, Jack A. "Private Sector Initiatives and Public Policy: A New Agenda," in *Meeting Human Needs*, pg. 6.

# 15

## WHAT ARE HUMAN RIGHTS?

*Human Rights Educators' Network of Amnesty International USA*

*Human rights are the rights a person has simply because he or she is a human being.*

Human rights are held by all persons equally, universally, and forever.

Human rights are inalienable: you cannot lose these rights any more than you can cease being a human being. Human rights are indivisible: you cannot be denied a right because it is 'less important' or 'non-essential.' Human rights are interdependent: all human rights are part of a complementary framework. For example, your ability to participate in your government is directly affected by your right to express yourself, to get an education, and even to obtain the necessities of life.

Another definition for human rights is those *basic standards without which people cannot live in dignity.* To violate someone's human rights is to treat that person as though she or he were not a human being. To advocate human rights is to demand that the human dignity of all people be respected.

In claiming these human rights, everyone also accepts the responsibility not to infringe on the rights of others and to support those whose rights are abused or denied.

### HUMAN RIGHTS AS INSPIRATION AND EMPOWERMENT

Human rights are both inspirational and practical. Human rights principles hold up the vision of a free, just, and peaceful world and set minimum standards for how individuals and institutions everywhere should treat people. Human rights also empower people with a framework for action when those minimum standards are not met, for people still have human rights even if the laws or those in power do not recognize or protect them.

We experience our human rights every day in the United States when we worship according to our belief, or choose not to worship at all; when we debate and criticize government policies; when we join a trade union; when we travel to other parts of the country or overseas. Although we usually take these actions for granted, people both here and in other countries do not enjoy all these liberties equally. Human rights violations also occur everyday in this country when a parent abuses a child, when a family is homeless, when a school provides inadequate education, when women are paid less than men, or when one person steals from another.

## THE UNIVERSAL DECLARATION OF HUMAN RIGHTS

Rights for all members of the human family were first articulated in 1948 in the United Nations' Universal Declaration of Human Rights (UDHR). Following the horrific experiences of the Holocaust and World War II, and amid the grinding poverty of much of the world's population, many people sought to create a document that would capture the hopes, aspirations, and protections to which every person in the world was entitled and ensure that the future of humankind would be different.

The thirty articles of the Declaration together form a comprehensive statement covering economic, social, cultural, political, and civil rights. The document is both universal (it applies to all people everywhere) and indivisible (all rights are equally important to the full realization of one's humanity). A declaration, however, is not a treaty and lacks any enforcement provisions. Rather it is a statement of intent, a set of principles to which United Nations member states commit themselves in an effort to provide all people a life of human dignity.

Over the past fifty years the Universal Declaration of Human Rights has acquired the status of customary international law because most states treat it as though it were law. However, governments have not applied this customary law equally. Socialist and communist countries of Eastern Europe, Latin America, and Asia have emphasized social welfare rights, such as education, jobs, and health care, but often have limited the political rights of their citizens. The United States has focused on political and civil rights and has advocated strongly against regimes that torture; deny religious freedom, or persecute minorities.

On the other hand, the U.S. government rarely recognizes health care, homelessness, environmental pollution, and other social and economic concerns as human rights issues, especially within its own borders.

Across the United States, a movement is rising to challenge this narrow definition of human rights and to restore social, economic, and cultural rights to their rightful place on the human rights agenda. The right to eat is as fundamental as the right not to be tortured or jailed without charges!

## A SHORT HISTORY OF HUMAN RIGHTS

The belief that everyone, by virtue of her or his humanity, is entitled to certain human rights is fairly new. Its roots, however, lie in earlier tradition and documents of many cultures; it took the catalyst of World War II to propel human rights onto the global stage and into the global conscience.

Throughout much of history, people acquired rights and responsibilities through their membership in a group—a family, indigenous nation, religion, class, community, or state. Most societies have had traditions similar to the 'golden rule' of "Do unto others as you would have them do unto you." The Hindu Vedas, the Babylonian Code of Hammurabi, the Bible, the Quran (Koran), and the Analects of Confucius are five of the oldest written sources which address questions of people's duties, rights, and responsibilities. In addition, the Inca and Aztec codes of conduct and justice and an Iroquois Constitution were Native American sources that existed well before the eighteenth century. In fact, all societies, whether in oral or written tradition, have had systems of propriety and justice as well as ways of tending to the health and welfare of their members.

## PRECURSORS OF TWENTIETH CENTURY
## HUMAN RIGHTS DOCUMENTS

Documents asserting individual rights, such the Magna Carta (1215), the English Bill of Rights (1689), the French Declaration on the Rights of Man and Citizen (1789), and the U.S. Constitution and Bill of

Rights (1791) are the written precursors to many of today's human rights documents. Yet many of these documents, when originally translated into policy, excluded women, people of color, and members of certain social, religious, economic, and political groups. Nevertheless, oppressed people throughout the world have drawn on the principles these documents express to support revolutions that assert the right to self-determination.

Contemporary international human rights law and the establishment of the United Nations have important historical antecedents. Efforts in the nineteenth century to prohibit the slave trade and to limit the horrors of war are prime examples. In 1919, countries established the International Labor Organization (ILO) to oversee treaties protecting workers with respect to their rights, including their health and safety. Concern over the protection of certain minority groups was raised by the League of Nations at the end of the First World War. However, this organization for international peace and cooperation, created by the victorious European allies, never achieved its goals. The League floundered because the United States refused to join and because the League failed to prevent Japan's invasion of China and Manchuria (1931) and Italy's attack on Ethiopia (1935). It finally died with the onset of the Second World War (1939).

## THE BIRTH OF THE UNITED NATIONS

The idea of human rights emerged stronger after World War II. The extermination by Nazi Germany of over six million Jews, Sinti and Romani (gypsies), homosexuals, and persons with disabilities horrified the world. Trials were held in Nuremberg and Tokyo after World War II, and officials from the defeated countries were punished for committing war crimes, 'crimes against peace,' and 'crimes against humanity.'

Governments then committed themselves to establishing the United Nations, with the primary goal of bolstering international peace and preventing conflict. People wanted to ensure that never again would anyone be unjustly denied life, freedom, food, shelter, and nationality. The essence of these emerging human rights principles was captured in President Franklin Delano Roosevelt's 1941 State of the Union Address when he spoke of a world founded on four essential freedoms: freedom of speech and religion and freedom from want and fear. The calls came from across the globe for human rights standards to protect citizens from abuses by their governments, standards against which nations could be held accountable for the treatment of those living within their borders. These voices played a critical role in the San Francisco meeting that drafted the United Nations Charter in 1945.

## THE UNIVERSAL DECLARATION OF HUMAN RIGHTS

Member states of the United Nations pledged to promote respect for the human rights of all. To advance this goal, the UN established a Commission on Human Rights and charged it with the task of drafting a document spelling out the meaning of the fundamental rights and freedoms proclaimed in the Charter. The Commission, guided by Eleanor Roosevelt's forceful leadership, captured the world's attention. On December 10, 1948, the Universal Declaration of Human Rights (UDHR) was adopted by the fifty-six members of the United Nations. The vote was unanimous, although eight nations chose to abstain.

The UDHR, commonly referred to as the international Magna Carta, extended the revolution in international law ushered in by the United Nations Charter—namely, that how a government treats its own citizens is now a matter of legitimate international concern, and not simply a domestic issue. It claims that all rights are interdependent and indivisible. Its Preamble eloquently asserts that:

> *[R]ecognition of the inherent dignity and of the equal and inalienable rights of all members of the human family is the foundation of freedom, justice, and peace in the world.*

The influence of the UDHR has been substantial. Its principles have been incorporated into the constitutions of most of the more than 185 nations now in the UN. Although a declaration is not a legally binding document, the Universal Declaration has achieved the status of customary international law because people regard it "as a common standard of achievement for all people and all nations."

## THE HUMAN RIGHTS COVENANTS

With the goal of establishing mechanisms for enforcing the UDHR, the UN Commission on Human Rights proceeded to draft two treaties: the International Covenant on Civil and Political Rights (ICCPR) and its optional Protocol and the International Covenant on Economic, Social and Cultural Rights (ICESCR). Together with the Universal Declaration, they are commonly referred to as the International Bill of Human Rights. The ICCPR focuses on issues such as the right to life, freedom of speech, religion, and voting. The ICESCR focuses on such issues as food, education, health, and shelter. Both covenants trumpet the extension of rights to all persons and prohibit discrimination.

As of 1997, over 130 nations have ratified these covenants. The United States, however, has ratified only the ICCPR, and even that with many reservations, or formal exceptions, to its full compliance.

## SUBSEQUENT HUMAN RIGHTS DOCUMENTS

In addition to the covenants in the International Bill of Human Rights, the United Nations has adopted more than twenty principal treaties further elaborating human rights. These include conventions to prevent and prohibit specific abuses like torture and genocide and to protect vulnerable populations, such as refugees (Convention Relating to the Status of Refugees, 1950), women (Convention on the Elimination of All Forms of Discrimination against Women, 1979), and children (Convention on the Rights of the Child, 1989). As of 1997 the United States has ratified only these conventions:

- Convention on the Elimination of All Forms of Racial Discrimination
- Convention on the Prevention and Punishment of the Crime of Genocide
- Convention on the Political Rights of Women
- Slavery Convention of 1926
- Convention against Torture and Other Cruel, Inhuman, or Degrading Treatment or Punishment

In Europe, the Americas, and Africa, regional documents for the protection and promotion of human rights extend the International Bill of Human Rights. For example, African states have created their own Charter of Human and People's Rights (1981), and Muslim states have created the Cairo Declaration on Human Rights in Islam (1990). The dramatic changes in Eastern Europe, Africa, and Latin America since 1989 have powerfully demonstrated a surge in demand for respect of human rights. Popular movements in China, Korea, and other Asian nations reveal a similar commitment to these principles.

## THE ROLE OF NONGOVERNMENTAL ORGANIZATIONS

Globally the champions of human rights have most often been citizens, not government officials. Nongovernmental organizations (NGOs) have played a cardinal role in focusing the international community on human rights issues. For example, NGO activities surrounding the 1995 United Nations Fourth World Conference on Women in Beijing, China, drew unprecedented attention to serious violations of the human rights of women. NGOs such as Amnesty International, the Antislavery Society, the International Commission of Jurists, the International Working Group on Indigenous Affairs, Human Rights Watch, Minnesota Advocates for Human Rights, and Survivors International monitor the actions of governments and pressure them to act according to human rights principles.

Government officials who understand the human rights framework can also effect far reaching change for freedom. Many United States Presidents such as Abraham Lincoln, Franklin Roosevelt, Lyndon B. Johnson, and Jimmy Carter have taken strong stands for human rights. In other countries leaders like Nelson Mandela and Vaclav Havel have brought about great changes under the banner of human rights.

Human rights is an idea whose time has come. The Universal Declaration of Human Rights is a call to freedom and justice for all people throughout the world. Every day governments that violate the rights of their citizens are challenged and called to task. Every day human beings worldwide mobilize and confront injustice and inhumanity. Like drops of water falling on a rock, they wear down the forces of oppression and move the world closer to achieving the principles expressed in the Universal Declaration of Human Rights.

# 16

## A MORE HOLISTIC UNDERSTANDING
## OF HUMAN RIGHTS

*Chandra Muzaffar*

Because Amnesty International is often equated with the worldwide human rights struggle, a significant segment of the intelligentsia in both Western and non-Western societies have begun to believe that what Amnesty International fights for or fights against is the sum total of the human family's human rights agenda. In other words, detention without trial, disappearances, torture, extra-judicial executions, capital punishment—this is what human rights is mostly about. Sometimes, one may choose to place all these violations within the larger context of the struggle to protect political and civil rights. In fact, human rights, as the intelligentsia and the middle and upper classes, as a whole, understand them, is synonymous with political and civil rights. Now and then, certain cultural rights, like the right to speak one's language or practice one's religion, would also be included in their definition of human rights.

It would be wrong, of course, to put the whole blame for this narrow understanding of human rights upon Amnesty International. Western governments with their liberal-democratic ideologies have, via pronouncements, policies, and practices, helped create the erroneous belief that human rights are essentially political freedoms and civil liberties. Given their overwhelming economic, technological, cultural, and political power at this juncture in history, they have succeeded in convincing people everywhere that human rights are equal to political and civil rights and nothing more.

### ECONOMIC AND SOCIAL RIGHTS

Needless to say, this has had some negative consequences for other equally legitimate dimensions of human rights. Economic and social rights have received much less emphasis than they deserve. The human right to food, to clothing, to shelter, to education, to health, to employment is fundamental to the very survival of the human being. For the vast majority of the human race, it is these rights that matter most. Of what use is the human rights struggle to the poverty-stricken if it does not liberate them from hunger, from homelessness, from ignorance, from disease? Human rights interpreted mainly in terms of political and civil rights will not satisfy the quest of the poor for human dignity and social justice. Life and liberty, food and freedom should go hand-in-hand if we want to develop a more holistic, integrated vision of human rights.

It is a pity there are very few groups, operating as human rights organizations, which are committed to a comprehensive view of human rights that embrace the different facets of human life. Most of them seek to defend political and civil rights, as they are conventionally understood. Thus, freedom of expression, freedom of association, the right of dissent, the rule of law, the independence of the judiciary are among their main—sometimes sole—concerns.

This widely prevalent perception of human rights is inimical to the interests of people in yet another way. Unlike Western governments which see human rights as rights revolving around the individual, there is in Asia and Africa in particular, a strong notion of the rights of the collectivity, the community, the nation. This has a lot to do with the colonial experience of Asian and African states. Subjected to alien, colonial rule for centuries, fighting for freedom for whole generations of Asians and Africans came to mean fighting for the freedom of their people. There is, therefore, a concept of collective freedom and the rights that go with that freedom in the historical baggage of the Asians and Africans. This explains why freedom for most post-colonial societies has been more than a litany of personal liberties. It is a collective ideal inextricably intertwined with the quest of whole communities, of entire nations for human dignity and social justice. Today, we are witnessing such a quest for collective freedom in the valiant struggles of the Palestinian people.

If the inherent rights of communities were given prominence, human rights movements would become more complete and comprehensive in their outlook.

### CONTROL AND DOMINANCE BY A FEW

Asserting the rights of the collective is not just a matter of developing a more complete perspective on human rights. It is a question of survival.

There is no denying that what has emerged in the course of the decades is an international system in which the poor and powerless who constitute the overwhelming majority of the human race have very little say over their own destiny. A system which virtually disenfranchises the majority cannot be democratic.

Authoritarianism at the international level, displays striking similarities to authoritarianism in national politics. At both levels, for instance, there is media manipulation and the abuse of political institutions and legal processes to serve the interests of those at the levers of power. In both national and international politics, elite control and dominance has resulted in the decline and denial of human rights. One wonders, therefore, why authoritarianism at the international level has escaped censure from conventional human rights groups in both the North and the South.

### GLOBAL CRISES

But sooner or later human rights groups in the North as well as the South will have to come to grips with the question of the international system and its impact upon human rights. For the oneness of humanity is becoming a reality in all sorts of ways. The environmental crisis, more than perhaps any other challenge confronting contemporary humankind, compels us to seek remedies from a global perspective. There is no national solution to the environmental crisis. We have to think, feel, and act universal in the truest sense of the word.

Once the importance of such an endeavor is understood, we will have to learn to view the whole of humanity as one single family. This is quite different from seeing human beings as citizens of different states in the international system. This is the approach adopted by human rights groups today. When we begin to appreciate the real meaning of this idea of 'humanity as a single family' we will find it intolerable that such a huge segment of the same human family does not enjoy basic economic, social, cultural, political, and civil rights. We will want to find out what the underlying causes are of this terrible injustice done to our brothers and sisters. We will seek to change social relationships, transform social structures in such a way that a more just and equal world emerges in which each and every human being exercises her rights and executes her responsibilities in consonance with her inherent human dignity.

That world awaits us. That world beckons to us. It is a world that we will not live to see. But it is a world that we must work to achieve. For it is a duty that we who live in the present owe to those who will inherit the future.

# BUILDING A MOVEMENT
# FOR HUMAN RIGHTS IN AMERICA

"Get up, stand up, stand up for your rights!"
—Bob Marley

Conventional approaches have failed to make a dent in economic inse-curity, poverty, and hunger in America. Anti-poverty policies have stigmatized the poor, emphasized their difference from other Americans, and offered them a combination of weak assistance and thinly veiled punishment. Rather than providing a way into the American mainstream, such policies—culminating in 'welfare reform'—have reinforced exclusion. We have ended up divided from one another, blaming and scapegoating the victims.

Under such circumstances, the resistance of structural poverty to change, even in times of general economic expansion and a 'healthy' economy, has led many to despair of ever finding true solutions. That despair has been a severe blow to the civil rights, anti-poverty, and union movements. As we move into a new millennium, the time has come for a fresh approach that can lift us out of our despair, renew our hope, and give us the energy to unite our movements in a common struggle.

We need to change the very way we, as a society, think about poverty. We must build on what we share in common: our essential humanity and dignity. In Part Four we have put forth human rights as just such a framework, one we can unite behind. But before address-ing movement building around human rights, it is worth reflecting on the lessons we can learn from what went wrong.

Progressive movements in America have for too long ceded the ter-rain of ideology to conservative and right-wing policy think tanks like the Heritage Foundation, and the Cato and American Enterprise Institutes. These media-savvy organizations have presented themselves as the defenders of family values and the work ethic. As progressives, we have let them seize the moral high ground as camouflage for their policy prescriptions to free corporations from public oversight. They have shifted the entire political environment to the right. Where massive cuts in public assistance would have been unthinkable two or three decades ago, in 'conservative America,' welfare reform passed with relatively little protest.

What the Right learned is that effectively addressing social and economic issues requires at least two elements. These are 1) moving the overall political environment, and 2) issue-based advocacy and lobbying. The conservative think tanks pressured the media and policy makers to use the language of efficiency, the work ethic, and conservative family values in policy debates. This opened space for grassroots organizing by the Christian Right, producing an outpouring of letters to elected officials and newspapers, as well as protests. They put forth church and other charitable organizations as the "thousand points of light" which would substitute for slashed federal program (and have not been up to magnitude of the task).

Meanwhile progressive movements were in retreat from so-called "ideological debates," choosing to focus on local community development and direct delivery of social services. While these are indeed important, the lack of attention to the overall political environment proved to be a recipe for sliding backwards. Each time a step was taken forward at the local level, the negative political environment usually dragged us at least two steps back, erasing the gains. We have seen this time and again.

We can offer an illustrative example. In 1997, U.S. food banks distributed $1 billion worth of food, a remarkable achievement. Yet it pales in comparison to the $4 billion cut in food stamps the same year. This is a case of one step forward and *four* steps back! Single-issue lobbying was able to restore some cuts—but not many—as lack of attention to the larger political environment by progressive movements has proven fatal. Now the time has come seize the initiative and take back the moral high ground. With value-based human rights arguments, we can shift the center of the debate back toward basic humanity, compassion, and opportunity for all. Human rights *are* family values.

The greatest strength of human rights is that they are universal. By simple virtue of being human, all share the same inalienable and indivisible rights to political suffrage, to be free from fear, and to have access to the basic necessities of life. Article 25 of the Universal Declaration of Human Rights (UDHR) states clearly that:

> Everyone has the right to a standard of living adequate for the health and well-being of himself [or herself] and of his [or her] family, including food, clothing, housing, and medical care and necessary social services, and the right to security in the event of unemployment, sickness, disability, widow-hood, old age, or other lack of livelihood in circumstances beyond his [or her] control.[1]

The right to an adequate standard of living underlies all economic and social rights. All people are assumed to be born with an equal right to human dignity. Making an adequate standard of living a right in no way means that governments themselves need provide all of the goods and services that go into such a standard, or that they must feed people directly. Rather it means that governments, including our own, must insure policy options that protect, respect, facilitate, and fulfill these obligations. By the same token they must reject policies that infringe upon these rights. We have highlighted throughout this book the myriad ways that our government, beholden to corporate interests, has implemented policies that undermine the basic economic human rights guaranteed by the UDHR. Those policies must be reversed, and we can achieve that reversal through an appeal based on human rights, if we build movements strong enough to do so. This is our challenge.

When the public is largely silent on trade, investment incentives, subsidies, and other policies that determine the direction of economic development, then the policy filter used by our elected officials is going to be that which is most convenient for their largest campaign contributors. The 'best policy' will be the one that freely permits untrammeled profit-taking, even if it means moving jobs out of communities instead of reinvesting profits locally to create more jobs, or failing to raise the minimum wage to keep up with inflation, or that rights of employed workers to organize in unions are eroded.

With a different policy filter—human rights—we might see those options rejected as inimical to the well-being of people and communities, and we might see alternative policies put in place which reward job creation and local reinvestment, while discouraging runaway businesses. It wouldn't be necessary to create new incentives, subsidies, or government expenditures. We could re-direct already existing subsidies and tax incentives—the kind of 'corporate welfare' that boosts profits at the expense of people—toward local economic development and the revitalization of communities across America.

Current federal priorities have meant an increase in child poverty and dilapidated schools, and a lack of affordable housing and health care. Corporate welfare today takes at least $448 billion per year from the federal budget, and costs about four times as much as what we spend each year on welfare for the poor.[2] Even after the end of the Cold War, the lion's share of our income taxes still go to the Pentagon. In 1998, military spending consumed nearly 43 percent of the total budget.[3] Are these really our priorities?

In order to move toward a human rights agenda for policy making in America, we need to take a page from the conservative think tanks and change the language that is used in the public debate. Every time a social or economic issue comes up for debate in the media, Congress, or city halls, we must ensure that human rights standards are discussed. If permission for a plant re-location is the topic, then we want the question asked, *what of the human rights of the workers to be laid off?* If the issue is food stamps, we want to hear, *what of the human rights of those who lose their entitlement to food and have no other alternative to make ends meet?*

If we were wealthy individuals or large corporations, we could use the power of our dollars to directly influence the media and policymakers, to have them say what we want. But we're not, so we must use the power of numbers. We must unite our movements behind human rights standards for all Americans. Labor rights, women's rights, discrimination based on ethnicity or religion, hunger, homelessness, low wages, and runaway businesses: these and many others *are* human rights issues. Human rights can unite us.

The power of our numbers can force the human rights perspective onto the agenda. We can follow the script used by the Right, but do it better. We should seize every opportunity to put forth human rights language, including letters to the editor, guest editorials, letters, faxes, and e-mails to elected officials, and protests of all kinds. The goal is to make asking the human rights questions an automatic reflex every time these issues come up.

Grassroots organizing must build political support for economic and social human rights. While there are thousands of organizations nationwide who address issues that clearly fall under the umbrella of human rights, their voices are dispersed. By adopting the human rights framework we can speak with a single voice, making our impact that much more powerful.

We must face the challenge of bringing local struggles for economic and social justice to the national policy level. We can build human rights alliances and coalitions to project these battles onto larger national and international stages, and force change in policy agendas from the bottom up. At the same time we need to bring existing human rights organizations, which in the past have focused almost exclusively on political and civil human rights, into economic and social rights struggles over poverty, homelessness, hunger, and social justice. We need to construct a larger shared agenda.

Hunger and poverty *can* be eliminated in America. There is no doubt that the resources *are* available in this wealthy nation to provide every healthy adult with a job that offers a life with basic human dignity, to provide every child with a home, education, and healthcare, and to guarantee that no one should ever have to live on the street because they can't afford mental health services or decent shelter. True American values demand that we find the political will to make such an America into a reality. America *needs* human rights.

1. United Nations Department of Public Information. *Universal Declaration of Human Rights* (New York: United Nations, 1993).
2. Zepezauer, M and A. Naiman. *Take the Rich off Welfare* (Tucson, AZ: Odonian Press, 1996).
3. Friends Committee on National Legislation. *Washington Newsletter, #631,* April 1999.

# APPENDICES

# APPENDIX ONE

## UNIVERSAL DECLARATION OF HUMAN RIGHTS

*Adopted by UN General Assembly Resolution 217A (III),*
*December 10, 1948*

PREAMBLE

Whereas recognition of the inherent dignity and of the equal and inalienable rights of all members of the human family is the foundation of freedom, justice, and peace in the world,

Whereas disregard and contempt for human rights have resulted in barbarous acts which have outraged the conscience of mankind, and the advent of a world in which human beings shall enjoy freedom of speech and belief and freedom from fear and want has been proclaimed as the highest aspiration of the common people,

Whereas it is essential, if man is not to be compelled to have recourse, as a last resort, to rebellion against tyranny and oppression, that human rights should be protected by the rule of law,

Whereas it is essential to promote the development of friendly relations between nations,

Whereas the peoples of the United Nations have in the Charter reaffirmed their faith in fundamental human rights, in the dignity and worth of the human person and in the equal rights of men and women and have determined to promote social progress and better standards of life in larger freedom,

Whereas Member States have pledged themselves to achieve, in cooperation with the United Nations, the promotion of universal respect for and observance of human rights and fundamental freedoms,

Whereas a common understanding of these rights and freedoms is of the greatest importance for the full realization of this pledge,

Now, therefore,
The General Assembly
Proclaims
This Universal Declaration of Human Rights

as a common standard of achievement for all peoples and all nations, to the end that every individual and every organ of society, keeping this Declaration constantly in mind, shall strive by teaching and education to promote respect for these rights and freedoms and by progressive measures, national and international, to secure their universal and effective recognition and observance, both among the peoples of Member States themselves and among the peoples of territories under their jurisdiction.

## ARTICLE 1

All human beings are born free and equal in dignity and rights. They are endowed with reason and conscience and should act towards one another in a spirit of brotherhood.

## ARTICLE 2

Everyone is entitled to all the rights and freedoms set forth in this Declaration, without distinction of any kind, such as race, color, sex, language, religion, political or other opinion, national or social origin, property, birth, or other status.

Furthermore, no distinction shall be made on the basis of the political, jurisdictional, or international status of the country or territory to which a person belongs, whether it be independent, trust, non-self-governing, or under any other limitation of sovereignty.

## ARTICLE 3

Everyone has the right to life, liberty, and security of person.

ARTICLE 4

No one shall be held in slavery or servitude; slavery and the slave trade shall be prohibited in all their forms.

ARTICLE 5

No one shall be subjected to torture or to cruel, inhuman, or degrading treatment or punishment.

ARTICLE 6

Everyone has the right to recognition everywhere as a person before the law.

ARTICLE 7

All are equal before the law and are entitled without any discrimination to equal protection of the law. All are entitled to equal protection against any discrimination in violation of the Declaration and against any incitement to such discrimination.

ARTICLE 8

Everyone has the right to an effective remedy by the competent national tribunals for acts violating the fundamental rights granted him by the constitution or by law.

ARTICLE 9

No one shall be subjected to arbitrary arrest, detention, or exile.

ARTICLE 10

Everyone is entitled in full equality to a fair and public hearing by an independent and impartial tribunal, in the determination of his rights and obligations and of any criminal charge against him.

## ARTICLE 11

1. Everyone charged with a penal offence has the right to be presumed innocent until proved guilty according to law in a public trial at which he has had all the guarantees necessary for his defense.

2. No one shall be held guilty of any penal offence on account of any act or omission which did not constitute a penal offence, under national or international law, at the time it was committed. Nor shall a heavier penalty be imposed than the one that was applicable at the time the penal offence was committed.

## ARTICLE 12

No one shall be subjected to arbitrary interference with his privacy, family, home, or correspondence, nor to attacks upon his honor and reputation. Everyone has the right to the protection of the law against such interference or attacks.

## ARTICLE 13

1. Everyone has the right to freedom of movement and residence within the borders of each state.

2. Everyone has the right to leave any country, including his own, and to return to his country.

## ARTICLE 14

1. Everyone has the right to seek and to enjoy in other countries asylum from persecution.

2. This right may not be invoked in the case of prosecutions genuinely arising from non-political crimes or from acts contrary to the purposes and principles of the United Nations.

ARTICLE 15

1. Everyone has the right to a nationality.

2. No one shall be arbitrarily deprived of his nationality nor denied the right to change his nationality.

ARTICLE 16

1. Men and women of full age, without any limitation due to race, nationality, or religion, have the right to marry and to found a family. They are entitled to equal rights as to marriage, during marriage, and at its dissolution.

2. Marriage shall be entered into only with the free and full consent of the intending spouses.

3. The family is the natural and fundamental group unit of society and is entitled to protection by society and the State.

ARTICLE 17

1. Everyone has the right to own property alone as well as in association with others.

2. No one shall be arbitrarily deprived of his property.

ARTICLE 18

Everyone has the right to freedom of thought, conscience and religion; this right includes freedom to change his religion or belief, and freedom, either alone or in community with others and in public or private, to manifest his religion or belief in teaching, practice, worship, and observance.

ARTICLE 19

Everyone has the right to freedom of opinion and expression: this right includes freedom to hold opinions without interference and to seek, receive, and impart information and ideas through any media and regardless of frontiers.

ARTICLE 20

1. Everyone has the right to freedom of peaceful assembly and association.

2. No one may be compelled to belong to an association.

ARTICLE 21

1. Everyone has the right to take part in the government of his country, directly or through freely chosen representatives.

2. Everyone has the right of equal access to public service in his country.

3. The will of the people shall be the basis of the authority of government; this will shall be expressed in periodic and genuine elections which shall be by universal and equal suffrage and shall be held by secret vote or by equivalent free voting procedures.

ARTICLE 22

Everyone, as a member of society, has the right to social security and is entitled to realization, through national effort and international co-operation and in accordance with the organization and resources of each State, of the economic, social, and cultural rights indispensable for his dignity and the free development of his personality.

ARTICLE 23

1. Everyone has the right to work, to free choice of employment, to just and favorable conditions of work, and to protection against unemployment.

2. Everyone, without any discrimination, has the right to equal pay for equal work.

3. Everyone who works has the right to just and favorable remuneration ensuring for himself and his family an existence worthy of human dignity, and supplemented, if necessary, by other means of social protection.

4. Everyone has the right to form and to join trade unions for the protection of his interests.

ARTICLE 24

Everyone has the right to rest and leisure, including reasonable limitation of working hours and periodic holidays with pay.

ARTICLE 25

1. Everyone has the right to a standard of living adequate for the health and well-being of himself and of his family, including food, clothing, housing, and medical care and necessary social services, and the right to security in the event of unemployment, sickness, disability, widowhood, old age, or other lack of livelihood in circumstances beyond his control.

2. Motherhood and childhood are entitled to special care and assistance. All children, whether born in or out of wedlock, shall enjoy the same social protection.

ARTICLE 26

1. Everyone has the right to education. Education shall be free, at least in the elementary and fundamental stages. Elementary education shall be compulsory. Technical and professional education shall be made generally available and higher education shall be equally accessible to all on the basis of merit.

2. Education shall be directed to the full development of the human personality and to the strengthening of respect for human rights and fundamental freedoms. It shall promote understanding, tolerance, and friendship among all nations, racial, or religious groups, and shall further the activities of the United Nations for the maintenance of peace.

3. Parents have a prior right to choose the kind of education that shall be given to their children.

## ARTICLE 27

1. Everyone has the right freely to participate in the cultural life of the community, to enjoy the arts, and to share in scientific advancement and its benefits.

2. Everyone has the right to the protection of the moral and material interests resulting from any scientific, literary, or artistic production of which he is the author.

## ARTICLE 28

Everyone is entitled to a social and international order in which the rights and freedoms set forth in this Declaration can be fully realized.

## ARTICLE 29

1. Everyone has duties to the community in which alone the free and full development of his personality is possible.

2. In the exercise of his rights and freedoms, everyone shall be subject only to such limitations as are determined by law solely for the purpose of securing due recognition and respect for the rights and freedoms of others and of meeting the just requirements of mortality, public order, and the general welfare in a democratic society.

3. These rights and freedoms may in no case be exercised contrary to the purposes and principles of the United Nations.

ARTICLE 30

Nothing in this Declaration may be interpreted as implying for any State, group, or person any right to engage in any activity or to perform any act aimed at the destruction of any of the rights and freedoms set forth herein.

# APPENDIX TWO

## THE INTERNATIONAL COVENANT ON ECONOMIC, SOCIAL, AND CULTURAL RIGHTS

*The Covenant was adopted by the United Nations General Assembly on January 3, 1976 and signed by President Carter on October 5, 1977 on behalf of the United States. However, the United States has yet to ratify this vital treaty.*

The States Parties to the present Covenant,

Considering that, in accordance with the principles proclaimed in the Charter of the United Nations, recognition of the inherent dignity and of the equal and inalienable rights of all members of the human family is the foundation of freedom, justice, and peace in the world,

Recognizing that these rights derive from the inherent dignity of the human person,

Recognizing that, in accordance with the Universal Declaration of Human Rights, the ideal of free human beings enjoying freedom from fear and want can only be achieved if conditions are created whereby everyone may enjoy his economic, social, and cultural rights, as well as his civil and political rights,

Considering the obligation of States under the Charter of the United Nations to promote universal respect for, and observance of, human rights and freedoms,

Realizing that the individual, having duties to other individuals and to the community to which he belongs, is under a responsibility to strive for the promotion and observance of the rights recognized in the present Covenant, Agree upon the following Articles:

## PART I

### ARTICLE 1

1. All peoples have the right of self-determination. By virtue of that right they freely determine their political status and freely pursue their economic, social, and cultural development.

2. All peoples may, for their own ends, freely dispose of their natural wealth and resources without prejudice to any obligations arising out of international economic co-operation, based upon the principle of mutual benefit, and international law. In no case may a people be deprived of its own means of subsistence.

3. The States Parties to the present Covenant, including those having responsibility for the administration of Non-Self-Governing and Trust Territories, shall promote the realization of the right of self-determination, and shall respect that right, in conformity with the provisions of the Charter of the United Nations.

## PART II

### ARTICLE 2

1. Each State Party to the present Covenant undertakes to take steps, individually and through international assistance and co-operation, especially economic and technical, to the maximum of its available resources, with a view to achieving progressively the full realization of the rights recognized in the present Covenant by all appropriate means, including particularly the adoption of legislative measures.

2. The States Parties to the present Covenant undertake to guarantee that the rights enunciated in the present Covenant will be exercised without discrimination of any kind as to race, color, sex, language, religion, political, or other opinion, national or social origin, property, birth, or other status.

3. Developing countries, with due regard to human rights and their national economy, may determine to what extent they would guarantee the economic rights recognized in the present Covenant to non-nationals.

## ARTICLE 3

The States Parties to the present Covenant undertake to ensure the equal right of men and women to the enjoyment of all economic, social, and cultural rights set forth in the present Covenant.

## ARTICLE 4

The States Parties to the present Covenant recognize that, in the enjoyment of those rights provided by the State in conformity with the present Covenant, the State may subject such rights only to such limitations as are determined by law only in so far as this may be compatible with the nature of these rights and solely for the purpose of promoting the general welfare in a democratic society.

## ARTICLE 5

1. Nothing in the present Covenant may be interpreted as implying for any State, group, or person any right to engage in any activity or to perform any act aimed at the destruction of any of the rights or freedoms recognized herein, or at their limitation to a greater extent than is provided for in the present Covenant.

2. No restriction upon or derogation from any of the fundamental human rights recognized or existing in any country in virtue of law, conventions, regulations, or custom shall be admitted on the pretext that the present Covenant does not recognize such rights or that it recognizes them to a lesser extent.

PART III

ARTICLE 6

1. The States Parties to the present Covenant recognize the right to work, which includes the right of everyone to the opportunity to gain his living by work which he freely chooses or accepts, and will take appropriate steps to safeguard this right.

2. The steps to be taken by a State Party to the present Covenant to achieve the full realization of this right shall include technical and vocational guidance and training programs, policies, and techniques to achieve steady economic, social, and cultural development and full and productive employment under conditions safeguarding fundamental political and economic freedoms to the individual.

ARTICLE 7

The States Parties to the present Covenant recognize the right of everyone to the enjoyment of just and favorable conditions of work, which ensure, in particular:
(a) remuneration which provides all workers, as a minimum, with:
   (i) fair wages and equal remuneration for work of equal value without distinction of any kind, in particular women being guaranteed conditions of work not inferior to those enjoyed by men, with equal pay for equal work;
   (ii) a decent living for themselves and their families in accordance with the provisions of the present Covenant;
(b) safe and healthy working conditions;
(c) equal opportunity for everyone to be promoted in his employment to an appropriate higher level, subject to no considerations other than those of seniority and competence;
(d) rest, leisure, and reasonable limitation of working hours and periodic holidays with pay, as well as remuneration for public holidays.

ARTICLE 8

1. The States Parties to the present Covenant undertake to ensure:
(a) the right of everyone to form trade unions and join the trade union of his choice, subject only to the rules of the organization concerned, for the promotion and protection of his economic and social interests. No restrictions may be placed on the exercise of this right other than those prescribed by law and which are necessary in a democratic society in the interests of national security or public order or for the protection of the rights and freedoms of others;
(b) the right of trade unions to establish national federations or confederations and the right of the latter to form or join international trade-union organizations;
(c) the right of trade unions to function freely subject to no limitations other than those prescribed by law and which are necessary in a democratic society in the interests of national security or public order or for the protection of the rights and freedoms of others;
(d) the right to strike, provided that it is exercised in conformity with the laws of the particular country.

2. This Article shall not prevent the imposition of lawful restrictions on the exercise of these rights by members of the armed forces or of the police or of the administration of the State.

3. Nothing in this Article shall authorize States Parties to the International Labor Organization Convention of 1948 concerning Freedom of Association and Protection of the Right to Organize to take legislative measures which would prejudice, or apply the law in such a manner as would prejudice, the guarantees provided for in that Convention.

ARTICLE 9

The States Parties to the present Covenant recognize the right of everyone to social security, including social insurance.

ARTICLE 10

The States Parties to the present Covenant recognize that:

1. The widest possible protection and assistance should be accorded to the family, which is the natural and fundamental group unit of society, particularly for its establishment and while it is responsible for the care and education of dependent children. Marriage must be entered into with the free consent of the intending spouses.

2. Special protection should be accorded to mothers during a reasonable period before and after childbirth. During such period working mothers should be accorded paid leave or leave with adequate social security benefits.

3. Special measures of protection and assistance should be taken on behalf of all children and young persons without any discrimination for reasons of parentage or other conditions. Children and young persons should be protected from economic and social exploitation. Their employment in work harmful to their morals or health or dangerous to life or likely to hamper their normal development should be punishable by law. States should also set age limits below which the paid employment of child labor should be prohibited and punishable by law.

ARTICLE 11

1. The States Parties to the present Covenant recognize the right of everyone to an adequate standard of living for himself and his family, including adequate food, clothing, and housing, and to the continuous improvement of living conditions. The States Parties will take appropriate steps to ensure the realization of this right, recognizing to this effect the essential importance of international co-operation based on free consent.

2. The States Parties to the present Covenant, recognizing the fundamental right of everyone to be free from hunger, shall take,

individually and through international co-operation, the measures, including specific programs, which are needed:

(a) to improve methods of production, conservation, and distribution of food by making full use of technical and scientific knowledge, by disseminating knowledge of the principles of nutrition and by developing or reforming agrarian systems in such a way as to achieve the most efficient development and utilization of natural resources;

(b) taking into account the problems of both food-importing and food-exporting countries, to ensure an equitable distribution of world food supplies in relation to need.

ARTICLE 12

1. The States Parties to the present Covenant recognize the right of everyone to the enjoyment of the highest attainable standard of physical and mental health.

2. The steps to be taken by the States Parties to the present Covenant to achieve the full realization of this right shall include those necessary for:

(a) the provision for the reduction of the stillbirth-rate and of infant mortality and for the healthy development of the child;

(b) the improvement of all aspects of environmental and industrial hygiene;

(c) the prevention, treatment, and control of epidemic, endemic, occupational, and other diseases;

(d) the creation of conditions which would assure to all medical service and medical attention in the event of sickness.

ARTICLE 13

1. The States Parties to the present Covenant recognize the right of everyone to education. They agree that education shall be directed to the full development of the human personality and the sense of its dignity, and shall strengthen the respect for human rights and fundamental freedoms. They further agree that education shall enable all

persons to participate effectively in a free society, promote understanding, tolerance, and friendship among all nations and all racial, ethnic, or religious groups, and further the activities of the United Nations for the maintenance of peace.

2. The States Parties to the present Covenant recognize that, with a view to achieving the full realization of this right:
(a) primary education shall be compulsory and available free to all;
(b) secondary education in its different forms, including technical and vocational secondary education, shall be made generally available and accessible to all by every appropriate means, and in particular by the progressive introduction of free education;
(c) higher education shall be made equally accessible to all, on the basis of capacity by every appropriate means, and in particular by the progressive introduction of free education;
(d) fundamental education shall be encouraged or intensified as far as possible for those persons who have not received or completed the whole period of their primary education;
(e) the development of a system of schools at all levels shall be actively pursued, an adequate fellowship system shall be established, and the material conditions of teaching staff shall be continuously improved.

3. The States Parties to the present Covenant undertake to have respect for the liberty of parents and, when applicable, legal guardians, to choose for their children schools, other than those established by the public authorities, which conform to such minimum educational standards as may be laid down or approved by the State, and to ensure the religious and moral education of their children in conformity with their own convictions.

4. No part of this Article shall be construed so as to interfere with the liberty of individuals and bodies to establish and direct educational institutions, subject always to the observance of the principles set forth in Paragraph I of this Article and to the requirement that the education given in such institutions shall conform to such minimum standards as may be laid down by the State.

ARTICLE 14

Each State Party to the present Covenant which, at the time of becoming a Party, has not been able to secure in its metropolitan territory or other territories under its jurisdiction compulsory primary education, free of charge, undertakes, within two years, to work out and adopt a detailed plan of action for the progressive implementation, within a reasonable number of years, to be fixed in the plan, of the principle of compulsory education free of charge for all.

ARTICLE 15

1. The States Parties to the present Covenant recognize the right of everyone:
(a) to take part in cultural life;
(b) to enjoy the benefits of scientific progress and its applications;
(c) to benefit from the protection of the moral and material interests resulting from any scientific, literary, or artistic production of which he is the author.

2. The steps to be taken by the States Parties to the present Covenant to achieve the full realization of this right shall include those necessary for the conservation, the development, and the diffusion of science and culture.

3. The States Parties to the present Covenant undertake to respect the freedom indispensable for scientific research and creative activity.

4. The States Parties to the present Covenant recognize the benefits to be derived from the encouragement and development of international contacts and cooperation in the scientific and cultural fields.

PART IV

ARTICLE 16

1. The States Parties to the present Covenant undertake to submit in conformity with this part of the Covenant reports on the measures which they have adopted and the progress made in achieving the observance of the rights recognized herein.

2. (a) All reports shall be submitted to the Secretary General of the United Nations, who shall transmit copies to the Economic and Social Council for consideration in accordance with the provisions of the present Covenant.
(b) The Secretary General of the United Nations shall also transmit to the specialized agencies copies of the reports, or any relevant parts therefrom, from States Parties to the present Covenant which are also members of these specialized agencies in so far as these reports, or parts therefrom, relate to any matters which fall within the responsibilities of the said agencies in accordance with their constitutional instruments.

ARTICLE 17

1. The States Parties to the present Covenant shall furnish their reports in stages, in accordance with a program to be established by the Economic and Social Council within one year of the entry into force of the present Covenant after consultation with the States Parties and the specialized agencies concerned.

2. Reports may indicate factors and difficulties affecting the degree of fulfillment of obligations under the present Covenant.

3. Where relevant information has previously been furnished to the United Nations or to any specialized agency by any State Party to the present Covenant, it will not be necessary to reproduce that information, but a precise reference to the information so furnished will suffice.

ARTICLE 18

Pursuant to its responsibilities under the Charter of the United Nations in the field of human rights and fundamental freedoms, the Economic and Social Council may make arrangements with the specialized agencies in respect of their reporting to it on the progress made in achieving the observance of the provisions of the present Covenant falling within the scope of their activities. These reports may include particulars of decisions and recommendations on such implementation adopted by their competent organs.

ARTICLE 19

The Economic and Social Council may transmit to the Commission on Human Rights for study and general recommendation or as appropriate for information the reports concerning human rights submitted by States in accordance with Articles 16 and 17, and those concerning human rights submitted by the specialized agencies in accordance with Article 18.

ARTICLE 20

The States Parties to the present Covenant and the specialized agencies concerned may submit comments to the Economic and Social Council on any general recommendation under Article 19 or reference to such general recommendation in any report of the Commission on Human Rights or any documentation referred to therein.

ARTICLE 21

The Economic and Social Council may submit from time to time to the General Assembly reports with recommendations of a general nature and a summary of the information received from the States Parties to the present Covenant and the specialized agencies on the measures taken and the progress made in achieving general observance of the rights recognized in the present Covenant.

ARTICLE 22

The Economic and Social Council may bring to the attention of other organs of the United Nations, their subsidiary organs and specialized agencies concerned with furnishing technical assistance any matters arising out of the reports referred to in this part of the present Covenant which may assist such bodies in deciding, each within its field of competence, on the advisability of international measures likely to contribute to the effective progressive implementation of the present Covenant.

ARTICLE 23

The States Parties to the present Covenant agree that international action for the achievement of the rights recognized in the present Covenant includes such methods as the conclusion of conventions, the adoption of recommendations, the furnishing of technical assistance and the holding of regional meetings and technical meetings for the purpose of consultation and study organized in conjunction with the Governments concerned.

ARTICLE 24

Nothing in the present Covenant shall be interpreted as impairing the provisions of the Charter of the United Nations and of the constitutions of the specialized agencies which define the respective responsibilities of the various organs of the United Nations and of the specialized agencies in regard to the matters dealt with in the present Covenant.

ARTICLE 25

Nothing in the present Covenant shall be interpreted as impairing the inherent right of all peoples to enjoy and utilize fully and freely their natural wealth and resources.

PART V

ARTICLE 26

1. The present Covenant is open for signature by any State Member of the United Nations or member of any of its specialized agencies, by any State Party to the Statute of the International Court of Justice, and by any other State which has been invited by the General Assembly of the United Nations to become a party to the present Covenant.

2. The present Covenant is subject to ratification. Instruments of ratification shall be deposited with the Secretary General of the United Nations.

3. The present Covenant shall be open to accession by any State referred to in Paragraph I of this Article.

4. Accession shall be effected by the deposit of an instrument of accession with the Secretary General of the United Nations.

5. The Secretary General of the United Nations shall inform all States which have signed the present Covenant or acceded to it of the deposit of each instrument of ratification or accession.

ARTICLE 27

1. The present Covenant shall enter into force three months after the date of the deposit with the Secretary General of the United Nations of the thirty-fifth instrument of ratification or instrument of accession.

2. For each State ratifying the present Covenant or acceding to it after the deposit of the thirty-fifth instrument of ratification or instrument of accession, the present Covenant shall enter into force three months after the date of the deposit of its own instrument of ratification or instrument of accession.

ARTICLE 28

The provisions of the present Covenant shall extend to all parts of federal States without any limitations or exceptions.

ARTICLE 29

1. Any State Party to the present Covenant may propose an amendment and file it with the Secretary General of the United Nations. The Secretary General shall thereupon communicate any proposed amendments to the States Parties to the present Covenant with a request that they notify him whether they favor a conference of States Parties for the purpose of considering and voting upon the proposals. In the event that at least one third of the States Parties favors such a conference, the Secretary General shall convene the conference under the auspices of the United Nations. Any amendment adopted by a majority of the States Parties present and voting at the conference shall be submitted to the General Assembly of the United Nations for approval.

2. Amendments shall come into force when they have been approved by the General Assembly of the United Nations and accepted by a two-thirds majority of the States Parties to the present Covenant in accordance with their respective constitutional processes.

3. When amendments come into force they shall be binding on those States Parties which have accepted them, other States Parties still being bound by the provisions of the present Covenant and any earlier amendment which they have accepted.

ARTICLE 30

Irrespective of the notifications made under Article 26, Paragraph 5, the Secretary General of the United Nations shall inform all States referred to in Paragraph I of the same Article of the following particulars:
(a) signatures, ratifications, and accessions under Article 26;
(b) the date of the entry into force of the present Covenant under Article 27 and the date of the entry into force of any amendments under Article 29.

ARTICLE 31

1. The present Covenant, of which the Chinese, English, French, Russian, and Spanish texts are equally authentic, shall be deposited in the archives of the United Nations.

2. The Secretary General of the United Nations shall transmit certified copies of the present Covenant to all States referred to in Article 26.

IN FAITH WHEREOF the undersigned, being duly authorized thereto by their respective Governments, have signed the present Covenant, opened for signature at New York, on the nineteenth day of December, one thousand nine hundred and sixty-six.

# APPENDIX THREE

## RATIFICATION HISTORY OF INTERNATIONAL
## HUMAN RIGHTS TREATIES

### INTERNATIONAL COVENANT ON ECONOMIC, SOCIAL, AND CULTURAL RIGHTS

Entry into Force: January 3, 1976
Signatories: 59
Parties: 136
United States Signature: October 5, 1977
United States Ratification: Not Ratified
Entry into Force (United States): Not in Force

### INTERNATIONAL COVENANT ON CIVIL AND POLITICAL RIGHTS

Entry into Force: March 23, 1976
Signatories: 58
Parties: 138
United States Signature: October 5, 1977
United States Ratification: June 8, 1992
Entry into Force (United States): September 8, 1992 with reservations

### INTERNATIONAL CONVENTION ON THE ELIMINATION OF ALL FORMS OF RACIAL DISCRIMINATION

Entry into Force: January 4, 1969
Signatories: 76
Parties: 148
United States Signature: September 28, 1966
United States Ratification: October 21, 1994
Entry into Force (United States): November 20, 1994 with reservations

CONVENTION ON THE ELIMINATION OF ALL FORMS
OF DISCRIMINATION AGAINST WOMEN

Entry into Force: September 3, 1981
Signatories: 97
Parties: 160
United States Signature: July 17, 1980
United States Ratification: Not Ratified
Entry into Force (United States): Not in Force

CONVENTION AGAINST TORTURE AND OTHER CRUEL,
INHUMAN, OR DEGRADING TREATMENT OR PUNISHMENT

Entry into Force: June 26, 1987
Signatories: 65
Parties: 102
United States Signature: April 18, 1988
United States Ratification: October 21, 1994
Entry into Force (United States): November 20, 1994 with reservations

CONVENTION ON THE RIGHTS OF THE CHILD

Entry into Force: September 2, 1990
Signatories: 140
Parties: 191
United States Signature: February 16, 1995
United States Ratification: Not Ratified
Entry into Force (United States): Not in Force

# APPENDIX FOUR

## ON MONOPOLIES AND SOCIAL JUSTICE
## AND THE ECONOMIC BILL OF RIGHTS

ON MONOPOLIES AND SOCIAL JUSTICE

*Excerpt from Franklin Delano Roosevelt's Campaign Address,*
*Chicago, Illinois*
October 14, 1936

The train of American business is moving ahead. But you people know what I mean when I say that if the train is to run smoothly again, the cars will have to be loaded more evenly. We have made a definite start in getting the train loaded more evenly, in order that its axles may not break again....

Because we cherished our system of private property and free enterprise and were determined to preserve it as the foundation of our traditional American system, we recalled the warning of Thomas Jefferson that "widespread poverty and concentrated wealth cannot long endure side by side in a democracy."

Our job was to preserve the American ideal of economic as well as political democracy, against the abuse of concentration of economic power that had been insidiously growing up among us in the past fifty years.... Free economic enterprise was being weeded out at an alarming pace.

During those years of false prosperity and during the more recent years of exhausting depression, one business after another, one small corporation after another, their resources depleted, had failed or had fallen into the lap of a bigger competitor.

A dangerous thing was happening. Half of the industrial corporate wealth of the country had come under the control of less than two hundred huge corporations. That is not all. These huge corporations in some cases did not even try to compete with each other. They themselves were tied together by interlocking directors, interlocking bankers, interlocking lawyers.

This concentration of wealth and power has been built upon other people's money, other people's business, other people's labor. Under this concentration, independent business was allowed to exist only by sufferance. It has been a menace to the social system as well as to the economic system which we call American democracy.

There is no excuse for it in the cold terms of industrial efficiency.

There is no excuse for it from the point of view of the average investor.

There is no excuse for it from the point of view of the independent businessman.

I believe, I have always believed, and I will always believe in private enterprise as the backbone of economic well-being in the United States.

But I know, and you know, and every independent businessman who has had to struggle against the competition of monopolies know, that this concentration of economic power in all-embracing corporations does not represent private enterprise as we Americans cherish it and propose to foster it. On the contrary, it represents private enterprise which has become a kind of private government, a power unto itself—a regimentation of other people's money and other people's lives.

## THE ECONOMIC BILL OF RIGHTS

*Excerpt from Franklin Delano Roosevelt's Annual Message to Congress* January 11, 1944

We have come to a clear realization of the fact that true individual freedom cannot exist without economic security and independence. "Necessitous men are not free men." People who are hungry and out of a job are the stuff of which dictatorships are made.

In our day, these economic truths have become accepted as self-evident. We have accepted, so to speak, a second Bill of Rights under which a new basis of security and prosperity can be established for all—regardless of station, race or creed. Among these are:

The right to a useful and remunerative job in the industries or shops or farms or mines of the nation;

The right to earn enough to provide adequate food and clothing and recreation;

The right of every farmer to raise and sell his products at a return which will give him and his family a decent living;

The right of every businessman, large and small, to trade in an atmosphere of freedom from unfair competition and domination by monopolies at home or abroad;

The right of every family to a decent home;

The right to adequate medical care and the opportunity to achieve and enjoy good health;

The right to adequate protection from the economic fears of old age, sickness, accident, and unemployment;

The right to a good education.

All of these rights spell security. And after this war is won, we must be prepared to move forward, in the implementation of these rights, to new goals of human happiness and well-being.

America's own rightful place in the world depends in large part upon how fully these and similar rights have been carried into practice for our citizens. For unless there is security here at home there cannot be lasting peace in the world.

# RESOURCE GUIDE

The organizations suggested here represent only a small portion of the many resources that can help you get involved with the struggle for economic human rights. Write or e-mail for more information.

**Alabama ARISE**
PO Box 846
Huntsville, AL 35810
Phone: (256) 880-6254

Fax: (256) 880-2781
Web: www.alarise.org

**Alliance for Democracy**
PO Box 683
Lincoln, MA 01773
Phone: (781) 259-9395

Web: www.eal.com/alliance
E-mail: peoplesall@aol.com

**American Friends Service Committee**
1501 Cherry Street
Philadelphia, PA 19102
Phone: (215) 241-7200

Web: www.afsc.org
E-mail: afscinfo@afsc.org

**Amnesty International**
600 Pennsylvania Avenue SE
5th floor, Washington DC 20003
Phone: (202) 544-0200

Web: www.amnesty-usa.org

**Amnesty International Educators Network**
53 W. Jackson Boulevard, room 1162
Chicago, IL 60604-3701
Phone: (312) 427-2060

Fax: (312) 427-2589
Web: www@amnesty-usa.org
E-mail: vcolucci@aiusa.org

**BOSS (Building Opportunities for Self-Sufficiency)**
685 14th Street
Oakland, CA 94612
Phone: (510) 663-6580

Fax: (510) 663-6584
E-mail: hno501@earthlink.net

**Bread for the World**
1100 Wayne Avenue, Suite 1100
Silver Spring, MD 20910
Phone: (301) 608-2400

Fax: (301) 608-2401
Web: www.bread.org
E-mail: bread@bread.org

**Californians for Justice**
161 Telegraph Avenue, Suite 206
Oakland, CA 94612
Phone: (510) 452-2728

Fax: (510) 452-3552
Web: www.igc.apc.org/cfj
E-mail: caljustice@igc.org

**Campaign for Labor Rights**
477 E. 32nd Avenue
Eugene, OR 97405
Phone: (541) 344-5410

Web: www.summersault.com/~agj/clr/
E-mail: clr@igc.apc.org

**Campaign to Abolish Poverty/Full Employment Coalition**
220 Golden Gate Avenue
San Francisco, CA 94102
Phone: (415) 928-1205

Fax: (415) 928-7252

**Center for Economic and Social Rights**
25 Ann Street, 6th floor
New York, NY 10038
Phone: (212) 634-3424

Fax: (212) 634-3425
E-mail: rights@cesr.org

**Center for Human Rights Education**
PO Box 311020
Atlanta, GA 31131-1020
Phone: (404) 344-9629

Fax: (404) 346-7517
Web: www.hrusa.org
E-mail: rosschre@aol.com

**Coalition for Ethical Welfare Reform**
2601 Mission Street, Suite 804
San Francisco, CA 94110
Phone: (415) 239-0161

Fax: (415) 239-0584
E-mail: coleman@sirius.com

**Coalition on Homelessness**
468 Turk Street
San Francisco, CA 94102
Phone: (415) 346-3740

Fax: (415) 775-5639
Web: www.sfo.com/~coh
E-mail: coh@sfo.com

**Food Not Bombs**
PO Box 422142
San Francisco, CA 94142
Phone: (415) 675-9928

**Franklin and Eleanor Roosevelt Institute**
801 2nd Avenue, 2nd Floor
New York, NY 10017-4706
Phone: (212) 907-1343

Fax: (212) 682-9185
Web: www.udhr50.org
E-mail: mcooper@unausa.org

**Free Speech TV**
PO Box 6060
Boulder, CO 80306
Phone: (303) 442-8445

Fax: (303) 442-6472
Web: www.freespeech.org
E-mail: fstv@fstv.org

**Greater Texas Workers Committee**
PO Box 3975
El Paso, TX 79923
Phone: (915) 533-9710

Fax: (915) 544-3730
E-mail: lamujerobrea@igc.apc.org

**Heartland Alliance**
208 South LaSalle, Suite 1818
Chicago, IL 60604
Phone: (312) 629-4500

Fax: (312) 629-4550
E-mail: heartlnd@mcs.net

**Human Rights USA Resource Center**
University of Minnesota Human Rights Center
229 Nineteenth Avenue South
Minneapolis, MN 55455-0444
Phone: (888) 473-3828

Web: http://www.hrusa.org

**Institute for Agriculture and Trade Policy**
2105 1st Avenue South
Minneapolis, MN 55404
Phone: (612) 870-0453

Fax: (612) 870-4846
Web: www.iatp.org
E-mail: iatp@igc.org

**Institute for Policy Studies**
733 15th Street NW, Suite 1020
Washington, DC 20005-2112
Phone: (202) 234-9382

Fax: (202) 387-7915
Web: ips-dc.org
E-mail: dorian@igc.org

**Interfaith Coalition on Immigrant Rights**
965 Mission Street, Suite 514
San Francisco, CA 94103
Phone: (415) 227-0388

Fax: (415) 543-0442
Web: www.igc.org/icir
E-mail: icir@igc.org

**International Forum on Globalization**
1555 Pacific Avenue
San Francisco, CA 94109
Phone: (415) 771-3394

Fax: (415) 771-1121
Web: www.ifg.org
E-mail: ifg@igc.org

**Jobs With Justice**
501 3rd Street NW
Washington, DC 20001
Phone: (202) 434-1106

Fax: (202) 434-1477
Web: www.jwj.org
E-mail: jobswjustice@jwj.org

**Kensington Welfare Rights Union**
PO Box 50678
Philadelphia, PA 19132-9720
Phone: (215) 203-1945

Fax: (215) 203-1950
Web: www.libertynet.org/kwru
E-mail: kwru@libertynet.org

**La Mujer Obrera**
PO Box 3975
El Paso, TX 79923
Phone: (915) 533-9710

Fax: (915) 544-3730
E-mail: lamujer@igc.apc.org

**Meikeljohn Civil Liberties Institute**
PO Box 673
Berkeley, CA 94701-0673
Phone: (510) 848-0599

Fax: (510) 848-6008

**Migrant Farmworker Justice Project**
PO Box 2110
Belle Glade, FL 33430
Phone: (561) 996-5266

Fax: (561) 992-5040
E-mail: hn2028@handnet.org

**National Law Center on Homelessness and Poverty**
918 F Street NW, Suite 412
Washington, DC 20004
Phone: (202) 638-2535

Fax: (202) 628-2737
Web: www.nlchp.org
E-mail: nlchp@nlchp.org

**National Lawyers Guild**
558 Capp Street
San Francisco, CA 94110
Phone: (415) 285-1055

E-mail: nlgsf@igc.org

**National Network for Immigrant and Refugee Rights**
310 8th Street, Suite 307          Fax: (510) 465-1885
Oakland, CA 94607                  E-mail: nnirr@nnirr.org
Phone: (510) 465-1084

**National Organization of Black Farmers**
231 Lafayette Street, Suite 669    Fax: (313) 226-2085
Detroit, MI 48226
Phone: (313) 961-5670

**People's Decade for Human Rights Education**
526 West 111th Street              Fax: (212) 666-6325
New York, New York 10025           E-mail: phre@igc.apc.org
Phone: (212) 749-3156

**POWER (People Organized to Win Employment Rights)**
126 Hyde Street, Suite 102         Web: www.fairwork.org
San Francisco, CA 94102            E-mail: power@fairwork.org
Phone: (415) 776-9379

**Program on Corporations, Law, and Democracy**
2115 Bradford Street               Fax: (508) 398-1552
Provincetown, MA 02657             Web: www.poclad.org
Phone: (508) 398-1145

**Project South: Institute for the Elimination of Poverty and Genocide**
9 Gammon Avenue SW                 Fax: (404) 622-7992
Atlanta, GA 30315                  Web: www.igc.org/projectsouth/
Phone: (404) 622-0602              E-mail: projectsouth@igc.org

**St. Anthony's Foundation: Justice Education and Advocacy Program**
121 Golden Gate Avenue             Fax: (415) 252-1635
San Francisco, CA 94102            Web: www.stanthonyfdn.org
Phone: (415) 241-2625              E-mail: juliet@stanthonyfdn.org

**Unitarian-Universalist Service Committee**
2000 P Street NW, Suite 505        Fax: (202) 775-2636
Washington, DC 20036-5915          Web: www.uusc.org
Phone: (202) 466-7400              E-mail: tsteege@uuscdc.org

**United for a Fair Economy**
37 Temple Place, 5th Floor
Boston, MA 02111
Phone: (617) 423-2148

Fax: (617) 423-0191
Web: www.stw.org
E-mail: stw@stworg

**Urban Justice Center**
666 Broadway, 10th Floor
New York, NY 10012
Phone: (212) 533-0540, ext. 318

Fax: (212) 533-4598
E-mail: ujc@dorsai.org

**Women's Economic Agenda Project**
449 15th Street, 2nd Floor
Oakland, CA 94612
Phone: (510) 451-7379

Fax: (510) 968-8628
Web: www.digital.sojourn.org
E-mail: weap@sirius.com

**WILD (Women's Institute for Leadership and Development)**
340 Pine Street, Suite 302
San Francisco, CA 94104
Phone: (415) 837-0795

Fax: (415) 837-1144
E-mail: wild@igc.apc.org

**Workers Organizing Committee**
PO Box 12292
Portland, OR 97212
Phone: (503) 236-0825

Fax: (503) 236-0835
Web:www.aracnet.com/~woc/
E-mail: woc@aracnet.com

**World Hunger Program**
Brown University, Box 1831
Providence, RI 02912
Phone: (401) 863-2766

Fax: (401) 863-2192
E-mail: Ellen_Messner@postoffice.brown.edu

**World Hunger Year**
505 Eight Avenue, 21st Floor
New York, NY 10018-6505
Phone: (800) 548-6479

Fax: (212) 465-9274
Web: www.worldhungeryear.com
E-mail: whyria@aol.com

**World Organization Against Torture USA**
1015 18th Street NW, Suite 400
Washington, DC 20036
Phone: (202) 861-6494

Fax: (202) 659-2724

# INDEX

## C

# NOW AVAILABLE

The video companion to the book, *America Needs Human Rights*

## America Needs Human Rights
A Food First Video

Fifty years after the Universal Declaration of Human Rights (UDHR) was adopted in 1948 by the General Assembly of the United Nations, America is still not living up to its commitments. Thirty million Americans go hungry—12 million of them children—despite abundant food. These universal and indivisible civil-political and economic-social rights are the rights of all people, rights that we must fight to move into reality.

Told in the voices of welfare mothers, homeless men and women, low-wage workers, seniors, veterans, and health care workers, *America Needs Human Rights* uses a human rights framework to portray the social ills of contemporary America and lay the basis for a powerful movement for fundamental change.

$19.95 VHS, color 23 minutes

# FOOD FIRST BOOKS OF RELATED INTEREST

*The Paradox of Plenty: Hunger in a Bountiful World*
Edited by Douglas H. Boucher
Excerpts from Food First's best writings on world hunger and what
we can do to change it.　Paperback, $18.95

*Dark Victory: The U.S. and Global Poverty*
Walden Bello, with Shea Cunningham and Bill Rau
Second edition, with a new epilogue by the author
Offers an understanding of why poverty has deepened in many
countries, and analyzes the impact of U.S. economic policies.
Paperback, $14.95

*Breakfast of Biodiversity: The Truth about Rain Forest Destruction*
John Vandermeer and Ivette Perfecto
Analyzes deforestation from both an environmental and social jus-
tice perspective.　Paperback, $16.95

*Education for Action: Graduate Studies with a Focus on Social Change*
Edited by Sean Brooks and Alison Knowles
An authoritative, easy-to-use guidebook that provides information
on progressive programs in a wide variety of fields.　Paperback, $8.95.

*Taking Population Seriously*
Frances Moore Lappé and Rachel Schurman
High fertility is a response to anti-democratic power structures that
leave people with little choice but to have many children. Instead of
repressive population control, the authors argue for education and
improved standard of living.　Paperback, $7.95

*BASTA! Land and the Zapatista Rebellion in Chiapas*
George Collier with Elizabeth Lowery Quaratiello
Examines the root causes of the Zapatista uprising in southern
Mexico.　Paperback, $12.95

*Benedita da Silva: An Afro-Brazilian Woman's Story of Politics and Love*
As told to Medea Benjamin and Maisa Mendonça
With a foreword by Jesse Jackson
Afro-Brazilian Senator Benedita da Silva shares the inspiring story of her life as an advocate for the rights of women and the poor.
Paperback, $15.95

*Dragons in Distress: Asia's Miracle Economies in Crisis*
Walden Bello and Stephanie Rosenfeld
After three decades of rapid growth, the economies of South Korea, Taiwan, and Singapore are in crisis. The authors offer policy recommendations to break these countries from their unhealthy dependence on Japan and the U.S.     Paperback, $12.95

*Kerala: Radical Reform as Development in an Indian State*
Richard W. Franke and Barbara H. Chasin. Revised edition
In the last eighty years, the Indian state of Kerala has experimented in the use of radical reform that has brought it some of the Third World's highest levels of health, education, and social justice.
Paperback, $10.95

Write or call our distributor to place book orders. All orders must be pre-paid. Please add $4.50 for the first book and $1.50 for each additional book for shipping and handling.

LPC Group
1436 West Randolph Street
Chicago, IL 60607
(800) 243-0138

# ABOUT FOOD FIRST

## (Institute for Food and Development Policy)

Food First, also known as the Institute for Food and Development Policy, is a nonprofit research and education-for-action center dedicated to investigating and exposing the root causes of hunger in a world of plenty. It was founded in 1975 by Frances Moore Lappè, author of the bestseller *Diet for a Small Planet*, and food policy analyst Dr. Joseph Collins. Food First research has revealed that hunger is created by concentrated economic and political power, not by scarcity. Resources and decision-making are in the hands of a wealthy few, depriving the majority of land, jobs, and therefore food.

Hailed by *The New York Times* as "one of the most established food think tanks in the country," Food First has grown to profoundly shape the debate about hunger and development.

But Food First is more than a think tank. Through books, reports, videos, media appearances, and speaking engagements, Food First experts not only reveal the often hidden roots of hunger, they show how individuals can get involved in bringing an end to the problem. Food First inspires action by bringing to light the courageous efforts of people around the world who are creating farming and food systems that truly meet people's needs.

# HOW TO BECOME A MEMBER OR
# INTERN OF FOOD FIRST

## BECOME A MEMBER OF FOOD FIRST

Private contributions and membership gifts form the financial base of the Institute for Food and Development Policy. The success of the Institute's programs depends not only on its dedicated volunteers and staff, but on financial activists as well. Each member strengthens Food First's efforts to change a hungry world. We invite you to join Food First. As a member you will receive a twenty percent discount an all Food First books. You will also receive our quarterly publication, *Food First News and Views*, and timely *Backgrounders* that provide information and suggestions for action on current food and hunger crises in the United States and around the world. If you want so subscribe to our internet newsletter, *Food Rights Watch*, send us an e-mail at foodfirst@foodfirst.org. All contributions are tax-deductible.

## BECOME AN INTERN FOR FOOD FIRST

There are opportunities for interns in research, advocacy, campaigning, publishing, computers, media, and publicity at Food First. Our interns come from around the world. They are a vital part of our organization and make our work possible.

To become a member or apply to become an intern, just call, visit our website, or clip and return the attached coupon to

Food First/Institute for Food and Development Policy
398 60th Street, Oakland, CA 94618, USA
Phone: (510) 654-4400 Fax: (510) 654-4551
E-mail: foodfirst@foodfirst.org
Website: www.foodfirst.org

You are also invited to give a gift membership to others interested in the fight to end hunger.

## JOINING FOOD FIRST

❏ I want to join Food First and receive a 20% discount on this and all subsequent orders. Enclosed is my tax-deductible contribution of:

❏ $100          ❏ $50          ❏ $30

NAME _____

ADDRESS _____

CITY/STATE/ZIP _____

DAYTIME PHONE ( _____ ) _____

E-MAIL _____

## ORDERING FOOD FIRST MATERIALS

| ITEM DESCRIPTION | QTY | UNIT COST | TOTAL |
|---|---|---|---|
|  |  |  |  |
|  |  |  |  |
|  |  |  |  |
|  |  |  |  |
|  |  |  |  |
|  |  |  |  |

PAYMENT METHOD:

❏ CHECK
❏ MONEY ORDER
❏ MASTERCARD
❏ VISA

MEMBER DISCOUNT, 20%         $ _____

CA RESIDENTS SALES TAX 8.25%         $ _____

SUBTOTAL         $ _____

POSTAGE: 15% UPS: 20% ($2 MIN.)         $ _____

MEMBERSHIP(S)         $ _____

ADDITIONAL CONTRIBUTION         $ _____

TOTAL ENCLOSED         $ _____

_____
NAME ON CARD

_____
CARD NUMBER                                    EXP. DATE

_____
SIGNATURE

MAKE CHECK OR MONEY ORDER PAYABLE TO:

**Food First,** 398 – 60th Street, Oakland, CA 94618

FOR GIFT MEMBERSHIPS & MAILINGS, PLEASE SEE COUPON ON REVERSE SIDE

**FOOD FIRST GIFT BOOKS**

Please send a Gift Book to (order form on reverse side):

NAME _____

ADDRESS _____

CITY/STATE/ZIP _____

FROM: _____


**FOOD FIRST PUBLICATIONS CATALOG**

Please send a Publications Catalog to:

NAME _____

ADDRESS _____

CITY/STATE/ZIP _____


NAME _____

ADDRESS _____

CITY/STATE/ZIP _____


NAME _____

ADDRESS _____

CITY/STATE/ZIP _____


FO

☐ Enclo

Plea

NAME _____

ADDRESS _____

CITY/STATE/ZIP ___

FROM: _____